Invitation to
RIDING

Sheila Wall Hundt

A FIRESIDE BOOK
Published by Simon & Schuster, Inc.
NEW YORK

Drawings by Gene Siegel

Copyright © 1976 by Sheila Wall Hundt

First Fireside Edition, 1984

Published by Simon & Schuster, Inc.
Simon & Schuster Building
Rockefeller Center
1230 Avenue of the Americas
New York, New York 10020

FIRESIDE and colophon are registered trademarks of Simon & Schuster, Inc.

Designed by Eve Metz

Manufactured in the United States of America

10 9 8 7 6 5 4 3 2 1 Pbk.

Library of Congress Cataloging in Publication Data

Hundt, Sheila Wall.
    Invitation to Riding.
    Bibliography: p.
    Includes index.
    1. Horsemanship. 2. Horse Shows. 3. Horses.
4. Fox-Hunting I. Title.
SF309.H78   798'.23   76-769

ISBN 0-671-54197-8 Pbk.

ACKNOWLEDGMENTS

A book such as this is never the effort of a single person, but rather the result of the skills and talents of many. First of all, I would like to acknowledge my debt of gratitude to the many superior horsemen who have helped me and the many horses I have had the pleasure to ride.

I would also like to express my thanks to the following people who have helped more particularly on this book: Alix Coleman, for her excellent photographs and general help above and beyond the call of duty; Lornie Forbes, Marge Campbell and Barbara Hammett, who expertly and patiently posed for most of the photos of work on the flat; Terry Rudd, whose sympathetic and accurate schooling is seen in most of the jumping photographs; and Stephen Barber, Mrs. John Franco, Jr., Major Jeremy Beale, Debbie Thorington and Maple Leaf Farm, Mrs. Alberta Bowen, Mary Hundt, George Hundt, Jr., Lester T. Hundt, Jr., John Saunders, Katharine Davis, Leonard Lee Rue III, Richard O'Donnell, and the many others who contributed in some way to the photographs.

Finally, I would like to thank Mrs. Ramsay Buchanan, Alexander Mackay-Smith, Major Jeremy Beale, David Wilson, V.D.M., and M. P. Lose, V.D.M., and particularly William Steinkraus, my editor, for reading and providing expert opinions about various parts of the book.

S.W.H.

Contents

Introduction   9

I. *PRELIMINARIES*
1. Getting Started   15
2. Grooming   22
3. Saddlery: Its Selection, Adjustment and Care   33

II. *BASIC RIDING SKILLS*
4. Your Basic Position, and How to Mount and Dismount   61
5. Signals and Controls at the Walk and Trot   71
6. Learning to Canter and Gallop   89
7. Trail and Cross-Country Riding   99

III. *SPECIAL RIDING SKILLS*
8. Learning to Jump   109
9. Basic Dressage   129
10. Longeing and Sidesaddle Riding   164

IV. *HORSE SPORTS AND COMPETITIONS*
11. The Background of Foxhunting   179
12. The Fox Hunt and Its Language   207
13. Horse Shows and Dressage Competitions   221
14. Combined Training and Hunter Trials   236

V. *OWNING YOUR OWN HORSE*
15. How to Buy a Horse   253
16. Keeping Your Horse at Home   261

Contents

17. Routine Health Care   281
18. Veterinary Notes   292

List of Sources   313
Bibliography   317
Index   321

8

Introduction

A virtual horse explosion has been taking place in the United States—and, in fact, around the world—during the past two decades. Our horse population, which contracted sharply between the two World Wars because of diminishing demand for work and remount animals, has now sharply risen, due to the growing demand for horses suitable for sport and recreation. Thus, many people who have never had much contact with horses before now ride and own them, and this book was written primarily for them.

More particularly, it was written for anyone who needs guidance in starting off with horses or one of the equestrian sports, from the complete novice who is contemplating his first riding lesson to the person who is well past that hurdle but now contemplates owning a horse, entering into some form of horse competition or taking up foxhunting.

Unlike Europe, where riding means much the same thing to all who participate in it, in the United States we make a sharp distinction between those who ride an Eastern (Hunter, "balanced," or English) Seat, those who ride a Western (Stock or Cowboy) Seat, and those who ride Saddle Seat, the native form of flat-saddle riding that developed in the South along with our Three- and Five-Gaited Saddle Horses and Tennessee Walkers. While there is still a substantial concentration of saddle-horse activity in the South and Southwest, Eastern and Western riding styles have both long since transcended their geographical boundaries and are now practiced in every state in the Union.

Introduction

This book is addressed primarily to those interested in Hunter Seat riding. This is perhaps the most versatile form, since it can be adapted, with suitable modification in stirrup length and inclination of upper body, to everything from trail riding and dressage to show jumping, foxhunting, and even point-to-point riding and steeplechasing. Since I am basically a Hunter Seat rider whose knowledge of horses comes mostly from the East Coast, my advice will inevitably have a certain "East Coast" bias, though I have certainly tried to keep other areas of the country in mind as I wrote. And anyhow, the basic principles of riding are the same no matter where they are practiced.

Good horse care also rests on the same basic considerations throughout the world, with the obvious adjustments for local conditions. Foxhunting admittedly does not exist everywhere, but the tenets of foxhunting apply equally to the hunting of coyote, which is the same genus as fox and has very similar habits. Some areas of the U.S. have neither foxes nor coyotes but practice drag hunting, in which the hounds follow an artificial line that simulates the run of the fox. Although the sport itself differs somewhat from hunting live fox, the demands on the horse and rider are much the same. A knowledge of "the real thing" will certainly add to the pleasure of those who participate in drag hunting.

My experience in the United States (as well as Ireland and England) has been broad and varied. If I cannot claim definitive expertise or national celebrity in any special equestrian discipline, I have at least enjoyed modest success and a great deal of fun from many of them: I have taught all ages of pupils on all qualities of horses since I was sixteen, hunted since I was ten with many American packs as well as English and Irish hunts, trained winning flat and hurdle horses, broken yearlings and remade spoiled racehorses, and won my small share in the show-ring, dressage arena and combined training. So I have, as it were, been through the mill, and my recommendations do not all come out of books. I can only hope that they will not only prove helpful but will stimulate the reader to seek further knowledge.

The following chapters have been organized in a progressive way. However, this does not mean that you must read from cover to cover to benefit from the information provided. I suggest that you flip through the pages, noting your areas of particular interest. Study the sections that are pertinent to your riding career at the moment and peruse the rest of the book at your leisure.

I cannot promise to let you in on any revolutionary discoveries; on the contrary, the tried and true methods described on the following pages have all proven their worth by their durability, and everything here has probably been told thousands of times before. I have stressed the basic principles involved, for I believe that for the fullest enjoyment of any sport, the participant must understand these principles and the theory behind them. Only by practicing these principles, while striving to deepen his understanding of their underlying theory, can the student develop his ability to carry them out.

This is of particular importance in the sport of riding, which obliges the rider to control not only his own body but the horse's as well. Added to the physical challenge is a psychological one, for horses are living beings with widely varying personalities and abilities, and they are not automatically programmed to respond in predetermined ways to a certain set of signals. In this mechanized age, one of the first things the novice rider must learn is not to expect the horse to react like a machine.

Hopefully, an understanding of the basic principles of riding will help the reader to avoid the unnecessary detours that occur when someone tries to learn mostly by the seat of their pants. True, some good riders have learned that way, and you will also occasionally see successful riders who appear to violate all the rules. You may be tempted to copy them, but beware! These riders possess enough talent to make up for the deficiencies in their form, and most of them would do even better if they rode in better form. Ordinary mortals will invariably progress more rapidly by trying to ride in good style.

Novice riders must beware, too, of free advice from various self-styled experts, if it contradicts what has been learned from more established sources. There are often parallel roads to success, but they never truly conflict, and good horsemen are rarely dogmatic. Unfortunately, many who talk a lot often know little, for a thorough knowledge of horses and horsemanship takes a lot of hard work and a great deal of experience that is not easily come by. In fact, complete knowledge is a never-ending search, which is part of the sport's fascination for the true horse lover.

Despite my emphasis on basic principles and established methods, I have tried hard to include in this book many useful little hints and details which more experienced horsemen and more advanced books usually take for granted. Between these two kinds of information I hope I have provided the kind of foundation from which you can develop your chosen horse activity safely, knowledgeably and pleasurably. If so, I am confident that your enjoyment of horses will only be matched by your growing skill in dealing with them.

SHEILA WALL HUNDT
Braeburn Farm
Malvern, Pennsylvania

I · Preliminaries

NOTE: Although most horse nomenclature isn't very complicated, the reader may encounter some terms for parts of the horse that are unfamiliar. In such cases, reference to the illustration of the horse on page 280 should eliminate any confusion.

1

Getting Started

You obviously have given some thought to getting started in riding, and more likely you have made some kind of start already, or you would not be reading this book. I trust your first experiences have already confirmed that your decision was a good one as time spent with horses is enormously rewarding. It is rich in simple pleasures, such as the involvement with one of God's most beautiful creatures and the enjoyment of the outdoors. It can be satisfying as well in the fulfillment that comes from achieving new skills and meeting new challenges, for the variety of things you can do with horses is almost limitless. Somewhere in that broad spectrum that ranges from a quiet hack in the country to the excitement of the chase, the show-ring or cross-country

Companionship is one of the many side benefits of riding.

course, there is a horse activity sufficiently daring, or tranquil, or aesthetic (as the case may be) to suit any taste.

Having already dealt with the most basic question of all, *Shall I take up riding?* and answered *yes,* your next question might be: *How should I start? In order to ride, do I need a teacher?* There are riders who are largely self-taught, but I certainly do not recommend the procedure to a beginner. In riding, as in most other activities, a competent teacher can save you a tremendous amount of time and effort and make the process of getting started immeasurably safer, swifter, and more pleasurable.

What if I only want to ride a little bit? Even in that case—even if you only want to go hacking or trail riding once in a while— you should learn how to control both your body and your horse. The quietest old dobbin can become a handful if a bee stings him, or a motorcycle suddenly approaches. Furthermore, if you learn to ride competently instead of just being a "passenger," your pleasure will be infinitely greater. *Where can I learn to ride?* This is often the most difficult question of all. What you want is a reputable teacher or riding school, but how do you find them? If you have experienced friends, all you have to do is ask them, but many beginners start with no contact with the horse community at all. The classified telephone directory can sometimes give you a start, not only in regard to riding stables, but tack shops and feedstores as well, and the personnel at the latter usu-ally have a pretty good idea of the standards maintained by the stables in their area.

If you are unable to find a knowledgeable local person who can advise you (and I stress *knowledgeable,* as someone who has only had a few rides himself may not be much help), then you should contact one of the sources discussed in the following paragraphs. Even if they are not situated near your area, they may well know of qualified teachers who are located near you.

Teaching Institutions. There are now several institutions in the country that teach and certificate riding teachers through courses that run from several months to a year or more. Among the more prominent are the Morven Park Equestrian Institute in Leesburg, Virginia, the Potomac Horse Center in Gaithersburg, Maryland, Meredith Manor, in Waverly, West Virginia, Pen-Y-Bryn in Chester Springs, Pennsylvania, and the Pacific Horse Center in

Elk Grove, California. Anyone who has acquired a teaching certificate from one of these institutions should be more than qualified to teach a beginner. Of course, anyone who has helped a well-known teacher or achieved an A or B Pony Club rating (see below) should also be qualified.

Other Organizations. Good sources of information for those under the age of twenty-one are the U.S. Pony Clubs and the 4-H Clubs, which can be joined for a nominal membership fee. Quite often the youngster must have his own horse to join these organizations, but their leaders should be good sources of information about where to obtain competent instruction. The Pony Club now has over 250 individual clubs and almost ten thousand members, and you can learn the location of your nearest club by writing the National Headquarters, U.S. Pony Club, in West Chester, Pennsylvania. The County Extension Service of your own State Department of Agriculture can provide information about your local 4-H Horse Programs.

On a somewhat more specialized level, the American Horse Shows Association, the U.S. Combined Training Association and the U.S. Dressage Federation all maintain lists of instructors and/or riding establishments. The AHSA's basic list of Riding Establishment Members is published in its annual *Rule Book,* and includes general as well as show-oriented establishments; the other two lists deal primarily with their particular disciplines, and are published separately. The addresses for these organizations will be found under the List of Sources at the back of the book.

SELECTING A TEACHER

In general, the beginner does not need to be taught by the most expert (and expensive) teacher; in fact, very few leading teachers have sufficient time to deal with novices at all. Therefore, do not feel slighted if a lower-level instructor is suggested. As long as they are well versed in the basics and have a good system of teaching, they are usually the most understanding of the problems of those just starting out with horses.

The range of charges for lessons varies somewhat from area to area as well as from stable to stable. As a rough guide, the head instructor may charge from $15 to $30 for a private lesson, while assistants receive from $8 to $15. Semi-private lessons are less, and class lessons are less again, of course.

Once you have selected a teacher, follow his methods faithfully. If after a time you are unhappy, then go to someone else, but do not continue lessons with a person if you cannot wholeheartedly cooperate with him. If you are sending your child for lessons, watch part of the lesson once in a while. Common sense will tell you if your child is getting adequate instruction. Lessons for younger children should not include more than a half-hour of actual riding time; it will mostly depend on how often the child rides and on his individual endurance as to when he is ready to take an hour lesson. When he does not want to get off the pony at the end of the half hour, the time has probably come for longer lessons.

Absolute beginners should have private or semi-private lessons until they can walk and trot in an enclosed area, and canter on the longe line. They should be able to do this in about a dozen lessons. By then a small group of their own age will probably be more fun, and they will learn faster when it is fun. This of course is only a rough guideline to help you know what to expect. Too often one runs into young people who have ridden two or three times a week for a couple of summers and who have not yet been taught how to canter. This is inadequate instruction!

Take a good look around the establishment you have chosen. The animals should be clean and healthy looking. The stalls should be clean and surrounding areas neat. A sloppy attitude around horses is dangerous. There should be a happy aura around the stables. Formal lessons should probably not start before the age of seven or eight unless the child is able to ride often for short periods. However, every opportunity should be taken to get the young ones acquainted with horses by popping them up on a quiet pony and leading them around for a few minutes.

RIDING APPAREL

Before you mount up for the first time two pieces of apparel are essential, even for the quietest kinds of riding: some sort of "hard

Debbbie is wearing a workmanlike outfit for everyday riding: velvet cap, jeans, chaps and jodhpur boots. She is riding her champion pony Rapunzel.

hat" to protect the head and a fitted, heeled shoe to protect the foot. Hard hats come in several shapes and forms but the most useful is the velvet or velveteen covered hunt cap. The purpose of a hard hat is to protect the rider's head in case of a fall. In order to do this the cap must have an unbreakable lining. To test for this, place the heel of each hand on either side of the hat and push; if the sides give very much under the pressure then the hat is not properly lined.

The hat must also fit properly so that it is not easily dislodged. Place the front edge of the cap on the middle of the forehead and pull the back down to a comfortable position. You should feel an even, slight pressure all around the inside of the hatband. Though, of course, the hat should not be so tight as to give you a headache. Be sure that your hair is arranged as it would be when you go riding. Never buy a hat for a youngster with the thought that he will grow into it. While he is growing it will not be protecting him adequately. An added safety precaution is a chin strap, which may range in type from a simple piece of elastic (which is useful if adjusted tight enough) to a complete harness. The U.S. Pony

Club requires that its members use a chin strap, and those participating in strenuous sports such as eventing and polo usually wear a chin harness of some sort.

Though it is *always* safer to wear a hard hat while on the back of a horse, it is up to the individual whether he invariably does so. An experienced rider working on the flat (not jumping) may elect not to wear one; after all, the odds that he is going to fall on his head are rather long. However, it is essential for children, novices, and all those who are jumping or taking any risk of a sharp fall to wear a hard hat.

To be appropriate for riding, shoes must have heels that will prevent the foot from sliding all the way through the stirrups. They should also cover the ankle in order to give it support and protect it from bruising and twisting. Jodhpur boots or shoes are the most appropriate, but oxfords are acceptable for the beginner riding under controlled circumstances. Sneakers, loafers and all shoes with heavy, ridged soles that might become stuck in the stirrup are unsafe and are unacceptable.

Many people ride happily in jeans or corduroy pants the year 'round. However, those whose skin chafes easily (which is most of us) will need chaps, jodhpurs or boots and breeches to be comfortable. Starting with the most informal, chaps are very convenient since they are worn over the jeans. They offer protection and a non-slip surface to the saddle. They must usually be custom-fitted to be entirely satisfactory. Jodhpurs are also comfortable and the stretch kind are easy to fit. Boots and breeches are ideal but require a substantial outlay of money and more upkeep. For a full description of formal attire see Chapter 11.

What and Where to Buy

Riding apparel comes in many qualities and price ranges. If you are going to do a substantial amount of riding, buy the best and you will be repaid with long wear and comfort. A medium quality can also be very satisfactory if carefully chosen, but the cheapest range is usually a poor economy, even in the short run.

Ask the advice of your instructor or experienced friends about where and what to buy. Sometimes good second-hand apparel is available locally. Even so, obtain and study the catalogues of the large harness companies, such as Miller's and Kauffman's so that you will become aware of what is available and what the average prices are. Their addresses are listed at the back of the book. This advice holds true for the horse's equipment as well.

Some people ride primarily to enjoy the fresh air and the countryside, while others enjoy the exercise and the fun of acquiring a new skill. Many ride in order to enjoy a sport, such as foxhunting or polo. A growing number ride to compete, either for the challenge it presents to themselves and to their horses or with the intention of reaching the top of their chosen field. Whatever your purpose in riding, be sure that it includes the elements of fun and appreciation of the horse. Then you will be well on your way to becoming a true horseman.

2

Grooming

Your horse will probably already have been groomed (cleaned) when you arrive for your first lessons, and in many stables you will seldom need to do this chore. However, take the time to learn how to groom and to know what a properly groomed horse looks like. A horse with a lustrous coat, mane and tail is a joy to the rider as well as the beholder. Knowledge of the background jobs, although not essential in learning how to ride, will add to your store of information about horses and will therefore help make you a better horseman.

Do not look upon grooming as just another necessary chore. Rather, view it as a chance to learn more about your horse, and as part of the general fun of riding. Certainly its main objects are to clean the horse and to prevent various skin diseases; however, it is also an opportunity to improve his appearance and, by a thorough grooming (strapping), even to improve his overall condition. Your horse will respond to a thoughtful grooming just as a dog responds to petting.

Practice good safety measures while grooming and tacking up. Consciously keep your feet away from your horse's hooves so that if he is startled and jumps a little to one side, or simply stomps at a fly, he will not step on your toes.

Whenever you walk behind a horse, you should employ one of two methods: either pass so far behind that you will be out of reach if the horse kicks, remembering that the horse has a long reach with his hind legs, or place a hand on his rump and pass

Keeping his feet well clear of the horse's hooves, Steve polishes off the coat with a short-bristle body brush.

very close behind his quarters. In the latter case you can push the hind leg away from you if he starts to kick. Be particularly cautious in fly season. When working around a horse's hindquarters, always stand slightly to one side, never directly behind. Never be tempted to kneel down next to the horse; you cannot get out of the way fast enough if something goes wrong. Although most horses would not intentionally hurt a person, they cannot be expected to look out for your safety when something is bothering them.

GETTING READY TO RIDE

To take your horse from the stall you will need a halter and a shank (lead rope). Halters and shanks may be made of leather,

23

rope or nylon webbing. All are useful, but for different purposes. The halter should be adjusted so that the noseband hangs a couple of inches below the cheekbones, and is tight enough so that a hoof cannot possibly be slipped through it while the horse is grazing.

The best halter is made of high quality leather with brass buckles and rings. It is good looking, durable, and most important, it is capable of being broken if the horse gets hung up on something. Less expensive leather halters are useful for turning out and other rough service, but special care must be taken with their fit, as they tend to rub.

The only advantages of a rope halter are low cost and toughness. Choose one if you need a halter that will not break for a particular purpose (such as cross-tieing a horse that tends to fly back and break leather halters). Otherwise they are not suitable for horses. A nylon webbing later is adequate if you keep in mind that it chafes easily and also is very difficult to break.

Never turn a horse out with a halter unless you can keep an eye on him from time to time. No matter how well it fits, the halter can become caught on something, and thus for normal turn-out a breakable halter may be preferred. Halters should be left on in the stall so that the horse can be quickly removed in case of fire. Of course, there should be nothing in the stall that the halter could get caught on. Pre-cut, synthetic sheepskin strips with Velcro fastenings are available to cover the parts of the halter that may rub. Though not necessary in the stall, these are advisable on long van trips and are easy to remove and wash.

Rope and nylon webbing lead shanks are inexpensive and suitable for most daily chores. Cotton rope is easier on the hands than hemp or nylon. A leather shank with a brass chain is needed to manage an unruly horse and for ponying (leading one horse off another). The chain can be run through the near (left) side ring, over the noseband and then attached to the off (right) side ring. It should never be allowed to hang loose over the nose as its action would be too severe and possibly cause injury. When handled with care, such a chain may be used to restrain a very fractious horse. Run the chain from the near side ring under the upper lip, and attach it to the other side ring. Make sure that the chain lies flat and is taut, so that it cannot slide down and cut the gum.

While working around your horse remember that he has only three natural defenses: running, kicking and biting. If he becomes frightened, he may revert to one of these defenses unless handled correctly. As you enter the stall, never slip in silently behind the horse; you may startle him and, in his fear, he may kick at you. Speak to him first, and wait until you have his attention. Then put the halter on, making sure the crownpiece is not twisted. Snap the shank to the round ring at the bottom of the halter. It is a good habit always to lead your horse with the shank as this provides better control than simply grasping the halter with your hand.

Always lead the horse from *your* right side, holding the shank a few inches from the snap with your right hand and holding the end of the shank with your left. If you make a loop to keep the extra length out of the way, never wrap the shank around your hand as you will be unable to release it quickly if the horse bolts or rears. Extend your right arm while leading, keeping the horse's head away from you so that he cannot step on your heels. If you face the direction you are going, the horse will follow right along with you.

You will sometimes see people facing the horse and tugging on the lead shank, unable to understand why he will not move. A horse will never step on you purposely; consequently he will not move forward if you are in front of him. If he does not wish to follow you for his peculiar horsey reasons, you will be unable to drag him forward. Circle or back him up a couple of steps to loosen his resistance.

When you are ready, open the stall door wide and lead your horse straight through, taking care that he does not hit his hipbones. Train your horse not to rush in and out of the stall. When you are returning your horse to the stall, always walk in with him so that he does not get in the habit of squeezing past.

The best way to fasten your horse for grooming is the cross-tie method. To do this, run ropes or chains from opposite walls to each side of his halter. This will prevent him from moving around too much. If you do not have the proper place for cross-ties, tie him to a ring or post, making sure that it is solid. Never tie him to a rail of a fence; if he pulls back suddenly he can break the rail, or even worse, drag it and badly injure or frighten himself.

To catch a horse that is turned out in a field, always take a shank and a few oats or carrots. If he is shy, keep the shank hidden behind your back and let him approach you the last couple of steps in order to get the feed. Then, quickly snap the shank on the back ring of the halter. Let him enjoy a couple of mouthfuls of oats, and he should never become a problem to catch. When turning your horse out to pasture, lead him through the gate and turn him around facing you. Unsnap the shank and encourage him to walk off quietly. It is awkward and dangerous if your horse tries to bolt out to the field the minute he sees the gate. Watch out for his hind feet as you release him, as horses often give a buck and a kick of joy at being free.

DAILY GROOMING

To clean a horse adequately you need five basic tools: a curry-comb, dandy (stiff) brush, body (soft) brush, comb and hoof pick. To this assortment you can add other tools and brushes of different textures as they suit your needs. Some stables also use a special horse vacuum cleaner as an efficient way of removing loose hair and dirt. In using this product, if it has a currycomb attach-ment, you use it in a circular motion; if it has a nozzle-type head, you use it back and forth with and against the lay of the hair after you have used an ordinary currycomb. Throw your weight behind your arm on the muscled areas so that you massage the horse as well as clean him. Always finish off with a body brush.

The first step in grooming is currying. Rubber currycombs can do the job of both cleaning the horse and cleaning the brushes; metal currycombs are used only to clean the brushes. The chief job of the currycomb is to loosen mud, sweat and hair. Use it in a circular motion, against the hair, starting up near the horse's ears and working backward. Use it gently over the bony areas which have no fat or muscle to protect them. There is a rubber mitt available which is very useful for replacing the currycomb on the head and legs.

Whenever you use a brush to clean your horse, use the currycomb in your other hand to keep the brush clean.

After currying, use the dandy brush, again starting at the head; use short, lifting strokes in the direction of the hair to remove the dirt loosened by the currycomb. You can also use the dandy brush to scrub the heavy dirt off the legs. Put the dandy brush in your working hand, or the hand closest to the horse's head, and the currycomb in your other hand. In awkward places, such as the inside of the legs, use whichever hand is convenient. After every two or three strokes with your brush, clean it by passing it over the currycomb. The currycomb is cleaned by knocking it on the floor, never on the walls.

When you are cleaning the legs, pay special attention to the back of the pasterns and the heels. Mud and water can collect in these areas and cause a condition called "scratches" which cracks the skin and can be very painful. Some horses have such fine coats and sensitive skins that the dandy brush and currycomb are annoying. Use them with discretion.

27

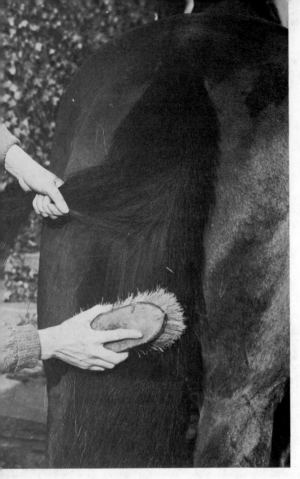

When behind a horse, always stand to one side, not directly in the line of fire. The dandy brush will both clean the tail and straighten the hairs, but if the tail is thin, it is better to pick it out by hand.

Now take your body brush; clean the horse's head well and polish the rest of him by working in the same direction as the hair in long strokes or large circles. Keep your elbow as straight as possible and put your weight behind your arm. Do not slap the brush down on the coat but rather use a massaging action. Remember to clean the brush often on the currycomb.

The equipment used for cleaning the mane and tail depend on their condition. If they are thick and tangled, start by separating the hairs with your fingers. If stuck with burrs, hold the burr with one hand and pull the hair away from it with the other. Then use a dandy brush to remove the worst of the tangles and mud. When the hair has become manageable, finish the job with a body brush, starting at the roots of the hairs and brushing down. Use a comb if needed. When using the dandy brush or the comb, hold the hair above it so that you are not pulling the hair out by the roots but pulling against the hand.

If you gently work one section of hair at a time, no harm will come from using these two implements, but with a fine-textured mane and tail, all that is needed is a body brush or comb. Finish the mane and tail off by wetting them slightly with the water brush. A water brush can be an old dandy brush that has lost its usefulness or one bought for the purpose made with plastic bristles. Do not use a good brush constantly as a water brush or you will rot the bristles out from the backing.

A dirty brush cannot clean a horse. Keep your brushes clean from dust, and when the dirt begins to accumulate, wash them. Immerse the bristles (not the back) in some ammonia and warm water, and let them soak for a few minutes. Then rinse thoroughly, again keeping the backing as dry as possible, and drain with the bristles down.

To complete this part of your grooming, wipe the horse's eyes, nostrils and dock of the tail with a clean sponge or towel and polish off the whole horse with a towel or rub rag.

The final task is to pick out the feet, checking for twisted shoes, loose nails and raised clinches (the part of the nail bent over on the outside of the wall) as you do it. A raised clinch is the beginning of a loose nail. If caught in time, the clinch can simply be hammered back down and will save a trip to the blacksmith.

To pick out the front feet, stand close to the horse's shoulder facing to the rear. Pick up the leg by taking the hand closest to it and running your thumb and forefinger down the tendon, pinching it gently if necessary. Do *not* try to pull the hoof up, as

Pick out the feet daily, particularly the clefts, in order to prevent thrush. At the same time, check for shifted shoes and loose nails.

To clean a hind foot, carry it back a step, and rest it in your hand on the inside of your leg between the knee and thigh.

the horse will simply pull back at you. If the horse resists picking up his hoof, push his shoulder with your shoulder, making him shift his weight to the other leg. As he picks up his hoof, slide your hand around toward the toe so the hoof rests in your palm. Take the hoof pick in your free hand and start cleaning from the heel, working toward the toe.

Pay special attention to the cleft on either side of the frog and the slight cleft in the middle as these are places where a stone may be caught or where thrush may start. Thrush is rotting of the frog which is caused by inadequate cleansing. (See page 292.) You will recognize it by its odor of rot and the unusual deepening of the cleft. When cleaning the clefts do not dig too energetically with the pick, especially if its point is very sharp.

To pick up the hind feet, stand close to the horse's hindquarters and run your hand down the inside of his leg. As he lifts his foot, pull it slightly forward, catching it with your outside hand. Be careful not to pull it out toward you as this will cause the horse to lose his balance and resist. To clean the hoof, take a step backward and rest the hoof in your hand on the inside of your leg between the knee and thigh. To kick with his hind leg the horse must first pull his foot forward, just as a boxer must draw his fist back to strike a blow, so there is little danger.

GROOMING AFTER THE RIDE

In the warm weather you will wish to give your horse a partial or complete bath after you have ridden him. You will need a bucket, a large sponge, a scraper and body wash. You may bathe the horse as often as necessary as long as you follow some commonsense rules. Use only the amount of body wash recommended; use lukewarm water; apply Vaseline to his heels if he shows any tendency toward scratches or mud fever. Keep his hooves as dry as possible during the bath and paint with a good hoof dressing if they are in bad condition before the bath so that the water runs off. Use plenty of water and do not forget to wash between the cheekbones and the hind legs. Geldings should periodically have their sheaths washed, too, but this can be tricky for a novice, and you should ask an experienced groom to show you the procedure before attempting it. Scrub the mane, tail, back and girth areas thoroughly. Scrape off as much excess water as you can, being careful of the bony areas. Then squeeze the excess water off the legs by running your hand firmly down from the elbows and hocks. With a towel or damp sponge, rub off the head and legs.

In the summer walk the horse until dry, preferably in the shade in order to keep the coat from becoming sunburned. A few nibbles of grass now and then will help the horse to cool out. In cooler weather wash only the areas that have become sweaty and cover the horse with a cooler to keep him from getting a chill.

In the cold weather after light work, simply rub the saddle and bridle areas vigorously with a rough cloth and knock off (a quick grooming) the rest of the horse. After hard work, keep in mind the basic principle that hot water opens the pores of the skin and cold water closes them. You do not wish to open the pores of muddy legs, which are cool, to bacteria so you wash them with cold water. You do not wish to shut the pores of a hot back on bacteria which may already have been introduced, so you wash thoroughly with warm water and antiseptic. When the back is dry you can then apply white lotion to cool it if it is tired from several hours of the saddle, or use alcohol, salt water or plain cold water to toughen it.

Do not groom a tired horse. Clean the essential areas, blanket and bandage the legs if necessary, and let him rest. Water is offered in limited amounts at intervals until he is no longer thirsty. Take the chill off it in cold weather. Hay may be given at once, but grain should be withheld for a couple of hours and then it should be given in some form of a mash.

STRAPPING

A thorough grooming (strapping) includes not only the above currying and brushing but also what is known as wisping, as in the old days it was done with a wisp made of plaited hay, doubled over and braided together until it formed a wad. However, it is time-consuming to braid a wisp and it does not last very long. An excellent substitute is a wad of horsehair covered with leather that has a hand strap attached to one side. You can also "wisp" a horse satisfactorily with a towel folded several times into a pad. The point of wisping a horse is to tone up his muscles and bring the oils of the skin to the surface. A horse that is regularly wisped should have a gleaming coat.

The correct method of wisping a horse is to take your wisp in your working hand, and pummel the horse's neck, chest, shoulders, back, barrel and quarters in a slow rhythm, throwing your weight behind a relatively straight arm. When the wisp hits the muscles they tense and as you draw back the muscle relaxes. Pummel the back and loin gently but hit the other areas as hard as the horse will allow. You will find that to wisp a horse five or six times in each area the first few days will take all your strength, but gradually you should work up to as many strokes as time allows.

In addition to the regular, every-day grooming activities, your horse will occasionally require to have his mane thinned, may sometimes need clipping, and if you hunt or show, will sometimes need to have his mane and tail braided. Novice riders are unlikely to be asked to help in these activities, and in any case, will want to see them done first by someone who knows what they are doing before attempting them. However, once you own your own horse, you may well be faced with the necessity of coping with them yourself, and so more detailed information is given in Chapter 16.

3

Saddlery: Its Selection, Adjustment and Care

For your first lessons your horse will probably be groomed and tacked up (saddled and bridled). Hopefully, your teacher will check to insure that the bridle is adjusted properly, that the girth is tight and that the stirrup leathers are the right length. However, once you have acquired some of the basics, you will not be so carefully watched over. It is human nature to assume that someone who shows a little knowledge, knows more than they actually do. Rightly or wrongly, the rider is ultimately responsible for checking that the tack is in serviceable condition and properly adjusted.

A good basic understanding of tack, its care and its adjustment and fitting can be obtained from this chapter. This knowledge will give you confidence and may keep you from any unnecessary fall, caused by a loose girth or a broken stirrup leather, or an unpleasant ride caused by an improperly adjusted bridle.

BRIDLES AND BITS

Your tack consists of a bridle and saddle and possibly a saddle pad, martingale and/or breastplate. Bridles are named after the bit used in them, i.e., a snaffle bridle is one which holds a snaffle bit. Bits may be sewn or buckled into the bridle, or, most commonly, attached by what is referred to as a hook or stud fastening. There are many different kinds of bits but they are all based on one of the following: snaffle, bit and bridoon (double) and pelham.

You may have a horse with a problem mouth, either due to mismanagement or malformation (parrot mouth, etc.), who does not go well in any of the bits we discuss. You will know you are dealing with a problem mouth when your horse consistently exhibits any of the following symptoms: head tossing, opening the mouth, carrying the head too low or too high, leaning on the bit, snatching at the bit and/or refusing to obey the signals sent to the bit. A problem mouth is caused by pain, fear, malformation or improper training, or any combination of these.

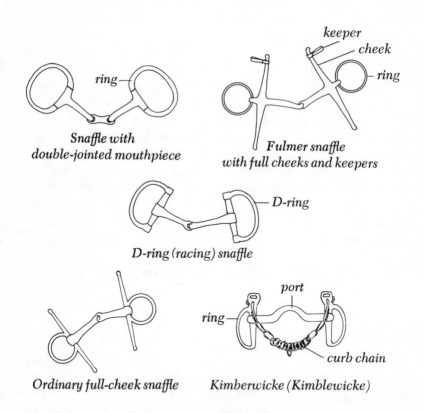

Snaffle with double-jointed mouthpiece

Fulmer snaffle with full cheeks and keepers

D-ring (racing) snaffle

Ordinary full-cheek snaffle   *Kimberwicke (Kimblewicke)*

VARIETIES OF SNAFFLE BITS

The first step in curing a problem mouth is finding the cause(s). Have a veterinarian check the mouth for sharp edges on the teeth, infected or wolf teeth, lesions, old scars on the tongue or bars or malformation. If any of these are found, ask his advice on dealing with them. It may be as simple as floating (filing) the sharp edges of the teeth or as complicated as finding a bit whose design allows for a tongue that is too large for its channel.

Once the mouth itself has been eliminated as the source of the problem, then you must discover whether fear of pain or bad (inadequate) training is the prime cause. Patient, tactful and yet consistent use of the bit will be helpful, but often extensive re-bitting, longeing, riding in a bitless bridle and general retraining are necessary. Seek the advice and guidance of an expert who can analyze the problem on the spot.

The Snaffle

The snaffle may have a jointed or rigid mouthpiece made of metal or hard rubber. The thicker the mouthpiece the milder the bit, as the thick mouthpiece does not dig as much into the bars of the jaw. (The bars are that space of gum on the lower jaw between the incisors and the molars.) A jointed snaffle is somewhat more severe than a rigid one due to its nutcracker action on the tongue, bars and lips. However, a rigid one pulls directly on the horse's tongue as well as on the bars and lips, and some horses avoid this by pulling the tongue back or flipping it over the bit. The same habits can be caused occasionally by a rubber-covered bit as some horses do not like the feel of it on their tongue. Some straight-bar mouthpieces have a slightly half-moon shape (Mullen mouthpiece) allowing more room for the tongue, and these should be preferred, since bad tongue habits should be avoided at all costs; they are very hard to cure!

Thus the mildest bit, though not necessarily the best, is the unjointed, rubber-covered snaffle. The next would be a rubber-covered jointed snaffle. Perhaps a better choice to make a young horse's mouth is a Fulmer snaffle. This bit has a jointed, thick metal mouthpiece but the nutcracker action is almost eliminated as the rings are not attached rigidly to the mouthpiece. It has full cheekpieces (bars of straight metal in front of the rings), the

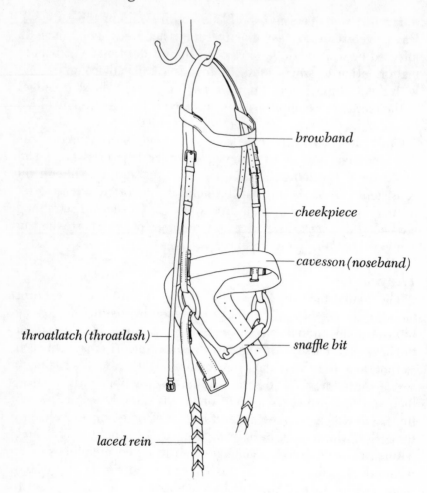

browband

cheekpiece

cavesson (noseband)

throatlatch (throatlash)

snaffle bit

laced rein

SNAFFLE BRIDLE

upper branch of which should be attached to the cheekpieces of the bridle by small leather keepers. This helps steady the bit in the horse's mouth and, in conjunction with a dropped noseband, encourages good mouth habits.

The shape of the rings has nothing to do with the action of the bit. However, when they are attached to the bit in such a fashion that they rotate in the mouthpiece, they have less of a nutcracker

A snaffle bridle with a dropped noseband, properly adjusted.

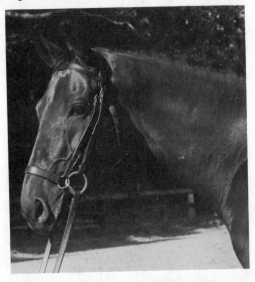

action than those that are rigidly attached. Cheekpieces prevent the bit from being pulled through the mouth. The straight side of a D-ring acts as a modified cheekpiece.

The snaffle will act on the lips, bars and tongue of the mouth of the horse that carried his head properly. If he raises his head out of position and slides the bit into the corners of his mouth, then the snaffle is not working properly, and both the rider and the horse will be uncomfortable. When this happens only occasionally, a running martingale may prove to be a solution. Otherwise the horse's mouth should be remade or another bit should be used.

The Kimberwicke (Kimblewicke)

The Kimberwicke has a straight-bar mouthpiece with a small port, D-rings and a curb chain. It allows the rider more control than a snaffle but less than a pelham or double bridle. The advantage of the single rein is the simplicity of its use, making it desirable for children and for fox hunters who often need a free hand. The disadvantage of this bit is its lack of flexibility. With the hands in proper position and a soft feel it acts like a snaffle; with the hands lower and a stronger feel it acts like a very short-shank curb. A pelham and a double bridle give the rider the

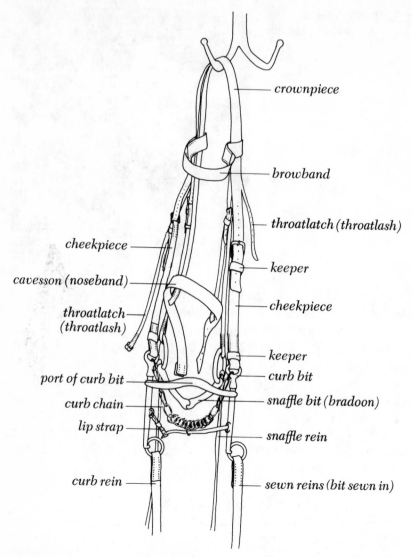

crownpiece

browband

throatlatch (throatlash)

cheekpiece

cavesson (noseband)

throatlatch
(throatlash)

keeper

cheekpiece

keeper

curb bit

port of curb bit

snaffle bit (bradoon)

curb chain

lip strap

snaffle rein

curb rein

sewn reins (bit sewn in)

DOUBLE BRIDLE

option of not using the curb rein at all while increasing the feel of the snaffle rein. The Uxeter Kimberwicke has two slots in the ring so that the rein can be attached high to give more of a snaffle action or low to give more of a curb action.

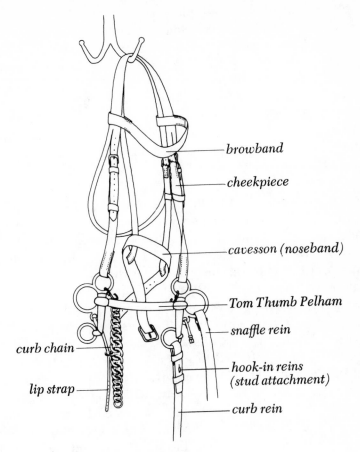

browband

cheekpiece

cavesson (noseband)

Tom Thumb Pelham

snaffle rein

curb chain

hook-in reins
(stud attachment)

lip strap

curb rein

PELHAM BRIDLE

The Pelham

The pelham combines features of the snaffle with features of
the curb, and is actually one bit with rings for two reins. The top
rein acts like and is called the snaffle rein; the bottom rein acts
like and is called the curb rein. The severity of this bit depends

on the thickness of the mouthpiece and the length of the shank. A couple of designs have a very high port intended to push on the roof of the horse's mouth. Avoid these at all costs. All pelhams have curb chains and, although they can be removed, it is best to use them; otherwise, the horse may learn to open his mouth and drop his jaw, thus avoiding the pressure of the bit when the curb rein is in action. Purists object to the pelham on the basis that it is hard to produce a pure snaffle effect. In practice, though, many horses go very kindly in a short-cheeked pelham, commonly called a "Tom Thumb."

Bit and Bridoon (Bradoon)

The bit (curb) and bridoon (snaffle) are the bits used in a double bridle. This bridle should only be used on horses that have already learned to accept the bit and by riders whose hands are independent of their seat and who have the finesse to use both bits properly. The bridoon is severe for a snaffle as it has a slender mouthpiece. The curb has a rigid mouthpiece with a port (U-shaped section in the center) which allows a little extra room for the tongue. Neither of these bits should ever be used alone.

The curb rein is attached to a small ring at the bottom of the shank of the curb, thus allowing the rider to exert a certain amount of leverage to the horse's jaw. The longer the shank, the greater the leverage. A curb chain is attached from one side of the top ring of the curb along the horse's chin groove to the other side of the bit. As the bottom of the shank is pulled backward by the reins, the top moves forward, bringing the curb chain into action. This action also exerts a slight pull on the poll, encouraging vertical flexion. The curb chain helps hold the bit in position and puts pressure on the chin groove.

The curb aids in teaching a horse collection so the most common uses of the double bridle are in the higher levels of dressage and in some of the sporting fields where added help is sometimes needed to keep an overly enthusiastic horse in control.

Curb Chains

Curb chains, in descending order of severity, are made of single-
or double-link chain, leather or elastic. A rubber sleeve is available
to cover those made of chain link. Curb chains are held in place
by a leather curb strap (except when used on a kimberwicke,
where the strap is not needed because of the design). The curb
chain comes into play as the top of the curb shank moves forward
when the curb rein is pulled. Except with the curb of the double
bridle, the chain can run through the ring of the bit and be hooked
outside it. This helps to prevent chafing and pinching. When link
chains are used, the hair and whiskers around the chin groove
should be trimmed for the same reason. The type and the tightness of the curb chain regulates its severity. The purpose of the
curb chain will be lost if it is adjusted so tightly that it exerts
almost constant pressure over a period of time, thus making the
jaw numb.

Martingales

Martingales are designed to help control the incorrect actions
of the horse's head. If your horse carries his head properly, then
you do not need a martingale except perhaps at times of stress.
For example, it is wise to add the control of a running martingale
to a young horse's equipment the first few times you take him
cross-country for foxhunting. He will have so many distractions
that he may forget parts of his training, some of it only recently
acquired.

The standing martingale runs from the back of the noseband,
through a strap (yoke) around the horse's neck which helps hold
it in place, to the girth. This martingale is effective on horses who
throw their heads up in the air. You may see, particularly at shows,
a standing martingale adjusted so tightly that it forces the horse
who wants to carry his head too high to carry it in the right position.
However, it is inadvisable to tie a horse's head down this tightly,
as you are limiting not only the upward movement but the forward and downward movements of his head that he may need to
balance himself under certain situations. A standing martingale
should be adjusted so that the slack will almost touch his throat
when his head is in the proper position. The adjustment of this

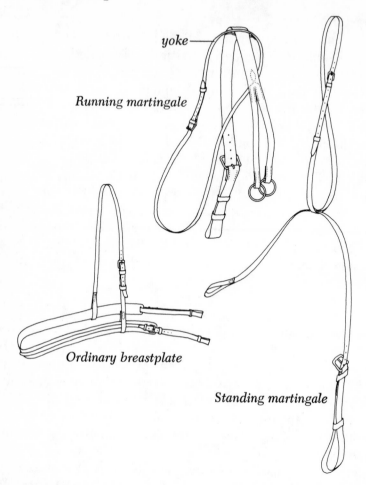

yoke

Running martingale

Ordinary breastplate

Standing martingale

martingale is thus somewhat dependent on the horse's conformation.

The running martingale starts out as one strap from the girth but then splits in half at the juncture of the yoke. Each strap has a ring on the end through which the snaffle rein of any bridle passes. When the horse raises his head too high, the martingale pulls the snaffle rein down, thus helping to keep the bit in position and allowing the rider quite a bit of leverage. The running martingale should be adjusted so that it has two to three inches of slack when the horse has his head in proper position. If this martin-

The rubber pelham bridle has rein stops on the snaffle rein in order to prevent the rings of the running martingale from catching on the studs. Pumpkin Light's girth is covered with a sheepskin in order to prevent chafing as she is overweight and unfit.

gale is adjusted too tightly it will cause constant pressure, or tug on the horse's mouth even when he is carrying his head properly. Whenever a running martingale is used on buckled or hooked reins, "stops" (small leather or rubber pieces) should be fitted to the reins to prevent the rings from catching. A standing or running martingale adjusted too loosely will be ineffective.

A hunting breastplate runs around a horse's neck between his front legs to the girth. On either side of the withers a strap runs from the yoke to the rings that are attached to the front of the saddle just below the pommel. These straps, plus the strap that attaches to the girth, keep the saddle from sliding back. This is necessary on horses with certain conformation faults, such as slab-sided (ribs not well sprung), herring-gutted (abdomen or barrel narrows sharply toward the flanks) or mutton-withered (meaty, ill-defined withers) horses. A running or standing martingale can be attached to the ring in the center of the yoke. In polo, steeple-chasing and show jumping, an ordinary breastplate is often used instead. This runs across the breast, being attached at each end to the girth, and held up by a strap running over the withers.

Nosebands (Cavessons)

Ordinary nosebands come in varying widths. The narrower the noseband and the lower and tighter it is adjusted, the more effective it is. There are three types of dropped nosebands listed here in order of effectiveness: the figure eight, the dropped noseband attached to the cavesson, and the plain dropped noseband most often seen in dressage work. They should only be used in conjunction with a snaffle and, as with all equipment on your horse, must be fitted properly.

The first two being the stronger are probably the most helpful in correcting already acquired bad habits. The plain dropped noseband is helpful in training the young horse's mouth because, when he experiments with the evasions of opening the mouth, crossing the jaws or various tricks with his tongue, it will exert pressure on his nose, lips and chin groove. The key word to be associated with a dropped noseband is "helpful." In itself it will not cure bad habits or force the horse to accept the bit. Only time and tact can do this. When the horse fully accepts the bit, the dropped noseband can be replaced by an ordinary cavesson.

SADDLES

Saddles used in so-called English riding are of two basic designs: forward seat (jumping) and dressage (polo). However, there are many gradations between the extreme forward seat with its pronounced cut forward at the knee, rather long twist (narrowest part of the saddle behind the pommel) and tilted upward cantle, and the extreme dressage saddle with its straight flaps, short, deep center close to the pommel, and thick padding under the cantle.

How do you choose between the many styles? First consider your style and type of riding and then the shape of the horse's back. Although most large saddlemakers are now producing a full line, it is well to keep in mind that the English and Italians are best known for their forward seat designs and the Germans for

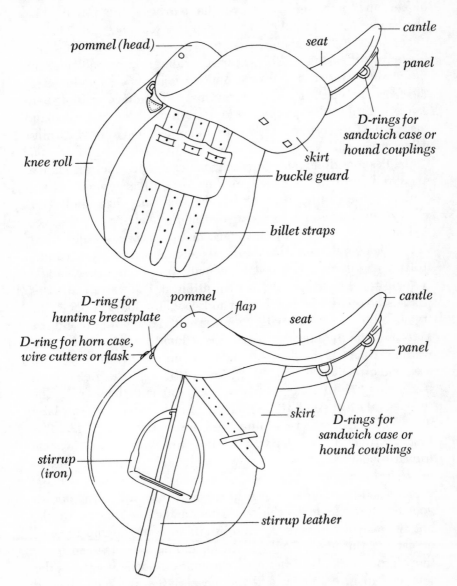

pommel (head)

seat

cantle

panel

D-rings for
sandwich case or
hound couplings

knee roll

skirt

buckle guard

billet straps

D-ring for
hunting breastplate

pommel

flap

seat

cantle

D-ring for horn case,
wire cutters or flask

panel

skirt

D-rings for
sandwich case or
hound couplings

stirrup
(iron)

stirrup leather

FORWARD SEAT (JUMPING) SADDLES

their dressage and all-purpose designs. Also remember that the higher and narrower the twist, the narrower the throat (the channel between the panels underneath the saddle).

For jumping you should examine the forward seat types; for foxhunting, hacking and cross-country riding, you would consider the modified forward seat or the all-purpose types; for dressage, the dressage types. If you are interested in combined training and cannot afford both a jumping and a dressage saddle, then look at the all-purpose types but be sure to select one in which the deepest part of the seat is well forward.

Saddles for adults range in size from sixteen to nineteen inches, measured from the nailhead in the side of the pommel to the center of the cantle. Style and maker influence size, and thus, while a seventeen-inch forward seat saddle may fit you perfectly, you still may need only a sixteen-inch dressage saddle. Most saddle dealers have a wooden saddle stand on which you can sit to try a saddle out. While it is difficult to tell whether a saddle is going to be right for you just by sitting in it for a few minutes in the store, it can be helpful if you know how to go about it. To try out a saddle, sit in it with your seat in the deepest part and the stirrups properly adjusted. Your knee should be close to the forwardmost part of the flap, whether straight or forward seat, with a couple of inches leeway. There should be approximately half a hand's breadth of space between your seat and the cantle. The twist should feel comfortably narrow between your thighs. Many new saddles feel rather stiff until they are broken in a bit, and it is best, once you have selected the style you wish, to borrow one from someone who has the same model and try it for a couple of hours, if this is possible.

Many saddles offer special features or options which can add to your comfort and make the saddle more suitable to your needs, but be wary of extremes. Knee rolls and padding behind the calf of various thicknesses help keep some riders' legs in position, though they are only an annoyance to others. Suede inserts on the skirt or seat give a softer and less slippery feel. Saddles that are thickly padded and have relatively deep seats are generally the most comfortable for those who ride for several hours at a time. Designs that employ a short girth, buckled low on the horse's barrel, eliminate buckles from under the rider's leg. However, these are not the strongest designs for hard usage, and require a collection of special girths if you use them on horses of different sizes. All in all, the best riders usually seem to pick the least "gimmicky" saddles.

The saddle must provide for the comfort of the horse as well as that of the rider, and the critical point here, especially with high-withered horses, is the pommel. You should be able to put two fingers between the pommel and the withers when you are in the saddle. The panels should be evenly stuffed and support the saddle over a long expanse of the horse's back. A saddle with a narrow twist will perch on a mutton-withered, broadbacked horse, and will tend to rock on a point just behind the withers. However, as it is desirable for the rider to have a narrow saddle on a broadbacked horse, this problem can sometimes be remedied by removing a little of the padding. A saddle with a broad twist may satisfy the rider if it is on a narrow horse and does not come down on the horse's withers. The addition of a little padding will help a borderline case.

Stirrups and Leathers

The best stirrups are made of stainless steel. Never-rust irons are adequate but require more care to maintain brightness. Those made of mixed metals are nice to look at but are unsatisfactory as they bend under stress; this is not the place to economize.

The basic stirrup useful in most types of riding is heavy in weight, and has branches (sides) that are uniform in length and a broad tread. A heavyweight stirrup is easier to keep on the foot than a lightweight one, and a broad tread provides the support which helps prevent fatigue during extensive galloping.

The offset stirrup is a variety of the basic design in which the outside branch is shorter than the inside branch, so that the stirrup tends to tip to the inside, and the tread is tilted backward. The theory is that this stirrup encourages the foot to stay on the inside of the stirrup and the heel to stay down, but for my money, whatever aid this stirrup is to the foot position is artificial, and it is not recommended.

A slim, lightweight stirrup is preferred by some dressage and show riders for its elegance and feel. A safety stirrup is one designed so that the metal of the outside branch is replaced by a heavy-duty rubber band fastened by a leather strap at the bottom and slipped over a metal hook at the top. This allows for another exit (the rubber band pops off easily) if the foot becomes caught during a fall. This stirrup is highly recommended for children.

Ridged rubber pads are available to fit into the treads of most stirrups. Their primary purpose is to help prevent the foot from slipping after the original tread has worn smooth, and, secondarily, to help keep the foot warm in the winter. Their primary function can be their greatest disadvantage as they can prevent the foot from coming out of the stirrup during a fall. However, they are an unqualified aid in dressage work in which the contact with the stirrup is light because of the length of stirrup leather; they help keep the rider's foot from slipping around or possibly out of the stirrup.

It is important that stirrups fit properly. They should extend from one to one and a half inches beyond the side of the sole of the boot; the larger the foot, the more leeway. They should be large enough for the foot to come out easily if necessary and yet small enough so that the whole foot cannot possibly slip through. Be particularly careful that children's stirrups fit properly.

Girths

Girths are made of leather, leather and elastic, linen, nylon cord, or mohair and plastic. Leather is the most durable and those with elastic at one end are easy to adjust, but the elastic must be replaced as it wears. String (cord) girths do not chafe and are popular with dressage riders, but are difficult to clean. Supplementary elastic overgirths can help prevent saddles from slipping during extreme exertions such as racing, and on problem or herring-gutted horses on whom it is difficult to keep the saddle in place.

Leather girths are made in three styles: (1) folded, which are made of a single piece of leather folded in three, which involves a little extra cleaning and chafes some horses; (2) shaped or Lonsdale, in which two pieces of leather are sewn together and slightly shaped away from the elbow area so that these seldom chafe; (3) Balding, in which one piece of leather is cut, over-

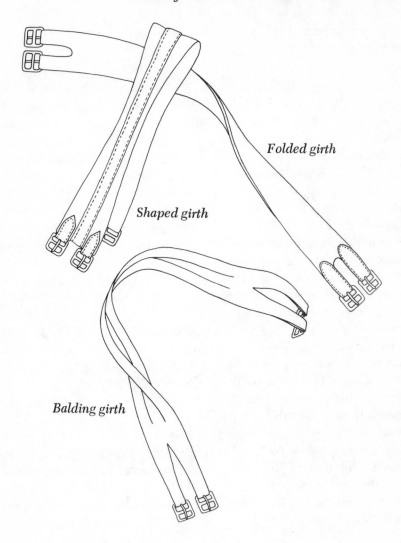

Folded girth

Shaped girth

Balding girth

lapped and sewn in the center to give even more shaping at the elbow. The Fitzwilliam girth is made of leather or webbing and consists of two girths. The broader, bottom one has two buckles and over it lies a second, narrower girth which provides a third buckle.

SADDLE PADS

A saddle pad or cloth is often used to protect the horse's back as well as the saddle during exercise, and it both simplifies tack cleaning and helps the saddle lining to wear longer. If your saddle fits properly, you can use a rub-rag of linen or toweling as a saddlecloth for everyday riding. However, some form of regular saddle pad should be used to equalize the pressure if the saddle is not quite right or if the horse has a problem back. Synthetic sheepskin pads are the easiest to keep clean and come in single or double thicknesses. The latter are usually more satisfactory. Unfortunately, some horses are allergic to them, and for them you may wish to try a real sheepskin pad. These can be used many times without washing if they are brushed when dry after each use. When they are dirty, they should be washed and dried as you would a good wool sweater.

Rubber pads are generally less desirable as they slip easily and heat up the horse's back. However, they do have a special purpose, as a hole can easily be cut in them to relieve the pressure over a sore. Felt pads fulfill all the qualifications of a good pad except that they are difficult to keep clean and soft. You should brush them when dry after each use; scrub the dirty side with soap and water when necessary. A pommel (wither) pad made for the purpose out of wool or improvised out of a folded stable cloth can be used in an emergency to keep the saddle from pinching the top or the sides of the withers. However, it cannot completely relieve the pressure, so eventually the saddle should be restuffed or replaced.

BUYING TACK

A good riding master will help you select and fit tack for yourself and your horse. Explain your needs and how much you wish to spend and be guided by him. Do not overlook secondhand tack, particularly saddles, but have them checked for wear and broken trees by an experienced person before purchasing. A high-quality, used saddle in good condition will give you more satisfaction than a poor-quality new saddle. Most local saddlery stores can carry only a few models of saddles. Look around carefully among stores and friends before you select the one you wish. Your local store can then order it for you.

There are three basic grades of leather, and first-quality differs substantially from third-quality in looks, price, workmanship and durability. You get what you pay for, and third-grade leather is a poor economy. If you are going to do a lot of riding, you can only afford the two better grades.

Most of the English and European leather sold in the United States is of the first and second quality, and it is difficult to tell the difference when the leather is new. If you wish the best and ask for the first- or top-line leather do not be satisfied with such answers as "This is good English leather," as both first and second grades are sold by the major manufacturers. When new, the first-line leather will have more body (be stiffer) and will be better finished with smoother edges and more stitches to the inch than the second-quality. When in use, the first-quality will soften nicely but retain better body and will darken to a better color than the second-quality.

The lowest or third-quality usually comes from Japan, Argentina, India or New Zealand and is quite soft and pliable even when new. Often the inside of the leather is not finished but rough or feathery and the stitching is coarse.

CARE OF TACK

Supple tack, gleaming from careful conditioning, adds to the general aesthetic appeal of a well turned-out horse and is unlikely to cause skin irritations. You should not ride in leather that has cracked or worn thin at the stress points, which are usually places where metal rests on leather. The prime places to check are the attachments to the bit, the leather around the girth buckles and the area of the leather where the stirrup rests.

Though many riding academies, hunt club stables and private

stables, too, are very careless about it, tack should be cleaned religiously after every use, just like brushing your teeth before you go to bed. There are two very good reasons for this: first, good tack is *very* expensive these days, and, though it will last almost indefinitely if cared for properly, its life will be short indeed if it is habitually neglected. Even more important is the safety factor, for tack failure—a broken girth, stirrup leather or rein—can cause a fall and serious injury. Even metal fractures will usually give some warning if the bit, buckle or stirrup is habitually inspected while it is being cleaned, and loose stitching or cracked folds in leather are also readily noticed if the tack is ever actually cleaned.

Make it a habit, whenever you untack a horse, to rinse the bit and rub off any hair and sweat from the bottom of the saddle and the girth while it is still wet, using a damp sponge, a towel, or even your hand. These simple acts will greatly ease your tack-cleaning chores later, for once sweat or mixed grass and saliva have been permitted to harden, they will take some elbow grease to remove.

A good tack hook suspended from the ceiling for the bridle and girth and a solid saddle rack are almost indispensable aids in getting the cleaning job done efficiently. The basic tools necessary are warm water (hot water dries the leather), a towel, saddle soap, steel wool and a natural sponge. Synthetic sponges are cheaper but unsatisfactory. It is also handy to have a nail brush to scrub at odd places and a second sponge reserved only for soaping.

There are many different saddle soaps and softening agents, often packaged with misleading directions, which causes confusion on the proper method to clean tack. Understanding a few basic principles will clarify the situation. Most saddle soaps are not "soap" such as you use to wash your hands, and do not contain the emulsifying ingredients necessary to lift the dirt. Rather they consist of one or more animal fats and are designed to replace the oils removed from the leather during use and washing.

Therefore, the tack must be clean before the saddle soap is applied. Ordinary sweat and dirt acquired in one or two rides can be removed by vigorously rubbing with a damp sponge.

Water removes oil from the leather so use as little as necessary. However, those items which do not receive daily cleaning, such as halters, can be soaked for a few minutes in warm water to which a small amount of ammonia has been added and then scrubbed with a nail brush and a mild soap such as Ivory or castile. Never use detergents. If the leather is wet, wipe it dry with a towel or chamois before applying the saddle soap.

You wish your leather to be supple but not soft. Daily applications of some products that claim to soften leather will actually do so to the point where you can scrape off layers of it with your fingernail! These products of course have their use: two or three applications can help to season new leather before use; occasional application can benefit leather both in and out of use when it appears dry, or when leather has needed a thorough washing, been soaped and allowed to dry overnight. Your saddler can advise you as to the proper uses of soaps and softeners.

My own method of keeping leather in good shape involves using glycerine bar soap (preferably imported), a bottle of Tanner's oil, a can of neat's-foot oil, a jar of Vaseline and a towel. Regular daily cleaning consists of wiping the hair and sweat off the girth and the bottom of the saddle with a towel, washing with a sponge all the leather surfaces, and then soaping the leather with glycerine saddle soap. Squeeze as much water as possible out of the sponge before applying the soap. Do not wring them, as they will rip. Rub any excess suds into the leather with your free hand. Reapply the glycerine to the sponge often. Make a particular effort to wash and soap those places where the metal rests on the leather.

Bits, curb chains and stirrups made of stainless steel need only to be washed and rubbed with a towel to be kept shiny. It is much easier to clean them if you always rinse them in a water bucket after you remove them from the horse's mouth. Steel wool may be used on heavy dirt. However, other metals will need the occasional application of metal polish. After about a dozen uses your tack should all be taken apart and the hard-to-get-at places completely cleaned and treated with Tanner's or neat's-foot oil. New leather treated with Tanner's oil two or three times before use will become more supple and start to acquire a good color.

Tanner's oil is a light enriching oil; neat's-foot oil is a heavy enriching oil. The practice of soaking a new piece of leather in neat's-foot oil is not recommended, as it saturates the leather and makes it greasy and overly soft. Tanner's or neat's-foot oil should be applied once a month to leather not in use. When you know leather is going to be out of use for more than a month, a thin application of Vaseline or dubbin will prevent mildew and dry rot.

TACKING UP

Once the horse is clean, and yet still tied or cross-tied so that he cannot move around too much, you can start to tack up. Place the saddle cloth or pad so that a couple inches will show in front of the pommel and make sure there are no wrinkles. Grasping the saddle by the pommel and cantle, set it gently on the withers from the off (right) side and slide it back until the front padding rests in the hollow behind the withers. Never slide it forward, as you will disturb the lie of the hair. Saddle sores, an irritated horse and an unpleasant ride will be caused by a badly placed saddle. Pull the pad up into the pommel arch to insure that there is no pressure on the withers and make sure it is square on the horse's back.

Attach the girth on the off (right) side and then go around and fasten it on the near (left) side. If the buckle guards are still present—which they should be—pull them down over the buckles. Do not attempt to tighten the girth all at once, as this will annoy the horse. If the horse moves around after the saddle has been placed on his back, make sure that it has stayed in the proper position.

Most saddles have three billet straps. Attach the girth to the front two if the saddle has a tendency to slip backward, to the back two if the girth has a tendency to pinch behind the elbow, and to the first and third if there is no problem. The girth should be long enough so that there are a couple of holes in the billet straps below the buckles and short enough that there are a couple of holes in the billet straps above the buckles on both sides. A girth that cannot be tightened as the horse works is a serious

By putting the bridle on this way, you can control the position of the horse's head with your right hand.

hazard. If you are using a folded girth, make sure the open edge is to the rear.

To put on the bridle, unhook the cross-ties or shank and, working on the horse's near side, put the reins over his head a bit behind his ears. You will then be able to hold him if he decides to move. Remove the halter and, facing the front, put your right arm around behind his head and grasp the top of the bridle with your right hand in front of the forehead. The noseband and throatlatch should be unbuckled and the curb chain, if any, unhooked. If the weather is cold, warm the bit in your hands.

With your left hand hold the bit between the thumb and forefinger or rest it in the palm of your hand, and press it gently against the teeth. Most horses will automatically open their mouths but, if one resists, press the lower lip over the bars with your thumb. As the horse opens his mouth, slip the bit in and lift the crownpiece up, first over his off ear and then his near ear, pushing the ears forward to do so. Pull the mane and forelock out from under the crownpiece, which should now lie in the hollow just behind the poll. Adjust the browband so that it is level and not pinching the ears. Straighten and fasten the noseband, throatlatch and curb chain and slide up the keepers. A plain, dropped noseband should be adjusted snugly with the nosepiece level with the juncture of the mouthpiece and ring of the bit (about three inches above the nostrils). The chin pieces are buckled below the bit in the chin groove.

Every part of the bridle has an important job to do when adjusted properly. The crownpiece holds the cheekpieces which hold the bit. The browband and the throatlatch help keep the bridle in place in an emergency. The browband should not be so loose as to sag in the middle nor so tight as to pull at the crownpiece. The throatlatch should be loose enough so that it will not cut the horse's breathing as he moves his head and as the windpipe expands when galloping. You should be able to insert three fingers vertically between the strap and the throat. The noseband should be low enough so that it will not rub the cheekbones and yet not so low as to pinch the corners of the lips when the bit is in action. It should be fitted snugly so as to discourage the horse from opening his mouth to avoid the pressure of the bit.

The curb chain should lie flat when the bit is in action. Always test by pulling on the curb rein and watching whether or not the sharp edge of the chain digs in to the chin groove. If it does, then unhook one end of the curb chain and make a half-twist in it backward before hooking again.

The bit is adjusted according to its type and the conformation of the horse's mouth. The mouthpiece of the bit should not project out more than one-fourth inch on either side of the horse's lips, but neither should it be so short that the rings pinch the corners of the mouth. A snaffle bit should hang in the mouth so that it is high enough to just touch the corners of the horse's lips, possibly creating one wrinkle. It should *not* rattle against the incisors or the tushes (the extra set of teeth behind the incisors of male horses and occasionally female horses), nor be placed high enough to pull on the corners of the mouth and rattle against the molars or wolf teeth (rudimentary teeth in front of the molars of male horses). If the horse has a tendency to get his tongue over the bit, the bit should be adjusted slightly higher than usual.

Remember that wolf teeth can be quite sore when they are being cut. If your young horse that has had a quiet mouth starts to fuss, be suspicious of the wolf teeth. Depending on the conformation of the horse's mouth and the bit used, the wolf teeth can also be in the way of the bit. If you suspect his teeth to be a problem, ask your veterinarian if they should be pulled. Remember also that the horse's upper jaw is wider than the lower jaw, so that only the inner edges of the upper molars and the outer edges of the lower molars receive any wear. Depending on the type of food and the consistency of the teeth, the other edges develop sharp points and should be floated (filed) at least once a year, or even more often if you suspect that sharp edges are chafing the horse's cheek or tongue.

A pelham or Kimberwicke should rest in the middle of the bars and just touch the corners of the mouth. On a double bridle the bridoon should be adjusted like a snaffle and the curb like a pelham. When you have adjusted the bit and it appears comfortable from the outside, then pull the horse's lips apart and see where it is resting inside his mouth. Then pull gently on the reins and see where it rests under pressure. A simple way to check whether a bit is too low is to push it gently up to the corners of his mouth; if the cheekpieces bulge out loosely, then they should be tightened.

II · Basic
Riding Skills

4

Your Basic Position, and How to Mount and Dismount

If you have tacked up your horse yourself, you *know* that the tack is safe and properly adjusted. Even so, the next step is to check the girth again for tightness before mounting. Most horses expand their bellies and resist against the pull of the girth; some do this so much that it can make a three- or four-hole difference in the adjustment of the girth. If you check the girth just before you mount, the horse will have had time to relax since the saddle was first placed on his back, and you can probably tighten it another hole or two.

You should check the girth again after you have been on the horse's back for a couple of minutes, and yet again after an hour's riding or before jumping. To check or tighten a girth while mounted, place your leg with your foot in the stirrup in front of the saddle flap, pull the flap up, and reach for the billet with one hand. Practice this operation until you can do it by feel without looking for the holes in the billets.

When someone else has tacked up your horse, inspect the condition and fit of your tack before mounting. The finer points of adjusting the saddle and bridle take time to learn but even a novice can check the essentials. Go to the off (right) side and check that everything is adjusted as described earlier in "Tacking Up"; lift the outer flap of the saddle to see that the girth is prop-

After tightening the girth, pull each of the horse's front legs forward to re-lease any loose skin that may be pinched under the girth.

erly attached, buckle cover down, and skirt lying flat. Repeat the procedure on the near side and check the girth for tightness.

When the girth is tight, it is a good idea to pull each of the horse's front legs well forward by facing him and grasping them firmly just below the knee. These actions will pull any loose skin that may be pinched under the girth, preventing galls (sores).

You can check that the length of the stirrup is approximately correct by placing the heel of your hand at the buckle, which should be pulled up tight against the stirrup bar, and measuring the leather along your arm. If the length is about right, the bottom of the stirrup should touch your armpit.

MOUNTING

Now you are ready to learn how to mount properly. Just getting aboard in a haphazard fashion may seem all right when you try it on a quiet, small horse on home ground. But if you try a clumsy technique on a fresh or nervous horse, or when you are out in the country and your horse is eager for a good canter, you may well become a horseless rider.

When preparing to mount, always stand the horse so that his legs are relatively square; if one leg is way out of position, you may throw him off balance in the act of mounting. Once your horse is standing more or less squarely, move close to his left shoulder, facing the rear. Then with your left hand gather up the reins, adjusting them short enough to prevent the horse from moving forward, and grasp the mane. (If the mane has been roached or clipped off, grasp his withers.) With your right hand, grasp the right branch of the stirrup, the one that is to the rear, and place your left foot in the stirrup, being careful not to dig your toe into the horse's side as you do so. Then grasp the cantle, or even better, the far side of the seat if you can reach it, with your right hand and swing up, springing off your right foot and pulling up your body with your arms. Keep your back as straight as possible. As you swing your leg over the horse's quarters, being careful not to kick him, move your right hand to the pommel for balance and gently ease your body into the saddle. Never land with a thump, as this is very hard on the horse's back.

If you are short and the horse is tall, you will find it difficult to reach the stirrup. Do not struggle, as this may make the horse fidgety. It is much better to let the stirrup leather down two or three holes; more than this would make it difficult for you to swing your leg over the horse's quarters.

Face the rear to mount, so that if the horse moves forward, he will help you swing up into the saddle rather than move away from you. Be careful not to dig your toe into his belly or to brush his quarters as you swing your right leg over.

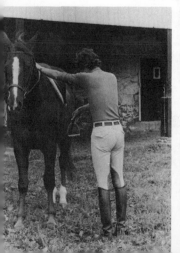
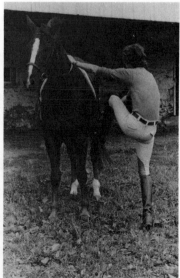

Once in the saddle, you should check the length of the stirrups. To find the correct length for ordinary riding, sit squarely in the center of the saddle, allowing your legs to hang straight down. If the bottoms of the stirrup irons touch the middle of your ankle bones, your stirrups are approximately the correct length for ordinary hacking. Of course, the correct length may vary a hole or two, depending on the conformation of the horse and the style in which you ride. You will usually need to shorten your stirrups a hole if you switch from riding a very broad horse to a narrow horse, and, if you are going to do any jumping, you want shorter stirrups than if you are only going to ride on the flat.

To adjust a stirrup, the best way for novices is to remove your foot and place your leg in front of the saddle flap. Pull the buckle well out from the saddle with the nearest hand and loop the reins over the other arm, freeing that hand. After making the adjustment, make sure that the buckle is pulled back tightly against the stirrup bar. Always make the horse stand straight and quietly while you are mounting and adjusting your stirrups and reins. To mount easily and correctly takes practice, but once you know how, you can mount any horse anywhere.

Once you are more at home in the saddle, you should learn to adjust the stirrups with one hand, which is actually easier. Do not remove your foot from the stirrup; simply bring your knee away from the saddle and reach for the free end of the stirrup leather, close to the buckle. Pull it away from the bar and *up*, and you will free the tongue; then by maintaining enough foot pressure to keep the leather stretched, you can adjust the buckle up or down with ease. When it is in the right position, use your index finger to push in the tongue, and then pull the buckle back tight against the stirrup bar as before. With practice you can adjust stirrups this way in a matter of seconds.

No matter how gracefully you mount, there is always some tendency to pull the saddle crooked in the process, especially if the horse has mutton withers. One solution is to have a groom or helper counterbalance your weight by pulling down on the off stirrup leather. After you are accomplished in the art of mounting, you can use a mounting block or convenient wall, or get a "leg-up." A leg-up means that someone grasps your left knee and

Getting a "leg-up" from a friend is helpful with a tall or restless horse.

ankle and quickly boosts you up while you spring off your right foot. Usually you make a little anticipatory hop to indicate that you're ready. Your hands and arms work as if you were mounting by yourself, and it is particularly important to keep your back straight.

As soon as you are "up" you should sort out the reins, making sure there are no twists. A help in learning to pick up the reins properly is to lay one rein at a time across the horse's neck, turn your knuckles up and then grasp the rein. If it is a single rein it should enter your hand either outside your little finger or between it and your ring finger, as you or your teacher prefers. (Some people believe that you have a more delicate feel if the rein comes to your ring finger.) The ends are grasped between your thumbs and forefingers. The bight, which is the center of the reins where they are buckled or sewn together, should hang down the horse's right shoulder inside the right rein.

If there are two reins, as with a pelham or double bridle, the snaffle rein should enter the hand outside the little finger and the curb rein should enter between the little finger and the ring finger. The thumb is kept firmly on the reins as they fall over the forefinger, preventing them from slipping and keeping their ends in place. The first time you use two reins they will seem like ten and you may feel that you will never be able to handle them. Nevertheless, you will become accustomed to them quite quickly and you should not avoid using a pelham bridle for this reason.

The usual way to hold double reins is with the snaffle outside the little finger, and the curb between it and the ring finger. (The bite of the reins should hang straight down in front of the saddle, not be curled up in a bunch like this.)

BASIC POSITION

With your reins under control you should next check your position to see if you are ready to walk. You should be seated in the deepest part of the saddle, which should be slightly forward of the middle, with your back straight, neither arched forward nor rounded backward. Your eyes look straight ahead, using the horse's ears as guideposts. Try not to look down, as this will make you lean forward and round your shoulders; instead, keep your head erect and draw your shoulders back to a comfortable degree. Your arms should drop naturally from your shoulders so that your elbows are bent and are slightly in front of your hips. Your forearms, hands and reins should form an unbroken line to the bit. In order to do this, your hands should be held three or four inches apart, just above the withers. The palm should be turned about ten degrees inside the vertical toward the horse. If the hand is held either absolutely vertical, or completely flattened so that the knuckles are up, it will tend to make your forearm stiff and will slightly break the straight line to the bit.

Your weight should rest squarely on your seatbones and then

A good basic position; the upper body is upright but supple; the leg is firm with the ankle nicely flexed. The hands could be a bit higher.

filter through your inner thigh, knee, calf and ankle to the heel. Your leg should not be clamped to the saddle, but should still cling firmly against it. The leg muscles will automatically tighten to hold you on the horse when necessary if the legs are in the correct position. Your lower leg must be drawn slightly back from your knee so that the stirrup leather hangs straight down. As you shorten your stirrups for jumping, the angle of the knee will close, but the stirrup leather must still remain absolutely vertical. Remember, your leg will give the greatest support and encourage the best balance in the upper body and the strongest seat if your heel is placed in the same vertical plane as your hipbone.

The ball of the foot should rest on the inside of the stirrup iron and the toe should point as nearly straight ahead as possible unless you walk like a duck. If your toes turn out they tend to pull the inside of your leg away from the saddle, and the grip moves toward the back of the leg. This you do not want. Of course, the opposite extreme is also wrong, for if your toes turn in too much, the ankle will be cramped and the lower calf will be loosened.

The position just described is the basic position that you will maintain while riding at a walk. At other times it is subject to many variations; as the horse's speed increases your upper body must incline progressively forward, and your seat will even leave the saddle for galloping and jumping; your lower leg will move further back to give certain signals, and should brace in front under other circumstances, such as a horse bucking with his head down. But this is the basic neutral position from which you move to other positions and to which you constantly return. You should feel relaxed and comfortable and should not feel any strain on any particular part of the body. Of course, until your muscles are conditioned you will have to exert a certain amount of effort, particularly in the thighs and calf.

How can you tell if your position is correct? A mirror or an instructor is ideal but not always available. However, there are many other ways of checking yourself. One way to put your seat in the right place in the saddle is to take your feet out of the stirrups and try to touch your knees over the pommel. Then drop your legs straight down without shifting your seat. To put your feet in the stirrups, roll your knee and thigh inward and upward into position until you can slip your foot into the stirrup without moving the leather out of its perpendicular line. Always make sure that the front edge of the leather and of the stirrup turn to the outside or the leather will dig into your shin and certain styles of stirrups will be in the wrong position. Grasp your inner thigh muscle from behind with your hand and pull it backward. If this is possible, that muscle needs further conditioning.

At the walk and halt you should be able to rise out of the saddle by leaning slightly forward and not using your hand for support. This is a good exercise for perfecting your balance and for pushing your weight all the way down into your heels. You should not be able to see your toes in front of your knees.

Now for some signs that your position is incorrect: as the horse moves out, if your upper body rocks forward or backward, if your hands jump up and down, if your legs move or flop around, if you feel uncomfortable, or if you tire or stiffen too quickly. But, remember, it takes some time to be able to maintain the correct seat even at a walk. At first, everybody slides around in the saddle and feels unsure. You will have to develop balance, relaxation and grip, all of which come from practice before you can gain confidence in yourself and the horse. Riding is a sport in which both the rider and the ridden must be athletes building their muscles, refining their coordination and learning their jobs together.

DISMOUNTING

To dismount: take your reins in your left hand with a short enough hold to prevent the horse from moving forward. Remove your right foot from the stirrup. Put your left hand on the horse's withers and your right hand on the pommel. Push your body up a little with your arms and your left leg. Swing your right leg over the horse's quarters, making sure not to kick him. As your leg clears the quarters, shift your right hand to the cantle to maintain your balance. Drop your right leg alongside your left and, shifting all your weight to your arms, slip your left foot out of the stirrup. Slide to the ground, pushing yourself slightly away from the horse. Run your left stirrup up to the stirrup bar on the inside of the leather, tuck the loose end of leather through the stirrup, and take the reins over the horse's head. Push the right stirrup up, and you are ready to lead your horse back to the cross-ties.

Always run your stirrups up as soon as you dismount because a horse can easily catch his teeth on a loose iron when biting at a fly and get hung up. Moreover, if he should get away from you, swinging stirrups tend to make him run farther and faster. As you are working around and leading your horse, keep the reins well clear of his front feet by putting your arm through the bight or holding it up with your hand. Remove the bridle by placing the reins up behind the horse's ears, undoing the throatlatch, noseband, and curb chain, lifting the crownpiece over his ears and waiting for him to drop the bit out of his mouth. Put on the halter, which you have hanging on your arm or nearby, tie your horse and remove the saddle by lifting, not dragging, it off his back. Hang your bridle on a convenient hook, quickly rinse the bit, and put your saddle on a saddle rack. If it is impossible to have a saddle rack available, then place the saddle very gently on a towel or pad with the pommel to the ground. When necessary, rest the cantle gently against the wall. Constant bruising of the leather across the pommel and cantle will cause it to split, ruining the tension across the seat and requiring a major repair job. Your saddle will be a good friend that will last a long time if treated with care. From here on, take care of your horse as already discussed in Chapter 2.

5

Signals and Controls
at the Walk and Trot

In riding, as in so much else, you must walk before you can run. The walk is the basic gait of the horse. The horse's feet all move independently of each other producing four distinct hoofbeats; only one foot is completely off the ground at a time. When the right foot is off the ground, the left rear is about to follow it, and it in turn is followed by the left front leg and finally the right hind leg. As it requires no effort on your part to stay on the horse's back at this pace, it gives you a good chance to learn about controlling yourself and the horse. Naturally, you are eager to get on with the more exciting aspects of riding. However, if you allow your teacher to help you acquire the foundation of good balance, a good seat and properly applied signals and controls, you will progress more smoothly and speedily at the trot, canter, etc.

Good teaching requires two-way communication, particularly during the first lessons when the teacher does not know the personality and physical capabilities of the student. Do talk to your teacher. Ask for explanations of terms and instructions you do not understand and tell him/her your problems. If you have a particular fear of falling or being stepped on or run away with, tell him. If your leg is being pinched, or you have a blister on your finger, or your hat is bothering you, or you are just plain tired, tell him. A good teacher can sense a lot of things but he is not psychic. Help him to help you.

THE WALK

To move from the halt to the walk, you must give your horse the correct signal, because, if he has been trained normally, he has learned to respond in certain ways to certain signals. The rider gives these signals mainly with his legs, hands, weight and seat. Occasionally, he uses his voice and/or a crop (whip) as reinforcement. If these signals are not given correctly or if the horse has not been correctly trained, he will not respond well and perhaps not at all.

Since you are just learning to ride, we will assume you have a quiet, normally trained horse and a controlled area such as a ring or paddock to work in. Under these circumstances you can practice the basic signals which will bring forth the desired response. As you progress you will learn more complicated sets of signals and controls (aids) to deal with more complicated situations.

Horses are individual personalities and not machines, and this distinction must never be forgotten. Even so, if you think of the various actions, familiar to most of us, that are necessary to drive a car, it may help you to understand more clearly the elementary actions that are necessary to "operate" your horse.

Before you can move a car, you must first turn on the motor. You must also "turn on" your horse before you ask him to move forward. You do this by establishing contact with his mouth by shortening your reins until you can feel a slight tension on the bit. Shorten your reins by grasping the right rein in front of the right thumb with your left thumb and forefinger; slide your right hand forward the desired amount. Then do the same with the left rein. Your reins should always be the same length. With the pelham bridle, the snaffle rein should be a little shorter than the curb rein unless you have a particular reason to use the stronger curb rein.

Establishing contact with the horse's mouth is the first in a chain of signals that tell your horse that there is something you want him to do. When he feels the light pressure of the bit his head should come into the correct position. If he is relaxed with his head down, he should raise it; if he is gazing around admiring the scenery he should straighten and lower it. How you complete the chain of signals tells your horse what particular action you wish him to take. As you become more accomplished in giving the right signals you may ask him to trot, canter, back or do various exercises from the halt.

Now we are going to ask him to walk straight forward. After you have turned the motor on, you put your car in gear to move forward. If your horse is standing with all four legs relatively square he is already "in gear." If he is resting a leg, or standing with one out of line, then squeeze your leg on the appropriate side to move the leg forward; keep the tension on the reins so that the whole horse does not move forward.

With car in gear, you release the brake and step on the gas to proceed. To move your horse into the walk you reverse this procedure. First you "step on the gas" by squeezing with both legs and at the same time you "release the brake" by shifting your weight *slightly* forward and giving (yielding) *slightly* with your hands. A properly trained horse will then move out promptly at the walk.

Unfortunately, not all horses are responsive, either from lack of training or from dullness, fatigue, or an inclination to ignore beginners. You will then squeeze harder with both legs; if this action does not get him into motion then you must give him two or three quick but definite taps with your lower leg in quick succession. This kind of pressure is called "intermittent." If this still does not move him forward he can be said to have "stalled" either from improperly applied signals or from some fault within himself. The instructor should tell you how to improve your signal giving or give you an "additive" in the form of a crop or spurs. Usually the novice should not use these artificial aids until he has learned to use his hands and legs independent of his body. However, some ponies and horses will respond more promptly if a whip is simply carried, not even used, or a pair of blunt spurs is worn to help get the message through a fat, furry side. Turning your heel in the horse's side, especially if you are wearing spurs, is probably the strongest way in which your legs can get his attention.

As the horse walks, his head moves forward and backward with each step to a greater or lesser degree depending on his conforma-

73

The whip is normally used to make the horse more responsive to the leg; therefore, it should be used on the horse's barrel, directly behind the calf of the rider's leg.

tion and the energy of his stride. If you keep your hands absolutely still he will then bump the bars of his mouth against the bit at each step, so your fingers and arms must give a little in rhythm with the swing of his head. The key to this soft contact with his mouth is the relaxation of your shoulders, elbows, wrists and fingers. Of course, the joints of your upper body cannot be steady and yet supple until your seat is secure from good balance supported by a firm leg lying flat against the horse with your weight sinking through your inner leg to the heel. Obviously, you will not develop a firm seat in a few rides so you will ride with your reins longer than ideal in order to insure that you will not hurt your horse's mouth. You will be riding in an enclosed area so that controlling your horse should not be a problem. But one of the first things you should practice is shortening your reins in quick, smooth motions so that you will be able to stop your horse if necessary.

As you are walking along, you should always look ahead in the direction in which you are going. Your shoulders will be still but your lower back and seat should move a little, not by their own will but rather following the motion of the horse. The legs will be still but will maintain a feel of the horse's sides. The lower leg should be ready to squeeze or tap if the horse slows down. To give "go forward" signals the position of the lower leg is "at the girth"; actually the foot is at the girth and the heel and lower leg are slightly behind it.

Constantly check your position at the walk, using the guidelines discussed in Chapter 4 under "Basic Position." Now add some new exercise, to increase your confidence, suppleness and balance: keeping the rest of your body still, turn your head as far as you can to the left and then to the right; take slow, deep breaths, lifting your diaphragm and stretching the top of your head toward the sky; alternating arms, make slow smooth circles in the air with them. If your horse is perfectly quiet at the walk (or if your teacher puts you on a longe line so that you can safely drop the reins and leave the horse's conduct to him) there are many other valuable exercises which you can practice to improve your balance and the independence of your seat: Rotate your shoulder by placing your hands on your hips and twisting your upper body to the left and then to the right; take your feet out of the stirrups and lift your whole leg away from the horse, keeping the toes pointed forward, starting with one leg at a time and working up to both legs at a time; keeping your knee firm, swing your lower leg back and forth rhythmically; work your feet around in circles to loosen your ankle joints; cross your arms on your chest and then lower your upper body back to the horse's rump; swinging the right arm in a graceful arc, try to touch your left anklebone and vice versa; looking forward but leaning backward on your hand, run it down the horse's rump to the base of his tail. (But make sure first that he doesn't object!)

Do these exercises and others that you think may help your particular problems, first at the halt and then at the walk. Obviously you will not wish to do all of them every time you ride but three or four at the beginning of your ride and again in the middle will prove helpful. As with all exercises, start with a very few and work up to five or ten each; mix the difficult ones with the easy ones; never push a muscle to the point of strain.

THE HALT

Once you have learned to move your horse forward, you must learn how to stop him, that is bring him to a halt. Ideally, this is accomplished by sitting deeper in the saddle (no longer following the motion of the horse with your seat), closing both legs on the horse's sides and at the same time fixing your hands (no longer following the horse's head but rather closing the fingers on the reins). The first question you will ask is: *Why do I squeeze with my legs to halt when I also squeeze with my legs to go forward?* The answer is that when you squeeze with your legs, the horse moves his hind legs more forward under his belly; this is necessary so that he can move forward. When he is moving and you squeeze with your legs but restrain his forehand by fixing your hands, his hind legs step further forward which puts him in a better balance to slow down and to halt. This is a good example of what is meant by the series of signals and how it is the combination of them that is important.

Let us review: To walk: 1) Establish contact with the mouth; 2) Squeeze equally with both legs; 3) Shift weight slightly forward and give slightly with the hands. To halt: 1) Close the legs (through using less pressure than for the squeeze to go forward) and sit deeper in the saddle, shifting the weight slightly backward; 2) Fix the hands and smoothly close the fingers. The second he obeys, relax the pressure on the bit to reward him.

What if you have faithfully applied all these signals in their proper order and coordination, but the horse has not come to a halt? There are two usual reasons for this lack of response from the horse to the novice rider. First of all, the rider probably has leaned forward rather than sitting more upright and more heavily in the saddle. Leaning forward at every change of pace, and at any little problem, is a common fault with a new rider and should be corrected as soon as possible. To the horse leaning forward even slightly lightens your weight on his back and means "go"; leaning backward, even slightly, means "stop." You must make sure that your upper body is really giving the correct signals to the horse. The second most common problem with the novice rider getting his

Holding the reins in one hand. Reins with rubber hand-parts like these are useful in sports in which the horse becomes heavily lathered.

signals through to the horse is that his reins are too long. Up to a point, this is unavoidable. Until your seat is secure and your upper body is supple you cannot maintain a contact with the horse's mouth without hurting him, but the problem is not serious.

We have described the ideal way to apply the rein signals to halt, but if they have no effect, because of the inexperience of the rider or the horse, then other steps must be taken. First, draw back both hands a couple of inches to the rear and then fix the hands and close the fingers again. If this has no effect, then the reins are too long and must be shortened and the above action repeated. The hands should move backward straight toward the waistline, neither higher nor lower, and should never end up in your lap; this is simply another sign that your reins are too long. When your horse has done what you have asked of him nicely, it's a good idea to give him an occasional pat or a rub on the shoulder or neck. You may carry your reins in one hand by (1) taking the other rein and placing it under the little finger or the ring finger (whichever is free) and laying it so that it comes over the fore-finger with the other rein or (2) taking the other rein and laying

The leading rein: the hand leads the horse in the new direction by moving away from the horse's neck.

it over the forefinger so that it comes into the hand from the opposite side and on top of the first rein. The second way is generally preferred.

Having discussed the very simplest aids at a walk and a halt, we can now do the same for the turn and for backing. Your brain and body can only absorb and apply so many lessons at one time. Your main concern during your first lessons should be to acquire some feeling of the horse and his reactions, confidence in him and yourself, and to establish the correct position. If you do not acquire a good seat (correct position) you will be unable to give elementary signals and controls consistently, much less the more advanced aids.

The leading or opening rein is the simplest for the rider to use and the horse to understand in order to make a turn. The rider takes the inside rein and, turning his thumb a little more upright, carries the hand sideways away from the horse's neck thus leading the horse's head toward the new direction. As the head turns, the outside hand advances slightly to allow for the bend in the neck. The further the hand moves away from the horse's neck, the more the horse's head will bend and therefore the whole horse will make a sharper turn or a smaller circle. The hand must not come up, pull back or move down but simply move straight away from the horse's neck. A common tendency and a bad mistake is to pull the rein down and back toward your knee. Once the horse has accomplished the amount of turn you have asked for, return the hand to its original position close to the withers.

78

When you feel confident in this rein use, you should start to think of where you should place your weight; on turns and circles it should favor the inside seatbone. You should always look in the direction in which the horse is moving, so your head should now be turned slightly to the inside. As you turn your head your outside shoulder and hand should advance. These two actions in themselves will shift your weight slightly to the inside. If you also think of sitting a little more heavily on your inside seatbone, you will have shifted your weight to the inside. To put it another way, your shoulders should follow the horse's shoulders: on a straight line a horse's shoulders are square to the front and yours should be, too; on a curved line the horse's outside shoulder is advanced further forward than the inside shoulder, and your shoulders should shift accordingly. When you return to the straight line, make sure you straighten out your upper body and hands.

At first you will find it necessary to think of each of these actions step by step but, if you truly work at it, they will quickly become second nature. Try hard to do them correctly, for it is easier to form good habits than to correct bad habits, and hence it is important for you to really practice these basic rein and weight aids at the walk. It will be much easier to get them working together now than later on, when you are involved with the more complicated actions and balances at the trot and canter. Then you will have more to do and less time to do it in. Riding circles, half-circles and serpentines will help you to develop your skills.

How not to bend your horse around the corner: Marge is looking down at the horse instead of in the direction toward which she wishes to move. Her high outside hand is pulling the horse to the outside, and he is both overbent and bent away from the turn.

You will discover that it is not easy to ride either a straight line or a round circle, even at a walk. You will find these patterns useful at the other paces as well.

REIN BACK

Although a horse must attain a certain level of training before he can move backward properly, the signals given by the rider are relatively simple; I will discuss them here in case you get into a situation in which you *must* back up for the horse's or your own safety. Otherwise, do not attempt to back your horse up until you have coordinated your signals and controls.

A horse should move backward by moving to the rear first one set of diagonal legs, and then the other in a measured, step-by-step fashion and in a straight line. The horse's head must not move out of its correct position, its body must remain straight and the legs must neither drag nor hurry to the rear.

In order to achieve these actions, the rider should first give the horse the signals to move *forward;* then as he lifts the front leg to do so, the rider directs that leg backward by taking a stronger feel of the reins. The rider's hands do not *move* backward and attempt to pull the horse to the rear. Rather, he asks the horse to move by closing his legs at the girth, remaining upright with the upper body but sitting a little lighter in the saddle and, in-

Posting on the right diagonal: Barbara is in the saddle as the right front leg and left hind leg are on the ground; she will rise as they rise. Note that very low hands tend to round the rider's shoulders.

stead of yielding (giving) with the hands (fingers) so that the horse may move forward, he then increases the tension on the reins so that the horse will move backward. If the horse resists, move him forward a couple of steps or just pat him on the neck and then ask again. If nothing at all happens, or you find your hands coming back toward your lap, then shorten your reins. Hopefully you are riding a horse that already knows the signals to back; to teach them takes some expertise, and if the methods described don't work, you'd better ask your teacher to help.

THE TROT

As soon as you are quite confident at the walk, it is time to think about trotting. Though the easy movement of the walk does not require any effort from the rider to remain on the horse's back, the trot poses more of a problem to the novice. The trot is a distinct two-beat movement in which one diagonal pair of feet, i.e., right front and left rear, is off the ground while the other diagonal pair of feet is on the ground. The swinging back movement produced by the stepping of alternate pairs of feet gives a distinct thrust to the rider's seat, depending on how high the horse lifts his legs from the ground, how fast he is trotting and how supple his back is. This thrust can give the rider quite a shaking up if he does not know how to synchronize with it.

The easiest way for the rider to avoid the bumps to his seat is to post or rise to the trot. The rider keeps time with one diagonal pair of legs; for instance he rises as the right front foot and the left rear foot leave the ground and he sits as they return to the ground. This should require very little effort as the thrust of the hind leg helps to lift him out of the saddle. The seat should rise as little out of the saddle as possible and still keep time with the movement of the horse's legs. The higher the horse steps, the higher the rider must rise. When you are starting to trot, just concentrate on the one-two, up-down rhythm.

Practice posting first at the walk. Shift your weight slightly forward and rising a little out of the saddle, by pushing down your inner thigh to your knee and then down into your heel. Do not pop yourself out of the saddle by pushing hard on the stirrup. At the walk, trot and canter the stirrup is merely a resting place for your foot. Sink back gently into the saddle, keeping your weight slightly forward and your shoulders slightly in front of the vertical.

When you have the feel of posting at a walk, then try it at a trot. Hopefully you will not have to worry about controlling your horse, so that all you need think about is getting the rhythm of the trot. Placing your knuckles just in front of the withers and leaning on them a little will make you more secure and help you to get started. Have someone call the right tempo to you (such as up-down or one-two) and repeat it to yourself. Once you get the rhythm, then raise your knuckles off the neck and carry them in the proper position, but still use a long rein so you will not bump the horse's mouth. Without the support of your arms you will find it more difficult to keep the rhythm, but do not be discouraged. It may take several rides before you can post with any regularity at all. If you completely lose the rhythm, replace your knuckles in front of the withers.

Once your body learns the trotting rhythm it will never forget. This goes for all the basic techniques of riding. Once you have learned them, you may stop riding for years and still take up where you left off except for a little unsteadiness and a sore muscle or two. Speaking of sore muscles, they are mostly caused by tension and overdoing. If you remind yourself often to relax and do not overdo each new step, you should never have an ache after riding.

Once you have confidence in your posting, it is time to check your position. It is bound to have gotten a little out of whack while you have been concentrating on getting the feel of the rising trot, and some details of the perfect position will probably have been ignored. Now is the time to correct any errors before you form bad habits. Are you looking straight ahead, not down or to the side? Are your shoulders square and is your back straight? Is your seat returning to the center of the saddle every time, and is your weight pushing down from your hips through your whole inner leg to the inner anklebone and then to the back of the heel? Is your foot at the girth and your lower leg just behind it? Is the ball of your foot square and to the inside portion of the stirrup?

Guard against leaning too far forward and pushing your seat to the rear. You will be able to post in this fashion but you will be out of balance with your horse. Check your hands. At the trot they should remain still, for the horse does not swing his head at this pace. At first your hands will move up and down as you rise and sit because your elbow joints are stiff. Place your forefingers on either side of the withers and feel the angles of your elbows open as you rise and close as you sit.

Whenever your hands start to move at the trot, replace your forefingers on the withers until they become steady. It will take quite a few rides for your hands to become consistently steady at the trot, because your seat will not be firm. Your seat will not be firm until your leg muscles are stretched and under control so that your leg remains steady at the girth, where it normally belongs. If your foot shoots out in front of the girth, the seat will drop toward the back of the saddle; you will find yourself heaving your upper body forward in order to keep up with the motion of the horse. If your foot slips behind the girth, your leg will not be in position to support your upper body and your knee will become your principal base of support. This position is both insecure and tiring.

Once you have mastered the basic mechanics of posting, it is time for you to take over the control of the horse. You move the horse from the walk to the trot with the same set of signals you use to move him from the halt to the walk. Shorten your reins until you have a light feel of his mouth. Shift your weight slightly forward and close your legs on the horse's sides with squeeze-hold motions, and yield a little with your fingers. If the horse does not take up the trot, then wake him up with an intermittent tap, tap of your lower leg.

When you are posting, you are rising and sitting in time with one pair of diagonal legs. If you are rising at the same time the right front leg is off the ground, you are said to be posting on the right diagonal; if you are rising when the left front leg is off the ground, you are on the left diagonal. You do not have to lean forward and look for the horse's knee to know which leg is up; simply glance at the shoulder without moving your head. When the point of the shoulder is forward, the leg is in the air; when the point of the shoulder is back (in its normal, standing position) the foot is on the ground.

Traditionally the rider posts on the outside diagonal in horsemanship classes and in the dressage arena when turning or circling, i.e., moving clockwise he should be on the left diagonal. There are arguments pro and con as to which diagonal to use on a circle, but the new horseman will always be safe posting on the outside diagonal.

It is important that the horse be worked equally on both diagonals so that both hind legs develop evenly. All green (unschooled) horses have a preference for one diagonal because one hind leg is stronger than the other. Some have such a strong preference that they are constantly trying to bounce the rider onto their favorite diagonal. When working in the ring, change to the new outside diagonal every time you change direction. You do this by sitting in the saddle for one beat and then rising with the other front leg. If you miss two beats and then rise, you will be back on the original diagonal. On straight lines, the diagonal use is less important. However, remember to change diagonals occasionally when riding cross-country and out foxhunting. If a horse has a rough diagonal, work on this one for a greater part of the time.

Just as a green horse has a favorite diagonal, he also has a side to which it is easier for him to bend, usually the left. The reason for this is believed to be that most foals lie in utero bent to the left. It is good for the rider to know the horse's "easy" side and plan his ride with it in mind. If the supple side is the left, then start riding him around the ring to the left. When he is warmed up and going well then circle him to the right. When you become more experienced, you will work on his stiff side until the horse eventually will bend to either side with equal ease. You too have a strong side and a weak side—you are either right-handed or left-handed. Hence you will soon find that it is easier to keep one leg firmer than the other and one hand more steady and relaxed than the other. You, too, must work on the weak side until it improves, for both your and the horse's stiff side will always need a little extra attention.

SITTING TROT

Not posting to the trot—sitting to it—is even harder for the novice than rising to it. At the sitting trot, the seat remains in the saddle and the lower back absorbs the thrust of the hind legs, instead of letting the seat rise to avoid this thrust. You should first try the sitting trot on a smooth-moving horse or pony that is willing to dog trot (jog slowly), until you get the feel of the movement. The reason the western riders can ride a "close seat" for hours is that their horses are bred to move at the trot with a very flat stride that hardly breaks at the knee. Most hunter-type horses bend more at the knee, their hock joints producing a bouncier trot. However, there is a wide range in the way horses move and once your seat learns to follow the movement, you can ride any horse at a sitting trot.

Move your horse out at a slow trot with your upper body upright. At first you may grasp the pommel lightly with one hand to help steady your seat. Thinking of the one-two motion of the trot, let your seat follow it by giving in your lower back. Make a particular effort not to become tense, as stiffness in the back or pinching with the knees and lifting the heels will make you bounce even more. Just let the horse carry you along. When in doubt, lean *back*—no matter what they say!

When you are confident, take your feet out of the stirrups, pull the buckle down a few inches from the stirrup bar and cross the stirrups in front of the pommel. The sitting trot without stirrups is the best exercise to get your whole leg long and flat against the horse. Do not let your toes hang down. Actually you will probably find it easier to practice the sitting trot without stirrups, as you will be forced to use your whole leg to stay close to the horse; when your foot is in the stirrup, there is a natural tendency to push on it with the ball of your foot. This actually pushes your seat up and away from the horse's back. So when you do take the stirrup back, be sure to duplicate the feel of the leg and the foot that you had at the sitting trot without stirrups. Your leathers will feel shorter than they did before you had ridden without them and you should take advantage of this feel by sinking your weight down

Practicing the sitting trot: the upper body is more upright than at the rising trot, the weight sinks through the inner leg, and your inside hand grasps the pommel lightly. When you catch the rhythm, remove your hand from the pommel and pick up both reins.

more into your heel and developing a springier ankle.

Be absolutely sure at all times that your stirrup leathers are of equal length. Until you have stretched and developed the leg on your weak side you may think that the leather on that side is longer and shorten it accordingly. This will make you shift your weight to the opposite side and certainly not strengthen your weak leg. Before mounting, check that your stirrups are level by running them down the leathers and, standing the horse squarely, step back facing the horse. If you are still not sure that the stirrups are even, then pull the leathers off the saddle and measure one against the other. New leathers will stretch several holes and the simple act of mounting will tend to stretch one leather more than the other. If this has happened, reverse the leathers and make a mark on the leather next to the holes that are equal, e.g., eight and nine, and adjust up and down from the mark, not from the number. Eventually if you keep checking, you can get the leathers the same length again.

TURNING

When you are describing the inside of the horse or the inside signals, you are speaking of the side toward which the horse is

86

bent; when bent to the right, the right side is the inside and the left is the outside. Once your seat is secure at the trot and your hands remain steady at the withers, it is time to learn a more subtle rein signal for turning which is called the direct rein or the direct rein of opposition. It is called the direct rein because your hand remains in position in a direct line to the bit and turns the horse's head by increasing the tension on the inside rein, while the hand on the outside rein yields forward just enough to allow the horse's head to bend the right amount for the size of the turn. You increase the tension on the rein by closing the fingers and fixing the hand.

If your reins are too long, as they probably still are, you will have to move your hand a little to the rear, toward your hipbone, to increase the tension, but do this gently. There is no need to pull the horse's head around; you simply wish him to look in the new direction. This rein is also called the direct rein of opposition as it opposes the hind leg on the same side. This means that it tends to slow down and direct the hind leg on that side to the outside. However, you do not wish the hind leg to do this. You wish the hind leg to keep up the same rhythm and continue to step in the marks made by the front foot on the same side. In order to insure that this will happen, you will increase the feel with your inside leg in a squeeze-relax motion. Your outside leg should slide a little

Turning with a direct rein: the inside hand squeezes the rein directly toward the inside hip while the inside leg squeezes at the girth. This encourages the horse to bend around the rider's leg and to step well under with his inside hind leg.

How not to execute a turn with the direct rein: Barbara is pulling the horse around with her inside hand and dropping her shoulder, causing him to lose his balance to the inside; her high outside hand is crossing over the withers, compounding the problem.

behind the girth and maintain a steady feel of the horse's side to prevent the hindquarters from drifting to the outside.

When turning, the inside hand tells the horse what direction to take. The inside leg remains at the girth and increases its feel to keep the horse moving forward and to encourage him to bend his body in the arc of the circle. The outside hand controls the amount of bend in the horse's neck and also his speed. Both hands remain at the same height at all times; watch out for unlevelness while turning.

You are now muttering to yourself that you cannot possibly remember to do all these things, and the horse turns just fine if you simply increase the feel of the inside rein. It is true that you will have to concentrate on coordinating these signals at first, but it will not be long before they become conditioned reflexes. Although your horse may not need all these aids to trot quietly around a large ring, he is going to need more instructions to canter, work in smaller circles, work without the guidance of a ring, etc.

Practice the signals first at a walk, first concentrating on the way that the hands are working together, then the legs. Ride in different patterns such as serpentines (making S-shaped loops), figure-eights and diagonal lines across the center of the arena in order to change direction, and alternate smaller circles with larger ones. When all your aids are working in coordination, then practice them at a trot.

6

Learning to Canter and Gallop

THE CANTER

The canter is a three-beat movement which can be started from either hind leg. *First beat* of the canter to the right from the walk: the left hind leg strikes off, remaining on the ground as the other three legs move into the air. *Second beat:* the left hind leg starts to leave the ground, the left front leg and right hind leg strike the ground and the right front leg starts to descend. *Third beat:* the right front leg strikes the ground, the left hind leg has left the ground and the diagonal legs start to leave the ground; this beat is completed when all the legs but the right front are in the air, and the full weight of the horse is supported on the right front leg. There is then a moment of suspension when all four feet are in the air before the sequence begins again as the left hind leg strikes the ground. The horse is now on the right lead.

This sequence of hoofbeats produces a smooth, rolling motion in contrast to the distinct two-beat movements of the trot. The rider needs only to sit in the saddle, his upper body upright, his legs clinging comfortably to the horse's side, his weight sinking into his heels and his whole body allowing the horse to carry him along. At first you should not worry about the exact signals to break a horse into a canter. If you are having a private lesson and the horse is on a longe line, the instructor will start the horse off. Put your reins in one hand and, grasping the pommel lightly, be

prepared to canter from the walk or sitting trot. As the instructor says canter, close your legs on the horse's sides and glue your seat to the saddle by sitting firmly on your seatbones and relaxing your lower back. The thrust of the driving hind legs must be absorbed in your lower back which yields to the front just as in the sitting trot. If the back is tense or rounded, you will bounce.

Be prepared to grip a little harder just as the horse strikes off as this is the most difficult movement to absorb. If you do not get bounced loose at the first stride, you should be able to rock along for several strides before you start to slide around. As soon as you lose the rhythm, bring the horse back to a walk and try again when you get organized. There is no benefit at these early stages of cantering in struggling to regain your seat because your bouncing on the horse's back will only upset his stride and make it more difficult for you to keep your seat.

Easy does it with all your new experiences. Tension, conscious or subconscious, is your biggest enemy. By grasping the pommel with one hand you can lean back slightly, keeping your body upright, thus allowing your weight to settle squarely on your seatbones.

The added security of holding onto the pommel will help to relax your lower back so that it can give with the swing of the horse's back, allowing the seatbones to slide fractionally backward and forward. Once you can feel the swinging movement of the

The horse's footfall when cantering on the right lead: from the walk, the horse strikes off into the canter from his left hind leg, pushing his weight onto the right hind and left fore. As the left hind leg leaves the ground the right front leg advances to take over the supporting duties. As the right front strikes the ground, the left diagonal leg begins to leave the ground. The right front leg alone takes over the duty of supporting the horse. The final stage is a moment of suspension, with all four legs off the ground. (We wish the rider's hands were a little lower and more yielding on these pictures.)

canter and can follow it without bouncing, it is time to let go of the pommel.

Without the security of holding onto the pommel, you must concentrate on sitting upright and allowing your seat to cling to the saddle. If you lean forward, you will lighten your seat and it will be bounced out of the saddle. Do not be disappointed if your ability to stick with the canter seems to degenerate without the aid of grasping the pommel. Keep seeking the feel of the canter when it was right and it will come back quickly. Of course, keep checking that your basic position is correct. When you are secure, shorten your reins until you have a light contact with the horse's mouth. At the canter the horse swings his head slightly forward and backward at each stride. Your fingers and arms must give and take in rhythm with this movement so that the tension on the reins remains even.

The rider is sitting well at the canter, but the horse demonstrates some resistance to the bit by his open mouth and tense jaw.

Striking off on the correct lead. Once you can control yourself and the horse at the canter, you must learn to give the correct set of signals to tell him which lead you wish him to take. When a horse is turning, he must always be on the inside lead, as all his weight is thrown in the direction of the leading front leg that is the sole base of support when the other three legs are in the air. He is obviously out of balance if he is on the outside lead while being turned to the opposite direction. (Try running around a tight circle while leading to the outside, and you will feel the problem.) If the horse is on the outside lead, he is also more likely to cross his legs and possibly trip, especially at speed or on sharp turns. The exception to the rule that the horse should always be on the inside lead when turning is a dressage movement called the counter-canter which requires the horse to canter on the outside lead. However, this exercise is beyond the scope of the novice as the horse and rider must be very well balanced to execute this exercise properly.

There are two principal sets of signals taught to horses to tell them which lead to take, and if you are riding a strange horse you may have to ask which way he has been trained. We will first discuss the set of signals in which the *diagonal aids* predominate. The outside rein and the inside leg give the primary instructions. The outside rein turns the horse's head slightly to the outside, thus freeing the inside shoulder and encouraging that front leg to lead.

The rider's inside leg is used in a driving manner in order to tell the horse that a faster pace is desired. The rider's outside leg remains at the girth with a steady feel of the horse's side ready to support the inside leg, if necessary. The rider's weight is on the inside seatbone. As soon as the horse strikes off with the proper lead, his head is turned in the direction in which he is moving. The advantage of using diagonal aids is that they almost force the horse to take the correct lead, no matter how badly balanced he is; the disadvantage is that the horse is not faced in the direction in which he is going to proceed. If you are interested in higher equitation or dressage, you will be teaching your horse incorrectly.

The best way to ask a horse to take the correct lead is with the predominantly *lateral aids*. The inside rein bends the horse's head very slightly to the inside and the rider's inside leg with a driving motion instructs the horse to take up the new pace. The outside hand prevents the horse from turning his head too much and the outside leg slides back slightly and with a steady feel keeps the quarters from drifting to the outside. The rider's weight is on the inside seatbone. At the moment you wish to take up the canter, use the outside leg in a push-hold motion to tell the horse that you wish his outside hind leg to push off into a canter.

"Working on the flat" is an expression used to describe a horse and/or rider striving to improve by concentrated work. "Hacking" is the expression used to describe a quiet ride along the trails. A ride cross-country would usually be understood to involve some galloping and jumping. Out hacking or riding cross-country, the canter is often developed from an ordinary trot, but when working on the flat, the horse should be asked to canter from the sitting trot or the walk, since at these gaits the rider has the full use of his seat and legs. It is easiest to start from the sitting trot and in a corner so that the horse is already bent in the right direction.

After you have established a good trot and have the horse's attention, ask him to canter. If he breaks into a rapid or an extended trot, bring him back to an ordinary trot before again asking him to canter. You do not wish the horse to fall into the canter simply from momentum but to break into the canter out of a balanced, rhythmic trot. The canter is not so much a faster pace as a change in the footfalls of the horse. The more rapid the trot, the more difficult it is for the horse to change the sequence of footfalls.

THE GALLOP

The hand gallop is simply an extended and faster canter. It is called the "hand" gallop because the horse is not asked for a full gallop at speed but kept "in hand." The horse's feet touch the ground in the same sequence as the canter, but the drive of the hind legs increases and the head lowers and stretches forward. At the canter the rider is in a full-seat or three-point position, that is, he is supported by his seat on the saddle, his legs against the side of the horse and his feet in the stirrups. At the gallop, the rider shifts his upper body somewhat forward, taking the weight off his seatbones and shifting it down through his knees into his heels. He has taken up a half-seat (two-point position); he is now supported only by his legs and the stirrups. The knee and ankle must now take on heavier duties than they had before. They must help carry the weight of the upper body and absorb the shock of the horse's increased momentum. The rider's joints have already learned part of this new job at the rising trot. However, the legs are not asked for sustained strength at the rising trot, for there usually is not much speed involved and the seat is out of the saddle only a second at a time. For the half-seat, the stirrup should be short enough for the knee to push down and forward while the ankle flexes and the heel sinks lower toward the ground.

Although the seat leaves the center of the saddle and moves more over the knees, it should not be raised so high that daylight is visible between it and the saddle. Shorten your stirrups one to three holes to gallop and jump, depending on how short you ride on the flat. There should be a definite angle created by the knee and thigh. If the stirrups are too long, you will feel that you are standing on your toes and your heels will be unable to sink down.

Take up the hand gallop from the canter. Shorten your reins, shift your weight forward off your seat onto your thighs, knees, calves and ankles and squeeze the horse forward with both legs into a longer and slightly faster stride. Keep a nice firm contact with his mouth, allowing your hands to follow his head forward. There will be a more pronounced swing to the horse's head the faster he moves, and your arms must give and take at the elbow in order to keep the reins stretched smoothly rather than flapping. The fingers and wrists must also act in a give-and-take motion.

Practice galloping at first on a straight stretch, preferably uphill. Ease the horse forward into the new pace and ease him down into the canter. As you feel him coming back to the canter, shift your upper body back to a more upright position. Do not expect to take back and pull up from the faster paces in one stride. This is hard on the horse physically and mentally. As your coordination and strength of your legs increase you will be able to ask for quicker stops and starts, but at first do everything gradually. If you or the horse is uncomfortable at a transition (moving from one pace to another), it is probably because you have asked for it too quickly.

After you are confident about hand galloping on the straightaway, practice in larger circles and up and down sloping ground. Then you are ready for a full gallop. This is not a run. Running is an entirely different gait and is only suitable for racehorses. At the full gallop the horse moves faster and with a longer stride

At the hand gallop, the horse extends his stride and stretches more into the bit. The rider shifts her weight off her seat and more into her thighs, knees and heels; her hands yield as the horse extends his neck, maintaining steady support.

than at the hand gallop. The rider's upper body is more forward and the reins are shorter. The horse is still under control at all times.

Consider your horse's condition and the footing seriously when you start galloping. He is not a machine that can go fast for any amount of time the driver wishes. He is made up of tissue and bone which must be slowly built up to withstand the strain. No matter how fit the horse is, traveling at speed over hard or very soft, rutted or rocky terrain is hard on his feet and tendons. Choose good footing for your galloping work. Of course, in the interest of sport, you will sometimes have to cover rough terrain at a faster than ideal speed, but always keep it in mind and save your horse as much as you can.

HANDLING SMALL EMERGENCIES

Once you start working at speed or out of a controlled area, a certain variety of problems will occur. What do you do if a horse stumbles, shies, wheels, bucks or bolts, or if you lose your whip, your reins, or your stirrups? First of all, do not lose your head.

There is a disastrous instinct in the majority of novice riders to lean forward and look down the minute something goes wrong. Unfortunately, this is the exact opposite of what they should do. Leaning forward tells the horse to go faster, and looking down bends the rider's upper body to one side and down toward the ground where he really does not want to be. So when something goes wrong, look up, sit up and lean back. Beyond this basic maxim each situation must be handled as it arises.

Stumbling is caused most often by carelessness on the part of the horse. It is also sometimes caused by long feet and by pain produced by a misstep or by sore feet. If your horse stumbles with regularity, have your veterinarian or blacksmith check his feet. A stumble is usually no problem to a rider who is sitting properly, but the horse should be punished immediately by a smack with the leg or the crop.

Horses shy and/or wheel (make a sudden half-turn) for many reasons, and the rider must know why the horse reacted this way in order to correct it. As a beginner, you should not have to worry about retraining the horse, but simply try to stay on him if he behaves abnormally. Ride with your reins at moderate length, never on the buckle, even when relaxing. Practice shortening your reins in quick, smooth movements and replacing your feet in the stirrups without bending over to look for them.

If your horse starts to buck, immediately try to get his head up and keep it up. To get in a really good buck, most horses need to get their heads down around their knees.

If the horse already has his head down, then brace yourself against being pitched over his shoulder by pushing your feet in front of the girth and, of course, pushing your shouders back. Use snatching motions with your hands to get his head up.

A horse bolts when he has been frightened and is not reacting sensibly. You must remain calm and do the thinking for both of you. Do not start hauling at the reins, as pain on his mouth will only make him run harder. Talk to him quietly and slow him down with a smooth tug-release action on the reins. If you are in an open area, pull on one rein and circle in a gradually decreasing spiral. If this is impossible, brace one hand on his neck just in front of the withers and use smooth, lifting tugs with the other. Alternate hands if necessary. Whenever a horse gets excited, the rider should keep cool.

Rearing is a dangerous habit as the horse can become unbalanced and fall over backward. Occasionally a horse rears when he is frightened but usually rearing is a resistance. The horse does not want to do something and up he goes.

If this ever happens to you, immediately throw yourself forward, grabbing the mane or wrapping your arms around the neck. This is one time in an emergency that you must go forward; hanging on the reins may pull the horse over. When the horse puts his front feet back on the ground, get off. A horse that rears once will rear again, and there is little a novice can do to prevent it happening. Let the instructor deal with him.

Rearing, when it has gotten as far as being a habit, is extremely difficult to stop. However, the young horse may experiment with these actions as they come naturally to him; rearing and striking are among his basic defenses. The experienced rider will feel that the horse is going to rear before he leaves the ground and will break his resistance by whirling him around in a tight circle or, if he thinks the horse is just having an attack of nerves, he may simply pat him and talk to him until he relaxes. When the horse is already up in the air, a couple of quick smacks across the ears may discourage a recurrence, although it may also make a very resistant horse worse. The habitual rearer needs the treatment of an expert.

The way to keep small emergencies small is to train yourself to react quickly and decisively. There is nearly always a warning that a horse is going to do something out of the ordinary if you are alert enough to catch it. For example, there may be only a few seconds in which you can take the simple actions of slowing down a horse that is galloping too strongly before that strong gallop becomes a runaway.

7

Trail and Cross-Country Riding

Once you have acquired the basic riding skills, you will undoubtedly wish to ride out on the trails and eventually cross-country, if this is available. One of the most delightful ways to enjoy nature is from the back of a horse. The horse will also benefit with a change from ring work.

For your first experiences outside the ring you should be mounted on a totally reliable horse and be accompanied by an experienced rider. A horse will seldom act the same out hacking as he has in the ring. The first thing you will notice with many horses is that when they are in front they will poke along, acting as if they want another horse to lead, but when another horse is in front, they are constantly pushing to get by.

Here are a few general principles to think about before you start your ride. A good adage to follow is "walk the first mile out and the last mile in." Do not take off at a canter or even a trot as soon as you are in the saddle. Give the horse time to "warm up," to get his blood circulating, to loosen his muscles and to adjust to the outside world after his stall. You would not wish to get out of bed and immediately run a mile in the heat or cold; then do not ask this of your horse. You will not improve his disposition and, under certain circumstances, you could cause serious physical ailments.

For the same reasons, never work your horse right up to the barn door. Give him time to relax and cool out. Then he will not try to jig or run to the stable every time you turn him in the general direction of home.

When you have been out a few minutes, and again after an hour or so, check your girth for tightness. Always carry a whip when riding out. Circumstances may arise where you will need to get your horse's attention and ride him forward quickly. The whip is carried with its end in the fork between your thumb and forefinger and its length along your lower thigh. It should be used just behind your calf as it normally is used to remind the horse to obey your leg. A long, dressage-type whip may be used without removing your hand from the reins; a short crop requires that you remove your hand from the rein to apply it behind your leg. Occasionally, you may use a couple of raps on the shoulder to distract the horse's attention from shying or to correct him from stumbling with his front feet. Look straight ahead, not at the whip, and apply it firmly once or twice. Practice transferring the whip from one hand to the other smoothly, as you must be able to use it on either side as needed.

Shying can be a problem with almost any horse ridden outside an enclosed area, particularly if he is alone or in front. There is no absolute solution. With some horses it is part of their personality and you must learn to live with it while at the same time keeping it under control. When starting a young horse, always take him behind a steady horse until he has gained confidence in himself. Try to understand why a horse shies at apparently innocent objects and noises. His instinct is to run away from anything strange that might be an indication of danger. Without this in-

After you have been out hacking an hour or so, remember to check the girth.

stinct he could not have survived, and it is your job to give him confidence that there is not danger behind every rock and every broken twig.

Keep your horse moving forward alertly on light contact even when relaxing. If he has nothing to occupy his mind, he will notice or even look for "spooks." If it is something truly frightening give it a wide berth so that he can study it without being forced to come face to face with it. On the other hand, if it is something that he has had experience with then turn his head a little *away* from the object and move him forward at a brisk walk or trot, at the same time giving him confidence with your voice, legs and hands. When your horse insists on shying at the same thing after passing it two or three times, then it sometimes helps to let him go up to the object and examine it. Otherwise, a couple of smacks with your crop as you approach should let him know that you have had enough of his antics.

To sum up about shying: you must first know *why* your horse is shying in order to handle it properly. If he is shying from fear, then you must do anything to give him confidence even to the point of dismounting and leading him. To punish him under these circumstances will only make him associate pain with the fearful object and make him more fearful. However, if he is shying from naughtiness and to test how alert you are, then a rap with your leg or crop should straighten out these notions. There are also those horses who shy from naughtiness but become worse if you punish them. With them, the minimum of punishment and fuss seems to be best.

Appreciate what a privilege it is to ride over other people's land. Always greet anyone you see about the property. Do not ride like a robot. Pick up dangerous objects that the next rider may not see, and break branches back; paths do not stay open without work. Volunteer for path-clearing parties. Never take a dog with you, or jump a fence, or open a gate without the specific permission of the landowner. If you involuntarily cause some damage, tell the owner and offer to repair or pay for it.

Keep off the paths when they are very soft. A few horses on soggy ground do more damage than a hundred on dry ground. Keep to the edges of all farmers' fields, even if you think they are

Cross-country and trail rides are among the greatest delights that riding affords, and make a welcome change of pace for both horse and rider after concentrated ring work.

unplanted. Make it a habit to keep off the worn paths except when they cross closely mowed places such as lawns. This will prevent the path wearing to the point of becoming a ditch. Treat other people's property better than you would treat your own, and you are likely to remain welcome on it.

Be considerate of your horse. He is not a machine—and even machines run better with good driving. Beware of hard, rocky or boggy places. Take them at a walk. The shock of pounding on a macadam road is bad for the horse's tendons and joints, although some walking and trotting toughens them. The pull of a boggy place is not only hard on his tendons and ligaments but often causes a lost shoe. The dangers of a rocky place are obvious.

Biting flies are a hardship to your horse and can ruin an otherwise pleasant summer ride. A thorough application of fly spray should protect him fairly well for a couple of hours unless he sweats heavily. You may also carry a fly whisk. The worst of the flies live in the woods and wetlands, so avoid these areas or move as quickly through them as the footing permits.

During a long ride your horse may be grateful for a few swallows of water from a clear stream. However, if he starts to paw, get him moving, as this is often a sign that he means to roll.

If your horse kicks, try to be the last one in line. Sometimes a good swat with your whip on the appropriate hindquarter will stop the habit. When you stop on a narrow path, turn your horse sideways so if he does kick it will only land harmlessly in some bushes. Even if he is not a known kicker, never allow anyone to ride on his tail. Do not be shy, but simply ask them to stay back a little. You will be much more embarrassed if your horse causes an injury, and the most patient horse in the world will kick if he is butted in the hindquarters. If you nevertheless end up with a kicker, tie a red ribbon on his tail and keep his armament aimed away from anything breakable. It is up to you to make sure that your horse does not kick, so take any necessary precautions.

Jigging is another bad habit which may show itself out hacking. Instead of walking flatfooted and keeping the distance of a length or so behind the horse in front, your horse takes shorter and shorter steps until he starts to fall behind. He then quickens these little steps into a jig. As with all bad habits, prevention is the best cure.

The minute he starts to lag behind, squeeze him forward in a strong walk or a definite trot in order to catch up. When constant repetition of this procedure does not help, enlist the cooperation of a good friend with a horse that does not kick. Every time your horse starts to jig, trot him forward until his nose almost touches the tail of the horse in front and then ask him to walk. It is very hard for him to jig under these conditions. If he starts to jig going toward home without anyone around, try trotting for a bit and/or make a series of very small circles and then ask him to walk. Repeat this procedure as often as necessary. If the horse is very excited, dismount and handwalk him until he settles down. Hopefully, he will be a different horse when you remount. But remember, *do not let the habit get started* as it is difficult to break.

Be decisive with leg and rein pressures when threading your way through woods. A horse will not bump himself on a tree, but he will not instinctively allow for the few extra inches of your leg, much less for your upper body. He will follow the horse in front, so if you wish to go another way, give him very clear aids.

Take a straight line up and down hills, particularly if the footing is slippery. The horse will tend to drift sideways in order to avoid jolting his front legs or pushing fully with his hindquarters, but this evading action greatly increases the chance of his feet slipping out from under him.

Help your friends to enjoy their ride. Do not allow your horse to lag behind or, conversely, to get too close to the one in front. Turn your head and give the traditional cry of "'ware hole," etc., to draw attention to dangerous objects. However, a voice warning is helpful only at the slower paces, as the caller's voice is often lost in the wind. It is frustrating for a follower to know he should be avoiding something, but not to know what or where. The most effective way of warning is to point at the object with your hand or whip. Calling "hold hard" or holding your hand up, palm forward, at shoulder level warns those behind of an abrupt stop.

When you advance to riding cross-country, you must be even more alert. Never move at speed unless you can see whether there are holes or wire ahead. There are two basic types of holes to watch out for: (1) *Blind.* These are unmarked by any disturbance in the ground around them and are doubly lethal in that they usually run straight down into the ground; (2) *Groundhog holes.* These usually come in pairs, plus a chimney hole; the entrance is marked by a pile of dirt and both it and the exit run into the ground at a 45-degree angle.

To avoid holes you and the horse need to be observant and to have a lot of good luck, plus the blessing of the Almighty. When galloping across an open field, maintain contact with the horse's mouth so that if he does stumble for whatever reason, he will have the smooth support of the reins and not just fall into space. The next thing to do is sit more upright and perhaps give a lifting tug with the reins if it is a front leg that has gone into a hole. Mostly you will have to rely on instinct to help the horse as much as possible. Do not fall forward, do not drop the reins, do not sit down in the saddle.

Learn to avoid holes and wire by looking well ahead. Always

A fun change from more serious riding is a bareback hack around the pasture. Bareback riding should be restricted to an enclosed area as you will have less control of your horse, particularly if you are not using a bridle.

follow the exact path of horses in front, especially if you do not know the country. Wire can be very hard to see if it is strung across the top of a fence or half buried in weeds. Even if you think there appears to be a better place to jump a fence or a closer gap in an old line of wire, follow where other horses have gone unless you know that you are safe. Learn to recognize signs of holes: mounds of fresh dirt, a suspicious mound of grass-covered earth, a patch of greener grass. Small honeysuckle patches are likely places for holes. When you see a hole, avoid it by several yards if possible so as to miss any auxiliary holes.

Be cautious on hard roads, particularly the smooth, high-crowned type, as they are slippery. If your horse is shod with borium, a hard metal applied to the shoe which gives added purchase, he is less likely but by no means guaranteed not to slip.

After all these cautions, it may seem that you will be constantly on the lookout for danger. Actually, all these precautions soon become second nature. So have fun and enjoy your ride.

III · Special Riding Skills

8

Learning to Jump

Most people who ride want to learn to jump. Soaring over even small fences is a special kind of thrill, and it opens up several equestrian sports if you become proficient. Let me emphasize, however, that if you are not interested in this aspect of riding, you should not feel pressured into trying it just because everyone else is doing it. To enjoy and be successful at jumping you must want to do it determinedly, without serious apprehensions. There are lots of other ways to enjoy horses without ever leaping over an obstacle if you feel uncomfortable about it.

If you are interested in jumping, watch good riders and horses at shows and while schooling. Notice the actions the horse makes to clear the fence and observe what the rider does to adapt his movements to those of the horse. As the horse approaches the fence he lowers his head, measuring the height and distance of the obstacle. His pace and length of stride should remain about the same, right to the takeoff point. However, if he is not going to meet the takeoff point comfortably, it is better for the novice rider to ask for a slightly faster pace rather than to try to restrain him, so that the horse can jump from a good, forward-thrusting movement.

As the horse reaches the point of takeoff, the front legs leave the ground and the hind legs come together and plant themselves more or less as a pair, providing a firm base of support for the thrust that propels the horse up and forward. The front legs leave the ground individually but quickly become a matched pair as they rise toward the top of the obstacle. They remain a pair until the horse is descending toward the ground when one front leg stretches out to strike the ground first. The head and neck remain stretched forward over the fence, reaching the most forward point of the stretch just before the front foot strikes the ground. As the hind legs strike the ground, the head returns to its normal position for the pace. The bigger the effort the horse makes, the more pronounced are his movements.

What does the rider do as the horse jumps? He simply follows the movements of the horse. As the horse pushes off the ground, the rider's upper body moves forward by bending from the hips with a straight back. As the horse's head stretches forward, the rider's hand follows it. As the horse's hind legs strike the ground, the rider's seat returns lightly to the saddle and his upper body becomes more upright. Of course, this sounds easier than it actually is, but if you proceed one step at a time and do not attempt to jump bigger fences or ride a more difficult horse until you are competent, your progress should be steady.

Two things are essential to start your jumping career off right: a good instructor and a steady horse. The instructor will help keep you from forming bad habits, which is really the easiest way to form good habits. The horse does not need to be a super jumper, but simply one that is absolutely reliable so that you can concentrate on controlling yourself rather than on controlling the horse. If you own a horse and know he has problems jumping, then learn on another. Get an experienced rider to straighten your horse out before you attempt to jump him yourself.

PREPARING TO JUMP

The rider may approach the fence in either the two-point (half-seat) or the three-point (full-seat) position. In the three-point position the rider has more control of the horse, but he also needs better timing and body control to be able to move forward with the horse at the exact point of takeoff. With the two-point contact the rider is already in the jumping position, which simplifies his

Trotting over rails on the ground is a good way to start jumping. Mary's lower leg has slipped back out of position from lack of drive down into her heel.

job, so this is the position the novice should take up until he is well along toward advanced jumping. The three-point contact should be used when the rider needs the aid of the seat to balance and control an inexperienced jumper or when approaching a difficult fence.

The first exercise you need to practice to prepare for jumping is to perfect taking up and holding the two-point contact, the "up" position of the rising trot. Remember, this simply means shifting your upper body slightly forward and shifting the weight off your seatbones and more on to your thighs and knees. Do not stand up in the stirrups, pushing your seat up out of the saddle. Rather, keep the crotch in light contact with the saddle. When cantering, take up the two-point or hand-gallop position. Continue your exercises of sitting and rising trot without stirrups.

Your first "jump" should be a rail on the ground. Shorten your reins until you have a nice feel of the horse's mouth and take up a good, energetic trot. Trot over the rail several times, looking across the top of the horse's ears. The rhythm of the trot should not change approaching or leaving the rail. Do not pull up immediately after the rail or turn, but trot straight ahead for several strides and then make a nice half-circle and come back the other way. Concentrate on keeping the horse straight and not looking down and to the side at the rail. After you have accomplished this in good order, do the same at the canter in the two-point position.

Trotting over cavalletti is a good way to establish rhythm and strengthen the legs. Again, Mary's lower leg has slipped back a bit, so that she is pivoting on her knee rather than clasping the horse's body with her whole leg.

If you do not have room to make an easy cantering half-circle in order to approach the rail from the opposite direction, then simply continue in a large circle and jump the rail from the same direction for a few times. Then take up the circle in the opposite direction. This is probably enough for the first day.

The next day do the same thing, but add the exercise of trotting over five or six rails that have been laid on the ground in succession, spaced four to five feet apart (depending on the length of the horse's stride). He should be able to trot over this series comfortably. Concentrate on looking over the last rail and keeping the horse straight and in the same trot throughout. The next step is to hold the rising position as you go over the rails. This will strengthen your leg muscles and teach you to keep your back straight but supple. As you approach the first rail, take up the two-point position and hold it until after the last rail when you resume the posting trot. If you start to lose your balance, place your knuckles on the horse's neck in front of the withers; do not support yourself by pulling on the reins.

Rails on the ground are a useful training tool, but they are easily dislodged. A more convenient form of this kind of training device is proper cavalletti, usually made of four-inch round poles attached to crosspieces so that they cannot be so easily knocked about. They are usually adjustable from six inches (for trotting) to nine inches (for cantering) high. Except for their heaviness, thin telephone poles lying right on the ground make excellent cavalletti. If cavalletti are available, practice trotting over them; cantering will come later. Their height will cause the horse to trot more energetically, and you will have to close your legs more firmly against his sides in order to keep your upper body steadily following his new rhythm. Check that your hands remain absolutely quiet. Keep at the rails or cavalletti work until you can follow the horse's motions consistently.

JUMPING LOW OBSTACLES

Now you are ready to tackle an obstacle that is just high enough to force the horse to make a jumping effort. Two rails crossed in the center at a height of about one foot make an attractive jump and encourage you to keep the horse straight. Take up a good rising trot, and two or three strides from the fence, hold the two-point position and place your knuckles about halfway up the horse's neck on his crest. Grasp the mane with one or both hands and keep the hands as close together as possible. This can be done easily if you simply grasp the mane between the thumb and forefinger. You are now frozen into a good jumping position and have nothing more to do than feel the motions of the horse. When he lands on the other side, remove your hands from his neck, sit a bit more upright, and resume the rising trot. The horse will make only a small hop over a fence this low.

During the approach, consciously close both your legs against

A good approach with the hands toward the pony's crest; this is enough contact for the learning stage of jumping. Having his foot all the way "home" in the stirrup prevents George, Jr., from putting more weight into his heel.

A nice position for this stage of learning, hands resting lightly on the pony's neck. Note how much rein the pony needs to stretch his head and neck.

the horse's sides as you take up the two-point position. This action should become automatic during the last two or three strides before a fence, no matter what gait you are at, how high the fence, or how willing the horse. A firm "wrap-around" leg, combined with a good drive from your hips down into your heels, will provide a secure basis for your upper body so that it can follow the motions of the horse. Also, closing your legs will encourage the unsure horse, keep the steady horse on his pace and quiet a horse that tends to rush his fences.

Another action you want to become absolutely automatic is to bend forward from the hips over the fence, keeping your back straight but supple. Do not bend at the waist, rounding only your back and shoulders. By placing your knuckles on the horse's crest and looking over the top of the horse's ears, you will put yourself in the proper position. You will also be training yourself to extend forward with your arms; the slack that will occur in the reins will allow the horse to move his head without any interference and will prevent him from being snatched in the mouth if something goes a little wrong with the jump. Trot over simple obstacles in this fashion for several days until all these actions become smooth and you begin to see and feel where the horse is going to take off each time.

The next step is to maintain the rising trot right up to the obstacle while still placing your knuckles on the horse's neck a couple of strides away. This will present a problem for your coordination, since fifty percent of the time you will be sitting in the saddle at the last stride. You will then have to rise into the two-point position as the horse takes off or you will be "left behind." When you are "left," your seat remains in the saddle over the fence. If your knuckles are on the horse's neck, you can grab onto a piece of mane, keeping your hands from coming back and your upper body a little forward, and you should have no real trouble. However, you will not really be with your horse; your seat will be in the saddle, putting the bulk of your weight behind the motion of the horse. Over larger fences, the weight of your seat will interfere with the horse's jumping mechanism. You want your weight off the horse's back during the jump freeing his muscles to perform their job.

When you can trot over fences, confident that you will not be left behind, do not place your knuckles on the horse's neck during the approach but do so just as he takes off. It is now important that you are not mentally or physically hanging back or you will end up being left behind and possibly hitting the horse in the mouth. Start to canter over the same low obstacles. Take up the two-point contact several lengths away and place the knuckles on the neck a couple of lengths away. Graduate to placing the knuckles on the neck at takeoff.

Before you think about jumping higher fences and taking over more control of the horse, correct any bad habits that have started. Are you being left behind? This is usually caused by not purposely thinking forward over the fence. The adage "throw your heart over the fence and the horse will follow" goes for the rider as well as his mount. Another cause is not following the motions of the horse. You must constantly feel what the horse is doing and, although you see where the horse should take off, you must follow his actions if he leaves the ground sooner or later than this point. When you can consistently feel when the horse is going to leave the ground, you are well on the way to building up his lines of communication which will enable you to tell him when and what you wish of him. For good communications between two parties, both must listen as well as speak.

Is your seat coming back into the saddle too soon, even before the horse lands? Be sure that your legs are firmly clasping the horse's side and your feet have not slipped forward. Is your face ending up in the horse's mane or turning to the side? Then you are bending too low over the fence and probably bending from the waist instead of just from the hips. This habit often comes from a rider's mistaken idea that he is helping a horse over the fence. Once the horse is airborne, there is almost nothing even the most talented rider can do to help him except change his direction. In fact, any added movement distracts him and disturbs his balance. Watch the good riders and notice how quiet they are, even over very large fences.

Are your heels flying up and your lower leg slipping backward? Then your weight is not truly sinking to your heels and your legs are not staying close to the horse's sides. Are your toes swinging out? Then you are gripping with the back of your calf rather than the inside of your thighs, knees and calves. Are your hands popping up, or is your chin jutting out? These habits come primarily from tenseness. Try anything that will help you relax— sing, whistle, take deep breaths during the approach. You can correct the chin problem by looking just behind the horse's poll instead of just ahead until the habit disappears.

Never look back at the fence. If you wish to see whether your horse knocked a rail down, wait until you have circled back. Everyone develops bad habits while riding; the only cure is to be checked often by a knowledgeable rider and to practice, practice, practice.

INTERMEDIATE JUMPING

One of the best exercises to develop balance and suppleness, once your seat is reasonably secure, is to jump without reins. Now is the time to practice, before you take over the complete control of the horse and take your hands off his neck to follow the motions of his head throughout the jump. Of course, you need a reliable horse and someone to longe you (see Longeing, Chapter 10), or an enclosed area or loose school in which your horse will happily

Jumping a grid without reins is an excellent way to develop balance and confidence. This grid is set no-stride, no-stride, one-stride.

hop over one or several low fences (a grid) without your steering.

The fences can be placed eight to nine feet apart for a cantering no-stride or bounce distance, and eleven to twelve feet apart for a cantering one-stride distance. You can try cantering over the single obstacle or the grid with your arms crossed on your chest, or extended out at shoulder height, or with your hands placed on top of your head or on your hips. Practice over a grid even if you cannot do it without reins as it is still a good exercise for you and your horse.

At the intermediate stage of jumping you still need a totally reliable mount. However, you should now take over his complete control, maintaining steady contact with his mouth throughout the jump and practicing over higher and wider obstacles. You will also begin to work seriously on your timing, which at this point involves seeing and feeling where the horse is going to take off and allowing your upper body to follow it smoothly, never ahead, never behind.

Start by shortening your reins so that your hands are in front of the withers when you have a nice feel of the horse's mouth. (As your body folds up over the fence, your hands will end up in your lap with your elbows sticking out if your reins are too long.)

A good approach for the intermediate stage of jumping, the horse moving well forward from the rider's leg. Terry likes to give horses lots of freedom, but we would prefer a little steadier contact with the bit.

Approach the fence in a half-seat, but instead of placing your hands on the horse's neck at takeoff, allow his mouth to draw your hands forward as he stretches his neck over the fence. Over a low obstacle he will hardly move his head, but this is not your concern. You are concentrating on keeping the light but steady feel of his mouth. In order to do this your hands must yield forward the same amount as his head moves or else you will be restricting the use of his head and neck which he needs for proper balance. However, you should not just shove your hands forward, independently of what the horse is asking. This is called "dropping" the horse, as you are dropping the steady feel of his mouth, thus disturbing his concentration and balance. The hand, just like the upper body, must *follow* the motions of the horse rather than following some arbitrary rule such as forward at takeoff, back at landing. The pace, the height and width of the jump and the horse's style vary the split-second timing, which must be carried out by feel not by some mechanical formula.

ADVANCED JUMPING

When the rider can consistently follow the motions of the horse over a series of moderate obstacles he is ready for more advanced

A straight but supple back, the seat lightly out of the saddle, a firm leg with the rider's weight nicely distributed produce a good fence.

jumping. We will define "advanced" as that stage of jumping at which the rider can (a) help the horse in the approach if necessary; (b) see where the horse will be taking off three or four strides from the fence and then shorten or lengthen the horse's stride if necessary; (c) jump more difficult obstacles set in more demanding courses; (d) jump over varying terrain and under stress, such as showing or foxhunting; (e) remain in a three-point position up to takeoff if it is necessary to steady a high-strung animal or drive on a lazy one.

The rider may now be mounted on horses that are not push-button. Some horses tend to rush their fences while others show little interest and approach lazily. The way in which the horse makes the approach determines the quality of the jump. If the rider allows a bad approach, he is asking for a bad jump or a refusal. Up to this stage a lucky rider will have had a reliable horse and an instructor doing a lot of his thinking for him.

At the advanced stage of jumping the rider must be tuned in at all times to his horse and should determine when and over what he should jump. Some basic rules: (1) Always warm up before jumping. Establish a good trot or canter and, if you cannot get it, then do not jump; a horse that is not working well on the flat will not jump well. (2) Start with low fences before moving on to higher ones. Even an experienced horse will stop (refuse) or duck out (run out to the side) if he is presented to a challenging obstacle without preparation. The rider must know his horse and feel his attitude to realize what is challenging. A two-foot white chicken coop which would be a warm-up jump for an experienced horse will present a challenge to a green horse or even one that is just feeling too good and has not yet settled down to his job. (3) Do not jump more difficult obstacles until you and the horse are consistently proficient at the easier ones. It is the old "one step at a time" that must be practiced.

If you try to skip a step, the existing problems will only become worse. Jump many small fences two to three feet high in order to build up confidence and harmony with your horse. At this height you will put less strain on the horse physcially and mentally while getting the most practice. Try not to bore him by jumping the same fence over and over. Signs of boredom are jumping sloppily and hitting rails. Vary the route and the approach. Jump some fences on angles from both the left and the right. Change the placement of the fences and the distance between cavalletti and combinations. A combination is a series of fences where there is not more than thirty-nine feet between each.

TYPES OF JUMPS

Jumps can be made of many materials but may be divided into four groups: (1) uprights or verticals, such as rail fences, gates or walls without any spread; (2) spreads which have width as well as height, such as an *oxer* in which the two top rails are at the same height but have a definite space between them, thus making a spread across the top; a *hog's-back*, which consists of two low rails with a higher rail between them; an *Aiken*, which is an upright with a pile of brush in front; a *triple bar*, in which the three top rails are spaced evenly and ascend as in a staircase; (3) banks which are obstacles that you jump on to and off of, (4) ditches or water, sometimes used in conjunction with one of the above.

Some materials used are natural rails, painted poles, oil drums, brush, boards and blocks painted to simulate gates, picket fences, or brick and stone walls. Wings, which are boards put together in such a manner as to help frame the fence and discourage the horse from running out, are not really necessary at home. In fact they can be detrimental as the horse and rider becomes dependent on their extra guidance.

SETTING UP THE JUMPS

Make sure the materials used are safe. For instance, a lightly made chicken coop can be punched through by the horse's hoof in the process of refusing, or tipped over when hit with the front legs, making it possible for the hind legs to hit the base as it turns over and produce a hard fall. The easiest and safest coop is actually half of one, angled against a rail. If oil drums are standing end up, be sure that rails are placed on top so that a horse cannot scrape his legs on the rim.

If the standards used depend on chocks or pins to hold the rails, rather than jump cups, always jump them with the rails on the far side of the standards. Then if the horse hits the rail hard it will come off without carrying both standards with it. The face of the jump should be at least ten feet wide, preferably twelve or fourteen feet. The rails should be heavy so that the horse will not become accustomed to flicking one off whenever he feels a little lazy.

Position and space your fences according to your horse's ability. An obstacle's difficulty is determined by its appearance and height, the terrain and footing around it, and its placement. More difficult placements are from light into shade (such as the edge of a wood), right before or after a turn, and combinations that are not exactly in the horse's stride. The shutter reflex of the horse's eye is slower than that of a human in adjusting from light to dark and vice versa, and the wise horseman will always keep this in mind. Do not try placing a jump off a turn or into a turn until you can keep the horse balanced and bent in the correct direction at the pace you are asking.

Some easy distances are: for trotting over cavalletti or single low rails to be approached at a trot, use nine feet to a fence which the horse will jump out of the canter stride; twelve feet between low fences for a bounce (no stride) at the strong canter or slow hand gallop; and for two fences (in and out) to be taken with one stride in between, use anything from twenty feet, for low ones to be taken at the canter, up to twenty-eight feet apart for those to be taken at the hand gallop. These are normal distances for normal striding horses. Obviously they must be shortened for ponies. They can be adjusted to help a horse with his problems. Shortening the distance will help you to get the horse that is heavy on his forehand back onto his hocks and will make him use himself more; lengthening the distance will get a horse to go forward more and stand back further and should be ridden at a stronger pace. If the horse is consistently reaching or shortening in order to jump a fence in a combination, then the distance should be adjusted accordingly.

How often and how many times a horse should jump is a question often asked that can really only be answered by using common sense. Many low fences can be jumped more often than higher fences. A fit horse can jump more fences than an unfit horse. The horse's legs will be less strained on springy footing than on hard or very soft going. If the fences and the area can be varied, more jumping can be accomplished without souring the horse.

STYLE OVER THE FENCE

A rider must keep the horse at the desired pace and in the desired frame (position of various parts of the horse's body in relation to each other). If the horse rushes or lags, if he raises his head or leans on the bit or deviates from the straight line, the rider should circle away and make another approach. This will not teach your horse to refuse if you make a decisive, smooth circle, alternating sides, and not a hasty, last-minute change of heart.

Remember to sustain the pace and decided direction after the fence until the point at which you wish to come back to the walk or halt or to circle or half-circle. The horse should not be allowed to rush on or just die back or cut off to the side. Jumping even little fences is serious work and should be carried out in an orderly fashion. If you want to relax, go out for a hack. If you are out for a ride and decide to jump, make sure the horse is prepared.

The approach is usually made at the rising trot or in the two-point position at the canter or hand gallop. However, the sitting trot or the three-point position at the canter will be used when the aid of the seat is needed to urge the horse forward. Also, some horses that rush can be calmed if the approach is made with a steady but supple seat contact which gives them confidence. It is more difficult to jump in good form from the three-point position as your seat must move off the horse's back at the point of takeoff. This must be done smoothly and quietly. Move too soon and you upset his balance, move too late and your weight interferes with his jumping mechanism.

You are now approaching the fence at a good canter in a half-seat, looking over the top rail. About four strides away you "see your distance," that is, you see where the horse's last stride will place him for the takeoff. If he is coming down to it right, he leaves the ground from a point that is approximately as far away from the base of the fence as the fence is high plus one third; for a three-foot fence, he should leave the ground approximately four feet away. Seeing the distance for a fence is a skill more easily acquired by some but not unobtainable by anyone. For many it takes a great deal of work and concentration, and they may never be able to see the distance from as many strides away as some others, but the result is worth achieving. You will have added confidence about jumping which you will transmit to the horse who will then perform better. You acquire this skill by constantly working at it.

On the flat at any pace, pick an object you see as three strides away and then the horse's forefeet should hit that point at the end of the third stride. The magic number seems to be three to begin with and only when you can consistently see this distance should you try to see longer ones. You will have days when you will have many more misses than hits but do not give up, because only when you can see that the horse's last stride is going to place him too close or too far away from a fence can you then lengthen or shorten the stride to get him to the right point.

Following are a few aids for developing your timing. (Do not use them too consistently or they will lose their value.) Ask someone on the ground to call the last three strides for you, counting backward, three, two, one, which should be takeoff. Also do it yourself once in a while. Lay a rail on the ground forty-eight feet from the fence and in three strides you should meet the takeoff point comfortably. If you don't, adjust the rail.

Once you get the feel of meeting the fence right, move the rail three feet closer and steady your horse by asking him to shorten his stride a little, then move it three feet back from the original position and ask him to lengthen his stride. When you have trouble with your timing go back to the basics. Are you relaxed and really in balance? Is the horse moving forward at a good pace? It is difficult to improve your timing during a meandering, dull approach.

Another help is to ask the horse to canter from a trotting approach when you see a certain number of canter strides ahead. Be careful not to look at the ground in front of the fence; this is easy to do when you are looking for the point of takeoff. You must train your eyes to stay up and take in the whole area. Timing is something you will work on your whole riding life. Consider it a challenge to be enjoyed and do not become frustrated if you have a bad day or even a week.

You are making the approach with a light hand contact with the horse's mouth and a firm leg contact with his sides that may vary from light to definite, depending on his personality. Without these contacts you are strictly a passenger and have regressed to the early intermediate stage of jumping. Of course many horses jump without contact, balancing themselves and adjusting their strides well, but then you are totally dependent on the horse's judgment and cannot help if he makes an error. As both the rider and the horse are hopefully going to make the jump, they must work together.

The rider's first responsibility is to make no movements that would interfere with the horse's jumping mechanism, and secondly, to adjust the horse's stride if necessary. Do not fall into the error of abandoning contact on a sensitive horse because he appears to resent it during the approach. If his flat work is correct, then he is rushing out of excitement, lack of confidence or actual fear. He, even more than his more stolid brothers, needs the light and steady contact of hand and leg.

With the horse that asks for a firm contact, be careful to maintain a forward, supple feel that does not degenerate into holding back. If the horse leans or pulls at your hands then circle away, and if he still does not get the message after several tries, then go back to cavalletti and trot-canter combinations. With most horses it is desirable to increase the leg contact during the last three strides even if the approach is perfect as it insures that the impulsion (forward, energetic drive of the hindquarters) is maintained. This action will increase the steadiness of your leg. If the horse will not permit stronger contact, then concentrate on sinking your weight from your hips down into your heels.

If you can see that the horse is going to hit the takeoff point too close to or too far away from the fence, then ask him to shorten or lengthen his remaining strides. Say that a hoofmark is six inches long, and you reduce or increase each of the last three strides by a hoofmark, then you will alter his arrival at the takeoff point by a foot and a half without a lot of dramatics. This does not mean that you should get out a slide rule, but rather points out that little adjustments can add up if made in time. Experience will teach you which to choose, but usually it is best to shorten his stride if he is moving long, lengthen his stride if he is moving short, and lengthen and quicken the pace a little if he is moving in his normal stride. If you are unable to see the distance or unsure what to do about it, then trust the horse to sort it out but keep the leg and hand contact and keep up the pace so that the horse will have some impulsion to work from.

As the horse leaves the ground, allow the thrust to carry your upper body forward the necessary amount, and follow his mouth with your hands. Be sure your hands allow his head and neck their full extension. It is better to lose contact with his mouth over the top of the fence, letting the rein go a little slack, than to keep too tight a contact and interfere with his balance.

If the approach has been normal, the rider makes no special actions to tell the horse to leave the ground except to be sure to keep the leg contact, which is easy to lose at this point. In fact, any unnecessary movement will only serve to distract the horse

Approaching a four-foot upright demands more concentration and control of the horse.

Terry sees her distance and eases gently into the saddle in order to maintain impulsion.

Although a steadier contact with the bit might be desired, Terry's supple seat and firm leg keep the horse well in balance and going forward during the last stride before the fence.

As the horse leaves the ground its front legs become a pair as they fold up and the hind legs plant themselves strongly, providing a firm base of support.

Terry is in perfect balance with the horse as he makes his descent. Too much release of the rein is preferable to too little.

It is important to maintain the hand-gallop position during the landing, keeping your weight off the horse's back.

from the job at hand. Of course, if he shows any signs of stopping, then you must use a driving leg or, if warranted, the crop. The crop must be used behind the rider's leg, and you will obviously lose some steering control while shifting the reins. So correct any minor hesitations quickly with the leg so that they do not develop into major hesitations. If the horse jumps sloppily, correct him immediately after the fence with your leg or crop, so that he knows he must pay more attention the next time.

It is important that you do not lose the hand contact just before the horse takes off, as both his balance and confidence will be impaired. At the earlier stages of jumping you had no contact and the horse was jumping on his own. But once you take up the contact, no matter how light, he becomes somewhat dependent on it and it will upset him if you drop it just before the fence.

Once his front legs leave the ground, his whole body is committed to the jump and he will not usually be upset by a little looseness in the rein. But the perfect jump is made when the rider's leg remains in position just behind the girth, the upper body moves quietly forward parallel to the horse's neck, the eyes look ahead and the hand yields smoothly forward, keeping a relatively straight line between the elbow and the horse's mouth. This perfection is worth striving for, and every time you achieve it, try to duplicate the feeling again. With every success it will become easier.

9

Basic Dressage

It is unfortunate that many people think the term dressage applies only to the performances of a highly trained Lipizzaner from the Spanish Riding School doing a series of airs above ground or an Olympic-caliber horse executing a Grand Prix test. Since they cannot visualize themselves or their horses achieving this level of art—and, in fact, are not even interested in trying—they are convinced that dressage has nothing to offer them. They are quite wrong, and are missing out on the most productive methods of training a horse.

In the first place, the apparently unattainable expertise of these great riders should no more prevent us from learning the basic principles of dressage than the tremendous performances of our Olympic riders over seven-foot walls should discourage us from learning to negotiate three-foot fences. Rather, let us admire and learn what we can from the finesse of the specialist dressage riders and be thankful to them for carrying on the traditions of classical riding as well as developing new traditions adapted to our modern horses and needs. Let us then study and apply the lower levels of practical dressage which are more relevant for most of us.

What then is dressage? The word is derived from the French verb "dresser," which means "to train" and is used most often in connection with animals. In its equestrian sense, however, the word dressage means something more precise than just what the word "training'" implies; we "train" our horse to accept human handling, to lead, to drive, to longe, to walk, trot, canter, gallop, jump, etc., but in basic dressage, we work to perfect our horse's basic mechanism and gaits, so that he can eventually do all of these things more correctly and thus more easily. The *Rule Book* of the American Horse Shows Association puts it very well: "Dressage . . . means the gradual harmonious development of the horse's physical and mental condition with the aim to achieve the improvement of its natural gaits under the rider and a perfect understanding of its rider." In competitive dressage this development is demonstrated by the performance of a predetermined ride or test in a rectangular arena of fixed dimensions. The perimeter of the arena is marked by letters and there are imaginary ones on the center line, and the required movements and transitions must be performed *exactly* at the indicated letter.

Eventually, some of us will accept the challenge of work on the flat as an end in itself and will move onto the higher levels of competitive dressage, but when we start our horse in dressage, most of us simply wish to improve his carriage and paces by increasing his impulsion. We teach him to be more responsive by striving for greater communication through the clarity of our aids, and increase his suppleness and balance through a systematic use of gymnastic exercises. We refine and coordinate our signals and controls until they truly become aids. In other words, we strive to improve the horse beyond simple usefulness.

The great emphasis on systematic training and development in dressage is reflected in the progressively greater demands made by the different levels of "tests," as the programs used in competition are called. Tests start with AHSA Training Level and go all the way up to the Olympic Grand Prix, but they all serve the same purpose: they test whether or not we have achieved a sufficient level of sound training to progress to the next more advanced level of training.

Even if you are not interested in ever riding dressage competitively, you will find it helpful to become familiar with the logical and systematic progression of training that is embodied in the AHSA tests at the lower levels, for the movements required of the horse through the Third Level are gymnastic exercises that will help his performance in any of the riding activities described

The horse is moving well on the bit at a good working trot. The rider's seat is excellent, but we would prefer her hands slightly lower and more level.

in this book. You can obtain copies of the various tests and a comprehensive *Supplement to Rules on Dressage* by writing to the AHSA (see List of Sources at the end of the book).

As we are dealing in this book mostly with initial experiences in the various aspects of horsemastership, in this chapter we will consider only the basic movements and principles of dressage training. Readers who are interested in riding in dressage competitions will find a further discussion of this aspect in Chapter 13.

Our first undertaking in dressage training is to teach the horse to accept the bit. This means that, although the horse's profile may be somewhat in front of the vertical, he accepts steady contact and offers no resistance to the bit. The head should be steady and the horse should neither fall behind the bit, by tucking his chin toward his chest, nor be above the bit, by raising his head and hollowing his neck. By the *First Level* the horse will be expected to show a greater acceptance of the bit and a greater degree of flexion (bend) at the poll, with the head now approaching the vertical, the head and neck somewhat raised, and again, not showing any resistances or evasions.

The poll, not the crest, is the highest point in the neck of a horse that has been put on the bit correctly by increasing the impulsion of the hindquarters. A lightness of the forehand and improved way of going will result. This increased lightness characterizes the "working" gaits, which the AHSA defines as those "in which an individual horse presents itself in the best balance and is most easily influenced and worked." In addition to the working trot and canter, the AHSA recognizes the "collected" walk, trot and canter, the "medium" ("ordinary") walk, trot and canter, the "extended" walk, trot and canter, and the "free" walk on a long or loose rein. In the collected gaits, the frame of the horse is shorter, its haunches lower, and its strides shorter and higher; in the extended gaits, the frame of the horse lengthens and the strides cover more ground. The medium gaits are intermediate between these two extremes.

At the *Training Level* the horse is asked to perform simple movements, large circles and gradual transitions. When a horse moves from one pace to another, i.e., walk to trot, trot to walk, or into or out of the halt, it is called a transition. The paces required are a working and free walk, a working trot, and a working canter. In all cases he will be expected to move absolutely straight when on a straight line and with the appropriate bend on curved lines, as well as to perform the movement at the designated letters, although slight inaccuracies will be forgiven if the horse is moving well forward into his transitions. The smoother and prompter the transitions, the better they are performed.

At the First Level, the above achievements will be expected plus lengthening of stride at the trot, ten-meter circles, half-circle at a trot, serpentines, and slightly more difficult transitions such as changes of lead in the canter through the trot in which the horse is allowed one to three trotting steps before being asked to take the other lead. Some simple exercises such as turn on the forehand or leg-yielding may be added to First-Level tests.

The points awarded in a dressage test are the total of the marks given for individual movements plus what are called the General Impressions which are multiplied by a coefficient of two to emphasize their importance. They are (1) gaits (freedom and regularity); (2) impulsion (desire to move forward, elasticity of steps, relaxation of back); (3) submission (attention and confidence, harmony, lightness and ease of movements; acceptance of the bit); (4) rider's position and seat (correctness and effect of the aids).

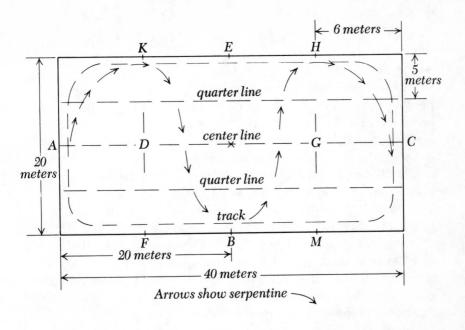

6 meters

5 meters

K   E   H

quarter line

A — *D* — *center line* — *G* — C

20 meters

quarter line

track

F   B   M

← 20 meters →

← 40 meters →

Arrows show serpentine ↘

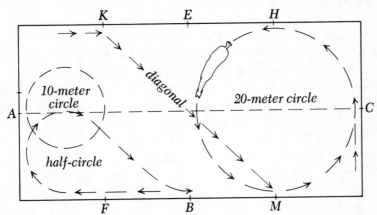

K   E   H

10-meter circle

diagonal

20-meter circle

A — — — — — — — — C

half-circle

F   B   M

POSITION AND SEAT OF THE RIDER

As the rider will be training the horse, let us take the position and seat of the rider first. Obviously the rider must be capable of improving the horse before he attempts to do so, or more harm will come than good. The rider must have confidence in himself and his horse at all gaits on the flat. He must have full understanding of the basic signals and controls and be able to use them independently but in coordination with each other. He must be able to maintain the correct position at all gaits.

If competent instruction is available on a regular basis, then this is the time to invest in as many lessons as possible. The instructor will then point out the obvious problems in the horse and the rider, and lay out a program of improvement. This also is the time for the rider to expand his theoretical knowledge. Some good books are recommended in the Bibliography, at the end of this book. Perhaps most important, the rider must now be willing to spend some time each day on the work of improvement. Your position will not improve if you think about it only once in a while. And obviously, it would be unfair and frustrating to ask a stiff horse to bend correctly on Saturday if you allow him to persist in his bad habits the rest of the week.

Now that you have made up your mind that you wish to improve yourself and the horse, let us check your basic position. For work on the flat, you wish to have as much contact through your seat and legs as possible with the horse in order to have maximum influence and communication with him; therefore lengthen your stirrups as far as you can while maintaining your security. (However, better a hole shorter than ideal than a pretty picture but an unsteady seat.)

To find out how long your stirrups should be, drop your leg down as straight as possible from your hip, turn your toe up and then roll your thigh and knee in and forward until you reach a comfortable position. Your thigh should create approximately a fifty-degree angle to your upper body. Adjust your stirrups to this length. Shorten them another hole if you find yourself losing the

A nice square halt: the rider displays a good basic position for dressage work, though hands are still slightly unlevel.

stirrups or you are unable to keep your weight down in your heel. It takes time and a lot of practice without stirrups to develop a "long leg," and this should be part of your daily regime. Grasp the pommel of the saddle lightly with one hand if you are insecure at the trot and canter.

The leg we aim to develop in dressage work has the following characteristics: the thigh lies flat on the saddle, the knee is pushed down as low as possible, the calf lies flat against the horse for as much of its length as is permitted by the conformation of both the horse and rider, the toe of the foot rests squarely on the inside of the stirrup, with a firm but not heavy pressure, and the foot parallels the body of the horse as nearly as it can without cramping the leg position. The weight of the rider pushes firmly and evenly down the inside of the leg to the inside of the anklebone and then to the heel. The whole leg is supple and sensitive with no added pressure at any point, such as the knee, the calf or the ball of the foot. The aim of developing this smooth, wrap-around leg is to increase the usefulness of our leg signals and controls. If the leg is cramped or pinched in at the calf (for example), then the calf will be unable to give signals as well as impairing the effectiveness of the rest of the leg.

The seat should be placed squarely in the deepest part of the saddle, which should be relatively far forward. The ideal saddle

(Left) The horse is not moving straight because the rider has collapsed her left hip and lifted her left heel, thus pushing the horse's haunches to the right. (Right) The horse is now moving straight, the rider having pushed his haunches to the right by carrying her right leg back a little.

for flat work is a dressage saddle; next to ideal is an "all-purpose" saddle. The weight of the upper body pushes down squarely onto the seatbones which rest comfortably wide apart on the sides of the saddle tree. The lower end of the spine is "at rest," neither pushed toward the back of the saddle as in a jumping position nor pushed forward as in a driving position. The hips should be square and level and in the same perpendicular line as the heels. The small of the back is supple, neither arched forward nor collapsed and rounded. The rib cage should be lifted (take a deep breath and exhale slowly) and the shoulders rotated backward, presenting an "open front." The neck should be without tension and the head level and square, eyes to the front and chin slightly pulled in. In other words, the rider sits tall in the saddle. One of the commonest faults is dropping the head and shoulders while watching what the horse is doing. If you must look, learn to glance down your nose.

The upper arm drops down from the shoulder close to the body and slightly in front of the perpendicular, with a bent elbow. The hands are slightly above the withers in front of the saddle and held three or four inches apart. Be careful not to turn the hands inward, thus breaking the wrist to the outside, while trying to maintain a steady contact. This can happen if your reins are too long. All the joints are relaxed and without tension. This position will be constantly modified, though only in very small ways, when the horse is in motion. These modifications, which up until now we have called signals or controls, will become in the more advanced rider true aids to the horse through their coordination, promptness, clarity and appropriateness.

REINFORCEMENTS OF THE AIDS

Once the rider has a secure seat, he will wish to use two artificial aids: a whip long enough to reach behind the calf without moving the hand, and spurs, usually of the short neck, blunt variety. The whip should be carried in daily rides to reinforce and keep the horse alert to the leg aids. The butt end of the whip is carried in the fork between the thumb and forefinger and, when not in actual use, the hand retains its normal position with the lower end of the whip resting across the lower thigh. A small flick of the wrist will then cause the proper whip to give a firm tap behind the calf.

An excellent leg position for flat work, providing strength without tension. The spur is properly adjusted, but the loose end of the spur strap would look neater if it were shortened.

Spurs are worn in order to extend the heel of the boot, not as a prod. They are usually positioned on top of the horizontal seam of the heel of the boot. Spurs can be particularly helpful when the conformation of the rider and the conformation of the horse are not entirely suitable, and with some horses whose sides are dull. However, they should always be used with discretion, particularly the more severe type, as they can be annoying to the horse or can encourage him to withdraw his ribs away from the legs. If you feel you need spurs to prod the horse along, perhaps you are not using your whip effectively or quickly enough when the horse does not respond to the leg aids.

The voice is an aid that the dressage beginner is not encouraged to use because it is prohibited in competition, and he tends to replace more important signals with it or uses it to no purpose at all. However, it can be an excellent tool with green horses. The words used are unimportant. It is the tone and emphasis which will communicate itself to the horse. Of course, repetition of the same word for the same act is helpful, such as "No" and a short, sharp tone for such naughtiness as bucking, shying, etc. Low, drawn-out words such as "Slo-oooow———" soothe and slow the horse.

THE AIDS

The Seat

The serious rider must learn to use his seat as an aid, not just as something to sit on. By now the seat should be secure and supple enough to maintain balance at all the horse's movements and in all of its positions. You have been constantly striving to develop feel and balance, mostly with a supple back which permits the seat to follow the movements of the horse. Now you must learn to use the seat as an active aid, principally through the act of pushing both seatbones forward and down to drive your horse forward or of putting more weight on the inside of a turn to encourage the horse to bend in that direction. The driving and bending actions of the seat support the driving and bending actions of the legs. As the horse becomes more responsive, less vigorous driving aids will be required.

You drive your horse with your seat to accelerate as well as to retard because both these actions require an increase in impulsion in order to be carried out in balance. The hands now must complete the line of communication by either yielding and allowing the horse to move forward, or by becoming fixed and thereby retarding the horse. We so constantly use the phrase "drive the horse forward," meaning push the horse up onto the bit with your seat and legs, that the rider may get the impression that this must be done with a great deal of energy. Not so. It should be done with as little force as necessary. If the horse does not answer to a light to moderate push, then he is not physically or mentally ready to do what you are asking of him.

A light to moderate push to the seat can be achieved by using principally the muscles of the lower back. You should not round your shoulders and back in order to drive harshly into his back. The seat is a powerful aid and should be used with discretion. Be aware that a horse can develop a hollow back as an evasion to improper or overuse of this aid, especially in the early stages of his training. Particular attention must be paid to how much pushing a young or green horse's back can take without creating resistances.

The Legs

The rider's legs activate and control the hindquarters of the horse, which really provide his motive power. They tell him when to start, to stop, to increase and decrease speed and when to "rev up," or in horseman's language, to increase impulsion. The other aids also play a part in all these actions but they should be secondary and supporting to the legs. To encourage the above actions the legs must act just behind the girth, not halfway back to the rib cage. When a leg is used farther behind the girth the hindquarters will move away from it, and it is used there to influence direction rather than impulsion.

The Hands

The hands receive the energy created by the legs. Therefore when you are working your horse on the flat or over jumps you must ride with constant light contact with his mouth. Otherwise the energy you are generating is mostly lost or, at the very least, lacks control. The hands also direct the forehand. Sympathy and accuracy in the use of the hands are what make the difference between their use as simple signals and controls or as true aids. A common fault is using too much hand and not enough leg.

We have already discussed the leading, direct and bearing reins in an earlier chapter. The only important rein effect that remains is the indirect rein of opposition, which is always supported by the outside rein to prevent over-bending (or worse, bending in the middle of the neck). The indirect rein of opposition opposes either the haunches or the forehand, depending on the placement of the rider's hand.

The *indirect rein of opposition behind the withers* is used to oppose the haunches, that is, to keep the haunches from drifting toward it, or to actively move the haunches away from that side, as in a turn on the forehand. The hand moves toward the center of the withers with a slight lifting motion toward the belt buckle of the rider. It should never cross over to the opposite side of the withers, and the feel should remain elastic. In this way the hand can support the leg in the control of the direction of the hind-quarters.

This horse is tilting his head instead of turning his body toward the new direction, usually a symptom of too much rein and not enough leg.

The *indirect rein of opposition in front of the withers* directs the forehand away from it, or prevents the forehand from falling inward. With a shortened rein, the hand moves in front of the withers toward the middle line of the horse. This rein is particularly useful to prevent the falling in of the forehand on a circle or its lagging in the leg yield. Beware of creating twisting in the head while using the reins of opposition. This occurs when the horse tips his nose to one side instead of properly bending at the poll and can be noticed immediately as one ear will drop lower than the other. When your hands become more educated, you will feel the beginnings of unlevelness through the reins. As in teaching all aids to the horse or rider, the rein aids will necessarily be more obvious during the learning process but will diminish to the point where the slightest twist of the rider's wrist or squeeze of the fingers will achieve the desired result.

Weight

Your weight gives the first signal to the horse that you wish him to increase or decrease speed, or to turn, and yet it is the most often neglected. The reason for this is that the rider subconsciously does not really think that his relatively small amount of weight is going to affect the relatively large bulk of the horse. But it does, particularly when it blends smoothly into the application of the other aids. For example, to make a downward transition the rider's weight stops following the motion of the existing pace as the rider "sits tall," stretching his spine upward, and bracing his back.

The expression "bracing the back" is more easily felt than explained. When the muscles of the lower back are relaxed, they allow the seat to follow the movements of the horse. When the same muscles push down and forward, they push the seatbones down and forward too, creating impulsion in the horse. However, when the lower back muscles brace they neither follow the motion of the horse nor do they push but rather they become taut in order to plant the seat firmly in the saddle (to combine two of Webster's definitions of "brace").

The rider's legs then close on the horse's side and his weight sinks from the seat of the saddle down through his legs into the stirrups. Then the hands squeeze the reins as the horse seeks this new balance. These aids follow each other in such quick succession that they seem almost simultaneous as the horse and rider become more experienced. Only when the simple aids do not get a response do the stronger aids of pushing with the seat and repeated squeezing of the rein and leg come into play.

To slow the horse, the rider's weight should stop following the pace and the rider should "sit heavy." To increase the pace or make an upward transition, the rider should sit more lightly. In dressage work at slow paces and on level ground this does not mean that the rider should lean forward, but rather that the rider should lighten the load of weight on the horse's back by shifting his weight to the forward edge of his seatbones. At the walk, trot, and canter on the flat the horse's momentum is too slow to necessitate leaning forward. In doing so the rider would lose much of the use of his seat.

The underlying principle in using weight as a directional aid is that the horse turns to the side on which added weight has been placed in order to compensate for it. The rider therefore places his weight on the inside seatbone, which is the side toward which the horse is flexed: the rider prevents the horse from "falling" to the inside by the active use of the inside leg at the girth with repeated squeeze-hold (pulsating) motions, which encourage the horse to bend his body and to support it with his inside hind leg.

These motions also drive the horse onto the outside rein so that the rider can control the amount of bend with the outside rein. The rider sits more heavily on the inside seatbone without dropping (collapsing) the inside shoulder or hip. This habit actually

Major Beale demonstrates the transition from trot to walk, the horse staying soft and in balance.

Here Major Beale demonstrates contradictory rein aids: the inside hand asks the horse to bend to the left, but it must pull instead, since the outside hand has crossed the withers and is flexing the horse to the outside.

shifts the weight to the outside; try it in an exaggerated manner and you will feel the weight shoot to the outside. When moving in a straight line, the rider's weight should be placed squarely on either side of the horse's backbone. It is easy to fall into the bad habit of sitting a little crooked.

BASIC PRINCIPLES

Properly timed aids are essential in truly helping your horse to carry out your wishes. Obviously one aid must not contradict another. Yet, obvious as this is, many riders inadvertently do just this, either by not understanding the effects of the rein, weight and leg aids and/or by not timing them correctly. As the calf muscles tighten to squeeze the horse forward, the hands must yield immediately, if only by a slight giving in the fingers, or the hands will have contradicted the signals given by the legs.

When moving or halting on a straight line the hands must be level and the reins of equal length. Only when the horse or part of the horse deviates from the straight line does the appropriate hand or leg change position to correct it.

For example, when a horse is traveling on a straight line and his quarters drift to one side, you should immediately slide your leg on that side slightly backward and, with repeated push-hold motions, direct the quarters back to the straight line.

143

On a circle the whole horse is bent from the poll to the tail so that his body travels the exact line of the arc. This is not easy for a horse until he is well muscled, balanced, and moving with good rhythm. His quarters will tend to drift to the outside while his forehand drifts to the inside. He does not want to bend in his spine or perhaps maintain the track with his inside leg.

Keeping this in mind, you will understand that the inside hand must be very soft, only indicating the direction by giving the flexion to the head or else the horse will be pulled into the circle. The outside hand controls the amount of bend and regulates the pace with the support of the inside hand if necessary. The inside leg indicates the amount of pace desired and also encourages the horse to bend with the rhythmic squeeze-hold motions of the calf. The outside leg is placed slightly to the rear of the girth with a holding pressure to encourage the quarters to keep to the bend of the circle. It becomes active if the quarters straighten or drift to the outside, and it returns to the girth in order to support the inside leg if necessary to maintain impulsion.

The balanced horse should work on the circle principally from the drive and bend given by the inside leg controlled by the outside rein. The second the horse is working on the circle (or anything else) to your satisfaction for the amount of training he has had, the aids stop being active and become accepting (holding). This is his reward. You accept his steadiness by being steady yourself. The moment some part of the horse or the pace becomes incorrect, it should be corrected by an active aid.

The basic position of the hands is just above the withers with the thumb pointing slightly toward the horse's mane. However, the hands should not break the straight line from the elbow to the bit. If the horse raises his head up out of position, the hands must follow it upward. The active leg aids will then be applied at the girth and, as the horse comes back up to the bit, the hands will yield downward. When the horse lowers his head, as in stretching exercises or for galloping, etc., the hands follow downward and forward.

However, if the horse leans on the bit by lowering his head, increase the impulsion with strong leg aids, and try light upward tugs with one hand, if he is boring on one side. If he leans on both hands, try vibrating the bit gently with your fingers by slipping it from one side of his mouth to the other with tiny sawing motions. If this does not seem to be the answer, try dropping the contact altogether, and then immediately drive with your legs and simultaneously pick up the contact again. As you drop the contact with his mouth he will lose his balance, and, after several repetitions of this, he should find it more comfortable to carry himself properly. The most important thing to remember is that you *do not* accept his challenge by fixing your hand when he leans.

Constant changes of direction, such as serpentines, and changes of pace will help improve both your hands and your horse's balance. You are pushing him up to and onto the bit and lightening the forehand by increasing the proper use of his hindquarters with your legs; he should not be throwing his forehand onto the bit. If he reaches, grabs or snatches at the bit you have an entirely different problem. This usually occurs in the downward transition if too much hand and not enough leg is used, and/or if the horse is asked to make transition more quickly than his training and development make comfortable for him.

As a general principle, you must keep constantly in mind that every positive aid must be followed immediately by a giving or yielding motion. This yielding motion of the rider often takes place, particularly with green horses, before the horse has yielded. The greener the horse, the more often the squeeze-give, take-yield, push-hold, drive-hold motions will have to be initiated to achieve the desired effects. It is nearly always more satisfactory to increase the number of times you use an aid rather than the strength of it.

This is where man's greatest aid comes into use—his intelligence. For it is through his intelligent understanding of his horse's mentality and capabilities, his anticipation and therefore his encouragement or correction of his horse's actions, and his control of his own emotions so that he can impose his will on the horse that a rider becomes a true horseman. A horse will forgive many technical errors if he is sympathetic to his rider, and this state of being is only achieved by man's use of his brain, not of his strength.

The pulsing, take-give feeling is essential to all the aids. The aids are accepting or holding when the horse has carried out what was asked of him. This acceptance is not an abandonment, but a quiet maintenance of the status quo which rewards the horse. Actually, there is only very brief acceptance in good dressage work; the rider is constantly asking for more or less pace, impulsion, bend, etc., so you are constantly using your lines of communication. Your motions must be smooth and supple and applied with as little strength as necessary. The "taking" part of the action should never be abrupt, and the yielding should still never lose contact with the horse. Imagine that you are squeezing a rubber ball without popping it out of your hand and relaxing without dropping it when you give retarding-yielding aids. Try to duplicate the elastic feeling of a rubber band, never letting it fall slack, when you wish to bend your horse.

The legs must close at the girth and the hands yield in order to move the horse forward. The push-relax motion of the seat will be applied in rhythm with the take-yield of the hands and the close-hold of the legs in a slightly slower rhythm than the horse's pace when you ask for a slower pace, a half-halt or a halt. A half-halt occurs when the rider asks the horse to halt, and just as the horse starts to accept this request (yields), the rider drives him on again.

The leg must never lose contact with the horse's side any more than the hand loses contact with the horse's mouth. However, the type of pressure and the placement of the leg indicate to the horse what is expected of him and, when properly applied, aid him to fulfill your wishes. To retard or gather your horse, apply both legs at the girth in drive-hold motions, thus encouraging his hind feet to move further forward under his belly. This is called shortening his base. Use both legs equally to encourage the hind legs to maintain their position, because in the effort to gather himself, the horse will often try the evasion of crookedness.

The ideal leg aid for moving forward is a squeeze with the calf. If the horse does not respond as quickly as his schooling should permit, this aid should be reinforced with the whip, just behind the calf. The tap of the whip should always be definite, never tentative, as a nagging action only annoys the horse. A driving leg is one in which as much of the lower leg as possible wraps around the barrel of the horse at the girth and, with a definite forward impulse, pushes with energy and releases, only to push again. It may help you to think of pushing the horse out in front of you. This driving aid is necessary to activate the impulsion in all horses sometimes, and in green horses more often, but be careful that your horse does not become dependent on it. Remember, the ideal is to have the horse respond to the almost imperceptible squeeze, push, tap.

Essential to developing this responsiveness in the horse is the timing of your application of the aids. If the horse is physically or mentally unprepared, even the clearest or strongest aids will not be effective. Therefore, the first step in applying your aids is to have your horse's full attention. If you have been in a relaxed attitude, the first way to get his attention is to put yourself in a working position, i.e., establish contact with your horse through your hands, seat and legs. In other words, assume the correct position. This alerts him that work is about to begin. If you are already at work and the horse is momentarily distracted, you must first regain his attention by the necessary corrective aids before you ask any more of him.

Not only must the horse be mentally prepared but he must be physically in a position to carry out your wishes. You must be able to feel where his hindquarters are and which of his feet are on the ground at any particular moment so that you do not ask them to move in an impossible manner. At first it may be difficult to feel the footfalls, particularly of the hind feet, but learning this is not a mystery, simply a matter of concentration and practice. It will help if someone calls out the footfalls for you or if you watch them in a mirror. The steps of the front legs can also be seen by watching the shoulders and felt through your thighs and legs as the horse's muscles swing back and forth. At the walk the push of the hind leg just before it leaves the ground and the swing as it moves forward are felt against your corresponding seatbone. Also the ribs of the horse swing out against the rider's leg when the corresponding hind leg is on the ground; they swing inward when that hind leg is in the air.

Because of the basic mechanics of the walk and trot, you will wish to use your leg on the side of the horse corresponding to the hind leg that is on the ground at that moment. When you wish to increase speed or impulsion, the horse is then able to put more thrust into the push off of the hind leg on that side. For example, if you wish to animate or lengthen your horse at the walk or trot, squeeze with your right calf when the right hind leg is on the ground and with the left calf when the left hind leg is on the ground, alternating for three or four times until the desired result is achieved.

How often should the same aids be applied in consecutive order before they lose their effectiveness? Remember that these various signals should be aids to your communication of the job at hand to the horse, not supports for the job itself. The horse should always carry you; you should never feel you are carrying the horse, nor should you allow yourself to be put in the position of "nagging" the horse along. Again, man's intelligence must come to the fore. He must constantly analyze his horse. A horse that is unfit or has a sluggish temperament will need stronger aids to get him to do his job. He will also put up with more repetition before becoming resentful.

A high-strung horse must be handled more carefully, even coaxed to put up with normal light aids. His exercises must be constantly varied to keep his mind active instead of fretful. He will probably learn his exercises more quickly and therefore will not need as much repetition. The sluggish horse tends to test your endurance; the high-strung horse, your patience and ingenuity. All horses need discipline, but the tug on the rein or the smack with the leg that will wake up your lazy horse may well shake up your sensitive horse. So a rule of thumb could be that if an aid repeated three times does not achieve at least some of its desired effect, then it and/or the exercise should be abandoned, if only for a few strides, before repetition. In the meantime, the rider should carefully think through *why* it did not work, starting with an analysis of his own application of the aid or selection of the exercise. Was the aid clear, was the horse prepared to receive it, does the horse have the proper groundwork to perform the exercise?

Because the propulsive mechanics of the canter are equally

Major Beale shows how to ride your horse forward between your hands. Notice the horse's impulsion.

shared by each leg in turn, there is no need to time your aid to the placement of a particular hind leg merely to ask for an increase in speed or a lengthening of stride. However, the timing you select must be consistent in the application of the aids. As most horses tend to become lazy with the inside hind leg on the bends and circles, it is better to apply your signal to move more forward when this hind leg is on the ground, which is also the same moment when the inside front hoof appears ahead of the shoulder.

WILLINGNESS TO MOVE FORWARD (IMPULSION)

Impulsion is that inner quality of the horse which enables him to carry out the job at hand in a lively manner. Basically, it is a willingness to move freely forward at any time. It is shown in the general alertness of the horse, in the lack of resistance at all gaits, in the freedom of the shoulders and the suppleness of the back and

Invitation to Riding

finally (and most important), in the rhythmic and powerful driving of the hindquarters. No matter what you ask of your horse he will be able to do it better as he develops more impulsion. Impulsion is not simply quicker steps nor is it a lengthening of the stride only by the front legs; in that case the horse would simply become heavier on the forehand. It is rather an increased use of the joints that occurs when the horse reaches with his hind feet well under his barrel and thus lowers his croup (engaging his hindquarters) and as a result, lightens his forehand.

A horse that has developed the proper impulsion for the job at hand will always be in balance. His hind steps will track truly the front steps. Before improved impulsion can be achieved, the horse must first be trained to move willingly forward at all gaits and even during his downward transitions. This is all that is required in the training tests. Starting with the First-Level tests, you are judged on real impulsion. You can practice this moving forward into the bit by working along straight lines and large circles.

General fitness and a good attitude are essential. These can be achieved by a hack through the countryside, working up and down hills, and consistent exercises such as lengthening and shortening of stride at all the paces and by varying your paces often. Work over cavalletti is excellent for development of the muscles and joints.

PACES

Your first efforts in training your horse will be directed toward establishing and improving his basic paces. Only after they can be performed with regularity and freedom will the development of contact and impulsion be possible. The horse that is tense and rushes his steps, or that is sluggish and drags his feet, cannot be put on the bit. Training a horse properly can be compared to building a brick wall. The foundation is the slowest but most important part of the job. If the foundation is unsound, no matter how beautiful the bricks built on the top of it look, the wall will crack and sag.

True, regular, free paces are the foundation of dressage; until these are established the horse should not be asked for a change

150

in head carriage or more difficult exercises. Then slowly one brick may be added at a time—first more impulsion, then more steadiness on the bit, then more accurate transitions and smaller circles.

Horses are not dumb, but they are slow to absorb new lessons, especially if they are taught more than one at a time. They learn by repetition and forget new lessons quickly. For example, a horse that has shown a few good steps of working trot has not "learned" to do a working trot. The exercise must be repeated for days, maybe weeks, on large circles before he can be asked to maintain it on smaller circles, straight lines and into transitions.

The Ordinary Walk

Too little attention is paid to the walk. It is the first brick in the foundation and of utmost importance. The ordinary walk should always be a four-beat gait. It should be lively without being tense, with free but definite, regular steps. The hind hoof should step in the print left by the front hoof. At the free walk, the horse's head should stretch well forward and the rider will allow this by lengthening the reins until there is almost no contact. The strides should be lengthened but the regular rhythm of the walk maintained. The hind feet should overstep the mark of the forefeet by at least a hoofprint.

A good walk: the horse is nicely stretched into the bit and moving with liveliness.

A good trot with the horse showing a nice outline, though a bit more impulsion might be desired.

The Working Trot

The working trot should always be a two-beat gait, the diagonals distinct and even, the hind feet stepping into the print of forefeet. It should be lively, regular and light.

The Working Canter

The working canter should always be a three-beat gait. (A four-beat gait can easily occur, especially if the horse is overly restrained, i.e., artificially pulled together by the hands rather than pushed forward into the bit by the legs.) This pace should be regular, balanced and light, with no tendency to fall on the forehand. This is perhaps the hardest pace at this level in which to preserve freedom as well as regularity and rhythm.

A good canter, the horse moving well through the corner.

CONTACT AND RELAXATION

At the Training Level the horse is expected to accept steady contact with his mouth and the rider is expected to maintain this contact. This contact must be maintained and accepted in a relaxed manner, and neither the horse nor the rider should show any tenseness.

OBEDIENCE, LIGHTNESS AND SUPPLENESS OF HORSE

In the First-Level tests, the requirement under General Impressions for contact and relaxation is taken for granted and is replaced by the requirement of obedience, lightness and suppleness of horse. Obedience means that more accurate transitions will be expected and any sign of disobedience will be more heavily penalized. As the demand for impulsion is also made at this level, so the demand for lightness naturally follows. The engagement of the hindquarters necessary in impulsion automatically lightens the forehand and thus lightens all the movements of the horse. The relaxation that the horse developed at the Training Level is now transformed into suppleness. This should be particularly evident in the transitions and smaller circles as there are no difficult exercises in First-Level tests to show this trait.

EXERCISES FOR THE HORSE

You may have thought to yourself several times while reading this chapter: "It's all very well to say 'establish the rhythm,' etc., but it's just not that easy." Obviously it is not. This is where knowledgeable help is of utmost importance. Every horse has his own small and/or large evasions and to propose solutions to them would take a book in itself. Therefore, ask someone who knows to help you analyze why your horse throws his head (hands too stiff and possibly too low), cocks his head to one side (one

153

hand heavier and not level with the other), switches his tail (heavily applied aids), carries his head too high (hollow and stiff back, needs suppling exercises), and so on, down the endless list of problems.

One suggestion for all is more longeing. First of all, longeing gives the horse an opportunity to work without having to balance the load of a rider and deal with the many distractions the rider presents. This is particularly true for a novice horse and/or a novice rider. Proper longeing with properly adjusted side reins (if anything, too loose rather than too tight) will teach the horse to bend and to accept the bit and provides a wonderful opportunity to study your horse and his reactions. Your horse will improve if he is longed correctly fifteen minutes every day before he is ridden and your riding will improve if someone longes the pair of you.

Your goals are set out for you in the tests. It is up to you to set up the daily pattern of work that will achieve them. A good regime is to start with work aimed at loosening the horse. For the first fifteen or twenty minutes either longe him, take him for a short hack, or work him on a fairly long rein on long straight lines and large circles. The object of this part of the exercise is to get the horse going forward. When he is relaxed, shorten the reins and start with a repetition of lessons already learned: straight lines, circles, half-circles and serpentines at all the paces in an area approximately the size of a dressage arena.

Trotting over cavalletti is an excellent exercise to increase the flexion of the horse's joints, to encourage him to lower his head, to improve his rhythm, and to lengthen or shorten his stride. The cavalletti should be sturdy and the spacing adjusted to your needs. Whenever the horse shows any signs of tiredness or resistance, walk on a long rein for a minute. Give him just long enough to relax but not so long as to cool off from the job.

EXERCISES FOR THE RIDER

The same advice applies to the rider. You will not help either yourself or the horse if you continue when you are tired or aching

How not to sit the trot: the rider's shoulders are rounded, the back is convex, the seat is pushed toward the cantle of the saddle, the hands are too low, the lower leg is pushed forward. The horse shows his discomfort with his tilted head, open mouth and poor impulsion.

from some tenseness in your joints or muscles. Walk, take deep breaths, rotate your feet out of the stirrups, your hands, shoulders or head, and analyze what was causing the tenseness. Were you dropping your head forward while watching your horse (making your neck and shoulders stiff), carrying one shoulder higher than the other (making your shoulders and upper arms stiff), sitting crooked and/or collapsing a hip (making your lower back stiff), or turning a foot in too much (making ankles stiff)?

As you begin to plan for competition, practice various sections of the test frequently, but ride the whole test only as often as necessary to get the feel and rhythm of it. Constant repetition of the whole test wil bore the pair of you and you will teach the horse to anticipate movements.

You can memorize the test away from the horse. Put down some sort of markers for the letters and walk it out on foot. Drawing the movements out on paper is another excellent way to get the feel of the test. Be sure you are totally familiar with the basic dressage terms used in this chapter and the additional information given in Chapter 13.

Only two arenas (enclosures), one twenty by forty meters, and

Invitation to Riding

the other twenty by sixty meters, are recognized for dressage tests: all Training and most First-Level tests are held in the small arena. (The letters remain in the same position; additional letters are added for higher-level work.)

The track is the path that follows the inside perimeter of the arena. When an instruction is given such as "take the track to the left," or "work on the left rein," you should know that your left hand is on the side toward the inside of the arena.

Vary the above exercises with a couple of turns on the forehand, several leg yields and shoulder-ins (when the horse is ready) from different positions and some lengthening of stride at the various paces. These exercises can be started as soon as the horse accepts the bit and works calmly.

TURN ON THE FOREHAND

In a turn on the forehand, the horse is asked to pivot around the front leg that is on the side toward the inside of the arena with his hind legs describing a half-circle. This exercise is done from the halt. When working on the track to the left, move off the track far enough from the side of the arena to insure that your horse's head and neck are not cramped from the movement.

Establish a square halt and be sure that you have your horse's attention and that he is accepting the bit. Then flex the horse's head slightly to the right. To flex a horse, you ask him to move his whole head to the left or right (lateral flexion) or backward to the vertical line (longitudinal flexion) by bending at the poll, never at the middle of his neck.

Put your weight on the right seatbone, which is now the inside seatbone because your horse is flexed to the right, and ask the horse to move his haunches sideways by moving your right leg behind the girth with push-hold motions, and by using the right indirect rein of opposition.

Your left leg is placed at the girth, ready to control the hind-quarters if they become hurried and to prevent any stepping backward. The left rein is ready to keep the head and neck from flexing too much or to prevent any forward movement.

The turn on the forehand starts from a square halt with the horse flexed slightly to the inside (right) and the rider's right leg slightly behind the girth, preparatory to asking the hindquarters to move to the left.

The right hind leg crosses over the left as the turn continues. The horse has come up off the bit a little, probably because his right foreleg is a bit stuck—it, too, should be stepping around at this point.

After three more steps of the turn on the forehand, the horse is now back on the bit and completing the turn nicely.

The whole exercise should be carried out in a calm, step-by-step fashion. In fact, it is the very deliberate nature of the turn on the forehand that is its chief benefit as it gives the rider time to coordinate his aids and time for the horse to understand and respond.

If during the movement the horse resists or starts to flounder, simply walk forward, and when calmness is reestablished start all over again. If he moves out of position (a small step backward is allowed, but none forward), or starts to turn on the center or on the haunches, then halt for a second and start again.

One practical use of the turn on the forehand is to open gates. Ride parallel to the gate with your horse's head at the opening. Lift the latch and execute a turn on the forehand as you swing the gate toward you.

LEG-YIELDING

Leg-yielding is the first lateral (sideways) movement the horse is asked to perform. It is less of a gymnastic effort but prepares the horse for the shoulder-in. The horse is straight rather than bent but he is positioned diagonally to the direction of the move-

Leg-yielding: the horse is moving forward and sideways on about a forty-five-degree angle in a good rhythm.

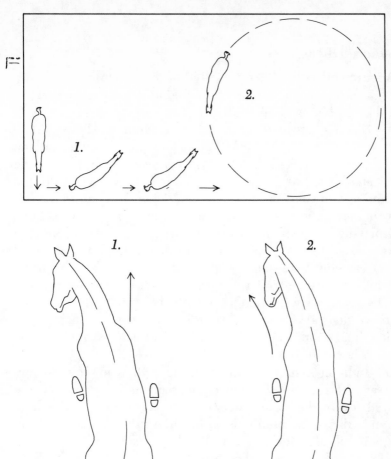

1. Shoulder-in   2. Circle to left

ment so that his body moves on a forty-five-degree angle forward and sideways at the same time. This is possible because the horse moves the one front leg forward and across the other and the one hind leg forward and across the other hind leg.

Leg-yielding is an excellent exercise to teach the horse the meaning of the lateral aids. As it may be first performed at the walk, it presents an opportunity for the rider to improve the application of his aids. When the rhythm and angle can be maintained at the walk for several strides and at will, then the exercise should be performed at the trot.

Leg-yielding can be done in different patterns. The easiest to begin with is probably to ask the horse to move down the long side of the arena (wall, fence) with his head facing toward the center and his tail to the wall. For example, take the track to the left, and as you come out of the corner, keep the bend to the left until the horse's forehand is off the track enough to put his body at a forty-five-degree angle to the wall. His head should be very slightly flexed to the left and you will direct him down the wall by (a) carrying both hands slightly to the right and (b) using your left leg just behind the girth to alternately give squeeze motions (when the left hind foot has left the ground, and therefore will move sideways away from your leg) and hold motions (when the left hind foot is on the ground) to direct his hindquarters sideways down the track.

Your right leg maintains contact at the girth, ready to make any necessary corrections. Your weight remains centered on the horse's back. As the horse understands what is being asked of him, the rein aids will be used only to put him in the proper position and then will all but disappear. The leg aids of course will also become less obvious, but they are still the dominant aids. After all, the point of the exercise is that the horse should learn to yield sideways from the pressure of the rider's leg.

Another pattern in which to ride the leg yield is across the diagonal from the corner marker to X with his body parallel to the sides, and then, as he meets the center line, to move straight ahead. As your horse becomes proficient in the exercise, he may be asked to leg-yield back to the next corner marker on the same side by changing his bending and your leg aids at X instead of moving straight ahead. The horse can also be asked to enlarge a circle by leg-yielding from a smaller one. This is an excellent exercise for horses that tend to fall into their circles.

Mix and match your patterns as the horse's ability demands. Be watchful for any loss of rhythm in his pace and always squeeze him forward with both legs on a straight line when the pattern is finished. A leg yield that loses forward impulsion is self-defeating.

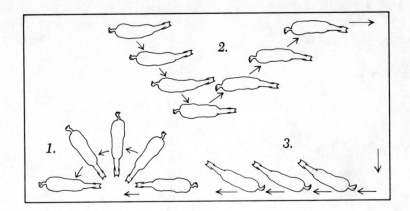

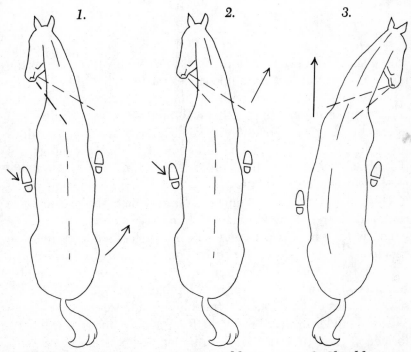

1. *Turn on the forehand*   2. *Leg yielding*   3. *Shoulder-in*

The easiest way to start a shoulder-in is out of the corner. The rider's inside leg is active at the girth.

SHOULDER-IN

In the shoulder-in the horse is asked to move his forehand to the inside of the track at an angle of approximately thirty degrees while proceeding forward with his hindquarters remaining on the track. Unlike leg-yielding, it is performed with both flexion and lateral bending, the horse being slightly bent around the rider's inside leg, i.e., away from the direction of the movement. It is a three-track movement, the horse's inside hind leg and outside foreleg sharing the same track.

This takes a definite gymnastic effort which the green horse cannot deliver, so you will first ask him only to do a shoulder-fore which is the same as a shoulder-in but of less angle. When the shoulder-fore can be performed without any loss of impulsion for several steps in either direction, you may then ask for more of a shoulder-in by moving the horse's forehand enough off the track so that his inside hind foot will track his outside front foot.

The shoulder-in may be taught from a walk but is mostly performed at the sitting trot and can be learned most easily out of a corner. If the horse flounders, ask him to move forward on a circle and then try the shoulder-in again when you reach the track. To perform the shoulder-in, take the track to the left. When the horse is moving with good impulsion and relaxation into the corner from the short side, maintain his bend to the left as you reach the long side until his forehand has moved slightly off the track. Keeping the bend to the left, push the hindquarters down the track and maintain the diagonal movement by using your left leg just behind the girth in the squeeze-hold motions, keeping rhythm with the stepping of the hind feet just as you did in a leg yield. Carry both hands slightly to the right.

The rider should look straight down the track and his right leg should be slightly back, bending the horse's quarters around his inside leg. The principal object of the exercise is to increase the flexion of the joints of the inside hind leg, which must step forward and sideways under the horse. The most common fault is for the horse to bend in the middle of the neck, causing him to shorten his stride and lose impulsion.

Let me offer some hints on teaching any of these exercises: start with the horse bent to the side on which he is less stiff, usually the left; wait until the horse is thoroughly relaxed but not tired; attempt the exercise only when the pace is correct and you have the horse's full attention; do not start a new lesson until the previous lesson has been well learned; be sure that your aids are sufficiently distinct and obvious until the horse understands what is wanted of him, when they should become minimal.

In this chapter, we have emphasized the independent value of basic dressage training for all horses and riders, quite apart from any competitive aspirations they may have. However, once they find out what it is all about, many riders become interested in gaining a little competitive experience, and this new challenge is especially attractive and valuable to those who are not interested in developing their jumping skills. Further information about dressage competitions will be found in Chapter 13.

At the shoulder-in the body of the horse forms approximately a thirty-degree angle to the track. The rider should be looking in the direction of movement.

10

Longeing and Sidesaddle Riding

LONGEING

Longeing is not exactly a part of the riding, but since it is an invaluable part of a young horse's training and can be an important part of an older horse's routine, it is a very worthwhile accomplishment to acquire. The process of getting a soft horse into condition can be accelerated by longeing him in the morning and riding him in the afternoon. It is also a way to exercise a horse that cannot be ridden for some reason, and a way to settle a fresh, fit horse to his work before you get on him, especially if you have no good provision for turning him out first.

Basic longeing is a skill that must be learned; longeing a horse in order to train him is an art that must be developed. The novice horseman should learn how to longe an experienced horse before he tackles a green one, as it takes a certain amount of dexterity to handle the line, the whip, and to keep the horse in a pace and position you wish.

The minimum equipment needed for longeing is a halter or longeing cavesson, a longe line at least thirty feet long and a longeing whip with a five-foot stock and a five- to eight-foot lash. A horse must be reliable to be longed with just a halter, as this does not provide much control if he decides to make a dash for freedom.

Longe lines, available at tack stores, are made of heavy tape

164

Longeing with a longeing cavesson: the shorter you keep the longe line, the more control you will have of the horse.

and have either a chain and snap or a leather strap and buckle at the end. A chain type is not suitable for use with the cavesson as the chain swings and rattles in front of the horse's nose and annoys him. Half-inch rope may be used as a longe line, but there is the danger of the horse getting a severe rope burn if he becomes tangled in it. In addition, it can be very hard on the hands. (Actually, it is always wise for the person doing the longeing to wear gloves, no matter what kind of longe line he is using.)

A proper longeing cavesson has several advantages over a plain halter: (1) it provides for greater control of the horse because the longe line is attached to a ring on top of the horse's nose; (2) side or running reins can be attached to the rings on the sides of the noseband; (3) it fits snugly; (4) in some models, a bit may be attached.

An ordinary snaffle bridle may also be used for longeing; the excess of reins is twisted under the horse's neck until there is no more slack and then the throatlatch is slipped through one loop and rebuckled. The buckle of the longe line is put through the ring of the bit and run up over the horse's poll and snapped at the top of the ring of the bit on the other side. Do not just snap the

Longeing with a snaffle bridle and side reins: the stirrups are firmly wrapped with the end of the stirrup leather so they cannot slide down and bounce against the horse's side. The longe line is run through the ring on the bit on the near side, over the poll and attached to the ring on the far side.

line on the ring of the bit on one side because it then will be constantly pulling the bit sideways through the horse's mouth and may give the horse a nasty jab if he starts to buck or run.

The horse may be longed with either a saddle or longeing surcingle. If a saddle is used, the stirrups must be secured by running them up and tying them with the excess of stirrup leather. A longeing surcingle usually has a buckle on the top so that the reins may be secured, and one to three rings on either side for the attachment of side or running reins at various levels.

Side reins should have an elastic insert so that they have a certain amount of "give." They are an aid to stabilizing the horse's head carriage and to encouraging him to accept the bit; on no account should they be adjusted tightly in an attempt to force the head into a certain position. Both reins should be the same length; do not shorten the inside rein in an attempt to flex the horse.

Start the longeing session with the reins longer than necessary and, as the horse starts to work well, shorten the reins gradually in order to establish more contact with the bit. One end of the side reins is snapped to the side rings on the cavesson for very young or green horses, or the ring of the bit; the other end is fastened to the billets of the saddle, or the girth, or the ring of the surcingle at the height desired.

166

The basic adjustment should permit the rein to run in a straight line from the horse's mouth back to the saddle when the horse is carrying his head properly. This adjustment varies according to the effect desired but both reins are always adjusted at the same height.

Seek an expert's advice on the adjustment of side and running reins. A running rein is a long rein which attaches to the surcingle at the height of the withers, is then run through the ring of the bit and back to the surcingle at a lower level.

If the horse is green, or just high-spirited, he should be longed with boots, at least on his front legs. Horses are more likely to interfere (strike one leg with the hoof of the other) during longe-

Properly adjusted side reins allow the horse normal head carriage and do not pull his nose into a vertical position. The horse should always wear boots during longeing.

ing than when they are being ridden or at liberty. Learn to handle the longe whip smoothly and quietly; one unintentional flick in the face can frighten a high-strung horse for weeks. Never use the whip to punish a horse and never hit him strongly in order to move him forward; a flick of the lash is usually sufficient for even the laziest horse.

Longeing at paces faster than a walk is hard work for the horse, so start with five-minute periods and build up to no more than half an hour. Change the direction in which he is being worked often. Be sure the longeing area has good footing and, if your horse is easily distracted, is quiet. A green horse will learn more quickly in an enclosed area, ideally a ring approximately sixty-six feet in diameter. If this is not available, use the end of a ring, indoor arena, or even a temporary fence of cavalletti along one or two sides.

Apply your full concentration and energy while longeing. Letting the horse putter along at the end of the line will not achieve much. The hand holding the longe line should maintain light, steady contact with the horse. A slack line indicates to the horse that this is not real work; it is also dangerous. Conversely, the horse should not be allowed to lean on the line; repeated light tugs will discourage this. The horse should be encouraged to use the full length of the line until he is fit and balanced; then his work can be made more interesting and more suppling by varying the size of the circles.

The hand holding the longe line should be held straight out from the body with a leading feel on the line. The whip should move from back to front toward the horse's hindquarters to ask him to move forward; it should be pointed toward his shoulders to ask him to stay out on the circle. The horse should obey the voice and whip commands promptly.

The voice commands should always be the same, given with the same intonation, and should not sound like one another. "Whoa" should be given in a slow, soothing tone to sound like "Ho-o-o." To steady a horse that is moving too rapidly, say soothingly, "slowly now," and give gentle tugs on the line. The command "walk-up," "trot-up," and "canter" should be given in a sharp tone of voice, accompanied by the whip signal.

Longeing without stirrups is a good way to develop a deep seat. Rest your hands lightly below the pommel of the saddle or on top of your thighs.

The horse should halt squarely on the arc of the circle. To prevent a horse from swinging in and facing you, walk toward him quietly, keeping the contact on the line, and repeating "Whoa." The rest of the time, the person longeing should pivot in the center of the circle. The majority of the work on the longe should be carried out at the trot. A young horse should not be asked for long periods at the canter until his balance is established; start by asking for only half a circle.

A horse can be taught to lower his head, use his back and lengthen or shorten his strides by longeing over poles and cavalletti. He should not be encouraged to shorten his stride, thus increasing the flexion of his joints, until his basic paces have been established. Longe a horse first over poles on the ground, starting with a single pole and building up to half a dozen, until he is working calmly and in rhythm.

Then advance to cavalletti, which should be no higher than twelve inches for a trotting cavalletto. Poles and cavalletti can be arranged in a straight line or in a semicircle like the spokes of half a wheel. The inside ends of the poles should be three to four feet apart while the outside ends should fan out to seven or eight feet apart. The horse can then be started through the distance that is comfortable for him and then gradually encouraged to lengthen his stride by easing him out on the circle where the poles are spaced farther apart.

The distances between poles and cavalletti for trotting should be four to six feet, and for cantering, nine to twelve feet, depending on the horse's stride. Very short-striding horses and ponies will need shorter distances. The horse should first be longed through distances that are comfortable for him until he can handle them in good rhythm on a regular basis. The distances can then be extended gradually to encourage him to lengthen his stride.

If you wish to longe your horse over straight lines of cavalletti or jumps, you must be willing to run. You must be careful not to get behind and end up dragging on the longe line or pulling the horse into a sharp turn after a fence. Side or running reins should be removed before asking the horse to jump. Set up a low, vertical fence nine to thirteen feet, after a series of trotting cavalletti or poles. A rail should be propped against the standard on your side to eliminate the danger of the line being caught on the top of the standard.

The cavalletti place the horse so that he takes one canter stride before jumping. When he can handle this situation well, remove all the cavalletti except the last and make the fence into an oxer. Eventually another oxer can be added, nine to twelve feet away for a bounce or eighteen to twenty-one feet for a one-stride. When measuring distances between fences, always measure from the landing side of the first to the takeoff side of the next.

The height of the fences should be well within the horse's capabilities so that he does not strain over them. The young horse should not be asked for more than a dozen or so jumping efforts in a day. When the horse is handling well the fences you present to him, then remove the last cavalletti so that he will have to place himself for the takeoff.

Horses love to play on the longe line and, although it is amusing to watch them have fun, it should be discouraged. They can fall or get a bad strain while bucking and turning in a tight circle and they can get a leg over the line as well. Also, some clever ones use a buck to get you off balance and then try to make a run for the open spaces.

Safety precautions must be rigidly followed, especially in an unrestricted area. It is easy to become a little careless, particularly when the horse is longeing well. Just as when he is ridden, the horse senses quickly any inattention and, if so inclined, will be quick to take advantage of it.

Keep the line away from the horse's and your feet. Never wrap the line around your hand or even carry a small loop that could be pulled tight. If the horse starts to pull or buck, brace your longeing hand, knuckles inward, against the back of your hip and tug at the line with your other hand.

Carry your whip properly so that you will not trip over it. If your horse is whip-shy, do not abandon its use; carry it butt forward, the lash pointing out behind your back. Introduce it toward the end of the lesson when he is relaxed and make all motions with it very slowly. In a few days he should realize that you are not going to hurt him. You need a whip to longe a horse properly so it is worth working to gain his confidence.

Horses learn to longe quickly when they are taught correctly and patiently. Choose a period of time when you can give a short lesson every day until he at least grasps the basics. An assistant and/or an enclosed area are a great help. The assistant carries the

An assistant is useful when you are training a horse to longe. Here the helper encourages the horse to move out in the circle and use the full length of the line.

whip and positions himself about halfway between the person holding the longe line and the horse, slightly to the rear.

Teach one pace at a time. Lead your horse around the circle and, a few feet at a time, ease toward the center. If he tries to stop he must be encouraged forward with the whip. However, when he succeeds in stopping and swings in facing you, the whip will be useless as he is facing the wrong direction and will not understand what you want of him.

He may become so confused that he tries to run backward, and this is a situation you want to avoid as you have lost your leverage on his head. A tug of war will then develop, and the stronger and heavier body always wins. The only thing to do when a horse swings into you is to go to his head, lead him back to the circle and start all over again.

After the horse walks in the circle and halts on command with little help from the assistant, he can be asked to trot. Once the horse has learned his lessons at the trot, the assistant can be omitted. The canter should not present any problems if the proper groundwork has been done and if it is only asked of the horse when he is physically capable. A great deal can be accomplished at the trot on the longe, so there is no hurry to start the canter.

You should be able to longe an unspoiled horse within a week without assistance. Avoid unhappy situations by remaining alert while longeing and you will not have to worry about retraining a spoiled horse, which can be a long and tedious experience.

SIDESADDLE RIDING

Riding sidesaddle is a much more specialized skill than longeing, and a much more limited one, since men are excluded to begin with, and even the vast majority of women prefer to ride astride. Nonetheless, the art of sidesaddle riding is currently experiencing something of a renascence, thanks largely to the horse shows. A number of our leading shows now offer a class on the flat open only to those riding aside, and this has encouraged many young people to essay this form of riding, even though they normally still ride astride. A few shows even offer complete divisions, including

Mrs. Bowen demonstrates correct attire for a lady hunting sidesaddle. The breastplate is too big for this horse.

classes over fences, and several exhibitors compete in dressage in skirt and veil.

It certainly makes a lovely picture, if the rider has a good seat and is mounted on a horse with an elegant head carriage and a first-class way of going. In sidesaddle riding, as in any other aspect of horsemanship, a good instructor is almost essential if the rider is to be successful. Therefore, we will only discuss the basic principles involved in order to acquaint those who might be interested in riding sidesaddle with both its attractions and its problems.

Sidesaddle attire is called a "habit" and differs from that worn astride chiefly in the skirt which covers the legs. For formal attire the coat, skirt and breeches should be dark blue or black and the headgear a derby or a silk hat with a heavy mesh veil fastened around the brim and covering the face. The sidesaddle itself is substantially heavier than an ordinary saddle, due to its greater size and amount of padding. There are as many differences in sidesaddles as in regular saddles and it is particularly important that the saddle fit the rider; an inch can be critical.

The panels are usually covered with linen, which is cooler on the horse's back than leather. The pommel provides a base of support for the right leg, the leaping horn for the left thigh, and the balance strap helps offset the additional weight to the left by

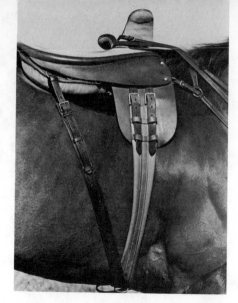

The fit of the sidesaddle is critical to both the comfort of the rider and the comfort of the horse. Note the balance strap that runs from a D under the seat of the saddle on the off side to a billet under the flap, and the special form of safety stirrup.

running from the right rear of the saddle, over the girth, and buckling to the left billet strap. A third strap runs over the balance strap to hold down the right flap. Most sidesaddles are built so that the rider's legs are carried on the near side, although off sidesaddles are available.

Those who prefer the sidesaddle praise its greater comfort for the rider on a long ride or hunt and its greater security for ladies who lack the muscular strength and long legs of a man. But certainly the twentieth-century woman, with her increased height and participation in sports, is more suited to riding astride than her grandmother. Some of the problems presented by the sidesaddle are that it is difficult to fit to many horses and that the rider has less control and "feel" of her mount. And though the rider may be less likely to be bucked or jumped off her mount, she is more likely to be pinned under him if he falls. It can also be difficult to keep your seat if your horse shies quickly, particularly when he ducks to the left.

Jumping can be an awkward experience if the horse does not go well forward into the fence and leave the ground smoothly. However, some old wives' tales are obviously false: the balance strap does not make a horse buck if he is properly introduced to it; the rider can be forward and with her horse over a fence; she is not likely to develop curvature of the spine!

A horse that has never carried a sidesaddle must be allowed time to become acquainted with it and with the different feel of the weight of the rider. Check the girth thoroughly before mounting, as it cannot be adjusted from the saddle. With the bulk of the skirt hanging over the left arm you can mount one of two ways. From a mounting block, face front and hop up, twisting slightly so that you land sitting sideways; then lift your right leg over the pommel. Alternatively, you may mount by using the stirrup, just as on an astride saddle, and then hook your leg over the pommel.

Once in the saddle, adjust the skirt over your right knee and hook the elastic under your right foot. In order to dismount, unhook the elastic and gather the skirt over the left arm. Remove the foot from the stirrup, throw your right leg over the pommel and slide down with your back to the horse.

The objectives of the sidesaddle rider remain the same as those of the rider astride: to direct the horse through his tasks with a balanced but firm seat in a controlled but relaxed manner. Obviously, with both legs on one side, the weight is not perfectly balanced and the rider must consciously make an effort to keep her upper body as square to the front as possible and not let the right side slide forward. The shoulders and hips must stay square and level, with the spine perpendicular to the horse's backbone.

It is important in riding sidesaddle for the rider's back to be perpendicular to the horse's backbone and her upper thigh to be parallel to it.

The right thigh lies across the top of the saddle supported by the pommel while the lower leg hangs straight down with the foot parallel to the ground. The left leg is in the same position as astride, which allows a little space between the leaping horn and the thigh, or the stirrup can be shortened a hole or two so that the top of the thigh contacts the leaping horn. The longer stirrup is most suitable for people with long legs and the shorter stirrup is most suitable for those with short legs who might lose the stirrup when gripping the horn. The rider never drives her weight down into the stirrup. The angle of the leaping horn can be changed to suit the rider's conformation and the length of the stirrup.

The upper body should be erect but supple at the walk, trot and canter and inclined forward, with the seat partially out of the saddle, to gallop and jump. Traditionally the sidesaddle rider sits to the trot. However, if you have a horse that throws you at the trot or are moving over rough terrain, there is no reason why you shouldn't post; do whichever is more comfortable and thus more elegant. The hands must be carried higher and somewhat farther back than astride but still in such a position that a straight line is formed from the elbow to the horse's mouth. At normal gaits the rider should not need to exert any real grip but should be carried along, sitting easily on top of the horse. This is why a sidesaddle rider particularly needs a horse that is a good mover: she cannot stand in the stirrups to avoid the jolt of a bad mover as an astride rider can. When necessary, the thighs close on the pommel and leaping horn, providing a really secure seat.

A horse that is responsive to the aids given astride should pose no problem when ridden sidesaddle. A long, dressage-type whip should be carried for training sessions to help replace the right, lower leg and to tune the horse into the new signals given by the right thigh.

If you are interested in this form of riding, by all means investigate it. However, just because you are a competent rider astride does not mean you can "pick up" riding aside. Do seek a knowledgeable person's help.

IV·Horse Sports and Competitions

11

The Background
of Foxhunting

Man has hunted animals with hounds since the beginning of recorded time and undoubtedly for many centuries before. His first purpose was to put food on the table, but even when this was achieved he still went hunting. Seeking, finding, following and accounting for a quarry with a pack of hounds while following on horseback is one of the most fascinating and challenging of sports. Nothing clears the head better on an early morning than the cry of the first hound as he strikes the line; nothing lifts the spirit more quickly than the music of the pack in full cry and the "gone away" blown on the huntsman's horn. No art lover appreciates a great painting more than a foxhunter enjoys the panorama of hounds and horses flowing cross-country after a straight-necked fox. The sportsman's soul is fully satisfied when his good hunter performs to the maximum and hounds alternately run full out on a good scent and then carefully work out the line as the fox doubles and twists and turns.

Organized foxhunting originated in England in the seventeenth century. As the country became agrarian the need to hunt for meat disappeared. As the forest dwindled under the farmer's hatchet, so did the wild boar; even deer became scarce. However, sportsmen found the fox an even more challenging quarry and today in England fox hunts outnumber stag hunts eight to one.

The sport was brought to America by English settlers in the late seventeenth century. It flourished principally among the landed

gentry of the eastern seaboard. Despite the vicissitudes of a growing nation, the sport never died out and by the middle of the nine-
teenth century it was as democratic as the country itself. There
were private packs, subscription packs, and farmers' packs, and
farmers with a few hounds that would join others with a few
hounds just to go foxhunting. The Rose Tree Foxhunting Club,
established in 1859, is the oldest subscription pack in the United
States and was the indirect successor to the Gloucester Foxhunting Club with whom George Washington was known to hunt.
These were both subscription packs.

The majority of hunts in America are found east of the Missis-
sippi and most of them hunt fox, although a few hunt coyote.
Some only drag hunt and others both foxhunt and drag. (Coyote
are of the same genus as fox and have much the same habits; the
same pack of hounds can hunt fox and coyote when they are
found in the same area.)

Drag hunting requires that the hounds follow a line of scent
laid by dragging a bag of fox urine or aniseed cross-country in
a line that simulates the run of a fox. As the pack does not have
to contend with the wiles and weaker scent of a real fox, they
can run faster, on average. The advantages of draghunting are: a
smaller pack is needed; the drag can be laid in country where foxhunting would be impossible because of major highways, housing
developments, etc.; sport is guaranteed every time; the drag can
be laid over the best footing and fences. The disadvantages of a
drag hunt are: its predictability; the loss of the competition between, on one side, man and his hounds, and on the other side, the
fox; not as interesting hound work; lack of the complete challenge
of a true fox hunt; it usually ruins a hound for foxhunting.

The most common misunderstandings about foxhunting come
from its English heritage. First of all, many people think that it is
a sport of only the rich and social. This is not so. Although it took
two world wars to democratize the sport in England, foxhunting
in America has belonged to all that were interested since the
Revolution. The other major fallacy is that a pack of hounds is
taken out with the express purpose of killing a fox who does not
have a chance against them. Again this is not so. The fox is not
released in front of the hounds but rather is sought for in his

natural habitat and must first be found before he can be hunted. A fox which is left alone can almost always outwit or outrun the pack of hounds.

In England and Ireland the fox flourishes to the point of over-supply. The apparent reasons for this are the mild winters, which guarantee a steady food supply, and the absence of two diseases: rabies, which used to be a periodic threat to the U.S. fox population, but is now controlled by vaccine; and mange, which periodically kills off many of our foxes and for which at this time there is no preventive. In England, where there is an overabundance of foxes, hounds are encouraged to kill. In America hounds are usually encouraged to kill only when (a) a farmer requests it, i.e., once a fox has discovered a hen house and has become a repeat visitor; (b) when a fox is injured or sick.

Foxhunting is a sport in which people, usually mounted, enjoy following a pack of hounds as they seek, hopefully find, and then chase the fox until he either eludes them, goes to ground in a hole, or they catch and dispatch him. The foxhunter's pleasure comes from riding a good mount, watching the pack work, first to find a fox and then to solve all the problems he creates for them, and listening to the music of the hounds which tells him the story of the hunt.

ORGANIZATION OF THE HUNT

Foxhunting as described below is the form in which it is carried on in the United States. There are slight variations in form in other countries. The hounds are either owned by an organization supported by membership fees, or by a private person who accepts a subscription fee or donations according to the ability to pay, or by a private person who may invite others to join him. The Masters of Foxhounds Association of America is the regulatory body which recognizes packs of hounds, sets up standards and regulations, and maintains the *Foxhound Kennel Stud Book*.

The country of one recognized pack never overlaps that of another. However, there are packs that are not recognized which hunt where and in what fashion they will, but who usually cooperate with the recognized pack in the area. Hunting is conducted from approximately the first of August to the first of April, weather permitting. Foxhunting has its own terminology and so that we will not have to interrupt our story too often, you will find a glossary of terms at the end of Chapter 12.

All hunts are headed by a Master or two or three Joint Masters. The Master is in charge of everything associated with hunting. The huntsman is responsible for hunting the pack of hounds. He carries a horn and by blowing certain calls on it and by using his voice, he indicates to the hounds when he wishes them to draw a covert, when he wishes them to come back to him and pack up, and, when they have found a fox, gives them encouragement. The Master is usually an amateur and the huntsman is usually a professional. However, some Masters may act as their own huntsman; in this case they appoint a Field Master, whose job it is to lead the Field as close to the hounds as possible without disturbing them. Masters who do not act as huntsman usually act as Field Master.

Depending on the structure of the hunt, there may be a kennel huntsman or kennelman who cares for the hounds. Of course, the Master supervises the breeding and the care of the hounds. One or more whippers-in help the huntsman control the hounds. They carry hunting whips with long thongs, wire cutters, hound couplings, and sometimes wear a spare stirrup leather buckled over their right shoulder. The whippers-in insure that the hounds obey the huntsman by sending stragglers on to him.

A good whipper-in seldom cracks his whip, but when he does the hounds know they have done something wrong (such as running "riot" which is following any animal that is not a fox). They also scout for the huntsman; at least one will ride to the far side of a covert hopefully to view a fox away and report its direction to the huntsman if the hounds don't strike the line promptly. A whipper-in is always on the lookout for riot; the scent of deer is stronger and easier to follow than that of fox and if the pack gets rolling on it, they can be very hard to stop. Of course, the hounds are trained not to hunt anything other than fox, but there are always a couple of puppies that are unreliable. The whippers-in must know the name of every hound so that they can call them by

On a misty morning the Master, horn in hand, listens to his hounds work out a line in the cornfield. Good field hunters are judged by performance, not by looks. This 17-hand half-pinto–half-Thoroughbred, Lord Knows, is also successful in the dressage arena and combined training.

name and report on their behavior when the huntsman cannot see them.

The secretary or a member of the hunt committee is responsible for collecting the capping fees of visitors and for reporting to the Master any damage to the property or any breach of hunting etiquette by any member of the Field. The hunt committee often assists the Master in policy making regarding the hunt and in maintaining the countryside.

It is a great honor to be asked to be a Master of Foxhounds, but it is also a great deal of work and, usually, expense as well. In the spring and summer, the Master sees that the hounds are properly exercised and that the puppies are walked and then introduced into the pack. He visits landowners and sees to it that fences are repaired and built. As the time to hunt approaches, he makes sure that the paths and fences are cleared. During the season, he decides when and where hounds will meet. This information is listed on the fixture card which is then sent to members of the Field.

Jointly with the huntsman he decides when and what coverts to draw and when it is time to take the hounds home. He must know every inch of the countryside, including where hounds and/or horses are not welcome; he must decide when to cancel a meet because of unsuitable conditions. He will try to provide the best possible sport without damage to property and is constantly trying to maintain good relations with the landowners. As a member of the Field, you owe him your utmost cooperation.

THE FOX

Both the red and the gray fox are native to America, although red foxes were found only in Canada and the northern United States until they were imported from the British Isles during the early eighteenth century to Maryland. Now both kinds of foxes thrive in most parts of the continent, although they are subject to the cyclical rise and fall of numbers that affect all wild animals. The gray fox is the smaller of the two and in most areas is not considered good sport as he usually runs in small circles, keeping to the covert, and pops up the first handy tree or down the first hole he finds. However, the larger gray fox of the south can be an exception and provide fairly good sport.

The wiliest, straightest running fox, the hero of fact and fiction, is the red fox, also known as Reynard and Charles James. Although he looks larger because of his luxuriant coat, most foxes weigh less than fifteen pounds, despite the occasional report of those weighing over thirty pounds. The color of the red fox can vary from a yellowish tan through bright red to such a gray-red that you must look twice to see that it is a red fox. They may or may not have a white ruff and/or a white tip on their brush (tail). Their legs

A vixen and her cubs enjoy the sun on the mound of earth outside their den.

are marked with black stockings and black hairs tip their ears and are often scattered over the rest of their body.

They each have their individual looks and ways of running and generally the huntsman knows his fox once he has seen him run. A fox establishes his home in a covert, usually taking over a groundhog (woodchuck) hole (earth) as a house for himself and his mate, and ranges out from there over a specific area for food. Foxes respect each other's holes and hunting ground. They prefer to hunt at night and sleep during the day, but luckily for fox hunters, they usually sleep above ground in such places as a sunny bank, on top of a fallen tree or in a cozy batch of honeysuckle. The hole is principally used for a quick retreat and as a place to have the family.

The eating habits of foxes are somewhat misunderstood. Although they are not above snatching a goose or a pheasant, they live principally off fruit, berries, rabbits, field mice and their kin. In fact, they eat almost anything from garbage to beetles. They prefer to stay away from man and his buildings, but if very hungry or if it is easily accessible, they will head for the chicken coop. However, they only kill to eat and will normally carry the chicken away to enjoy it in peace or to take it back to the hole for the family. The farmer who finds several dead chickens in his yard should not blame a fox, but rather a weasel or skunk. Another predator that will carry the chicken off is the raccoon and he can open many types of latches with his paws.

Those who like to shoot pheasants have felt that foxes keep the pheasant population down. However, researchers have proven several times over that the rise and fall of the pheasant numbers is not tied to the number of foxes in the area but rather to the natural law that decrees a cyclical rise and fall in the numbers of all wildlife. In fact, when foxes have been carefully removed from an area, the pheasant population has suffered from the imbalance in nature.

A dog fox (male) goes looking for a vixen (female) to mate with in December and January and he may range as far as twenty miles in the search. Some of the best hunts occur during the cold weather when hounds find him away from his home country and chase him many miles back to his hole. Once the fox has won his mate, they work as a team, seeking food and avoiding the enemy. When the vixen comes close to whelping or has already had her cubs, the dog fox, on hearing hounds or other enemies, will do all he can to attract their attention and lead them on a merry chase as far away as possible from his mate and the den.

Vixens have their cubs, averaging four to a litter, in March and April and most hunts stop at the end of March to avoid the chance of killing the cubs when they are old enough to come out of their holes, but too young to run from the hounds. The parents bring food back to the family and teach them how to hunt and avoid the many dangers that surround them. When they are old enough, the parents send them off to find their own holes and country which they often do in pairs. Eventually, these pairs separate at the onset of the mating season.

Most foxes like to run or else they would just slip down the

As the cubs mature they leave the family den, usually in pairs, to find their own den. They play and learn together.

nearest hole and would not provide any sport. Some consistently run better than others. When a fox shows a tendency to go to ground too soon the huntsman can do one of several things to outfox the fox: (1) stop (block up) the hole while the fox is out hunting; (2) send a whipper-in to stand by the hole in order to turn the fox away; (3) dig the fox out and send him on his way; (4) send a terrier down the hole in order to bolt the fox out the other end. In the latter two cases, the huntsman takes the pack away a distance and gives the fox a fair start. Usually, if you can get a fox to stay up and run well once, he will continue to do so.

How does a fox stay ahead of a pack of twenty couple (forty) hounds? The hunted always has an advantage over the hunters as he can choose where he wishes to run. Reynard is substantially smaller than a hound and can slip through places such as thick brambles and wire fences which slow the pack almost to a standstill. The hounds chase the fox by following his scent with their noses. As the fox hunts his own prey with his nose, he has strong instincts about scent and how to foil it (make it difficult to smell).

The fox's scent glands are in his pads (feet) and under his brush. He will run through cows, sheep, pigs, freshly spread manure, or after a deer knowing the stronger smells will mask his. He will run hard roads and dusty paths knowing they do not hold the scent well, and he will run streams and muddy fields knowing water and mud kill the scent. The fox's scent is strongest when he is running well; it is weakest when he is moving slowly, and it will sometimes disappear temporarily if he is badly frightened. Therefore, a fox may squat (lie still) or walk slowly out of a covert, even though the hounds are quite close, hoping they will pass him by.

The stratagems of the wily fox are legend and no man knows them all. Every old fox hunter will have his favorite tale, such as the one in which hounds would run a certain fox very well but would always lose him in the same farmyard. Where he went was a great mystery, until one day the farmer admitted that every time this clever Charles James had run up the ladder into the hay mow. However, there are certain tricks he uses consistently besides the ones already mentioned and the one that is hardest to solve is the double-back. When the fox is far enough ahead of the hounds, he will make a sharp U-turn running back directly the way he came for a distance before branching off in a new direction. Hounds naturally cast to the front and sides when they lose the scent of the fox and so Mister Fox will gain a good deal of time and perhaps "win the hunt" by fooling them altogether.

When hounds run backwards on the line of the scent it is called "running heel." Normally they are whipped off, so that it takes a good huntsman and whippers-in to know exactly where the fox had run when there is a chance of him doubling back. Reynard will also make sharp right-angle turns, twists and loops and cross his own line. A good fox does not make too much use of these ruses, but runs relatively straight ahead, earning him the accolade of a "straight-necked" fox.

These are Penn-Marydel foxhounds, taking a minute's romp before packing up. The Penn-Marydel was developed particularly for voice and nose and for moderate size that enables them to work through thick brush and wire fences.

THE HOUNDS

The hunt is only as good as its hounds, for the best running fox can provide no sport if the pack does not hunt him well. Hounds, never called dogs, have been bred expressly for hunting the fox for the last three centuries. The three main types of hounds used by organized packs in America are English, American, and cross-bred. All hounds are bred with the intention of producing the following characteristics: a good nose which can smell scent under varying conditions; drive, which is that urge to push forward on the line; for sense, which is the strong desire to find and hunt only fox; pack sense, which keeps the hound working as part of the team; cry, which is the tone and volume of tongue (never called bark) thrown by a hound; stamina, which implies good

conformation that enables a hound to move with efficiency and
stay sound; and, last but not least, sufficient speed to stay with the
fox in the country to be hunted.

The different types of hounds are bred with emphasis on one or
more of the above characteristics in order to make them particularly suitable for the terrain and scenting conditions of the area
in which they are to hunt. Without going into the finer points of
hound breeding, it can generally be said that the English hound
is known for his speed and drive, the American hound for his nose,
voice and ability to hunt without repeated help from the huntsman, and the cross-bred (English and American) hound is bred
with the intention of getting the best characteristics of both types
of hounds.

The American hound is descended from the English, Irish and
Welsh, and was selectively bred to hunt in the new continent with
its difficult scenting conditions and thick cover that often prevented the huntsman from getting to his hounds. Two main
strains of American hound have been developed: the Virginia
and the Penn-Marydel. There is not a great deal of difference
between them, but the Penn-Marydel is bred to be smaller, with
particular emphasis on voice and ability to hunt a cold line. These
characteristics make it easier for them to hunt through the page
wire and thick underbrush found in southeastern Pennsylvania,
Maryland and Delaware. Their marvelous voice is not only a
delight to the ear, but helps the huntsman and the Field know
their whereabouts at any given time.

A hound hunts from training, instinct and imitation. In the
summer of their first year, puppies are "walked" either by the Staff
(huntsman, whippers-in) or by individuals who take them to
their farms. They are taught the fundamentals of life, such as answering to their names and overcoming the urge to chase cats
and chickens. In the summer of their second year they are introduced to the pack during daily exercise, with the Staff first on
foot and then on horseback. They are often coupled by a leather
attachment on the collar to an older hound until they understand
the basic facts of life.

Cub hunting (cubbing) starts in August. The huntsman takes
the hounds out early in the morning for gradually lengthening

periods of time, the principal objective being to train the cubs (young foxes) to run and the puppies to hunt. Formal hunting starts in November when the worst of the heat is over and hounds are fit and ready to run as far as a fox will take them.

The puppies will be divided into three groups by now. Those in the quick group that have learned their lessons and are hunting well with the pack will be entered, that is added to the list of hunting hounds. The second group will be under the huntsman's careful scrutiny because they have certain problems such as: (1) babbling: speaking (tonguing) when not on the line of a fox; (2) loafing: not hunting until other hounds have opened up on a line or not casting after the line has been lost; (3) swinging: ranging far away from the body of the pack while drawing or wildly overrunning the line; (4) dragging: not keeping up with the pack. All these problems lie in the questionable category. It is the huntsman's dilemma to decide on how long he should give a puppy to enter or whether he should be drafted (removed from the pack). Then there is the third group of puppies, hopefully non-existent, whose problems were so severe during cubbing that they are no longer under consideration.

On a typical hunting day, hounds will be taken to the place of the meet and will pack up (gather closely) around the huntsman's horse, waving their sterns (tails) in expectation until given the signal on the horn, which is one medium-length note, to move off. The huntsman will then move the hounds as a pack to the first covert and, with his voice and horn, encourage them to fan out and draw the area. If the covert is small, this is a relatively simple procedure; if it is large, the huntsman will draw with the pack spread out around him in a pattern that will assure no part of the area is missed (remember the squatting fox), but at the same time emphasizing places that he knows from experience or intuition that a fox will most probably lie. During the draw you will hear him give encouragement with his voice and an occasional short note on his horn.

A word about hound language. The huntsman communicates with his hounds through his horn and spoken words. There are traditional notes and calls for all the important occasions during the hunt, but every huntsman has his own interpretation and one seldom sounds much like another. Therefore listen to your hunts-man and learn to interpret his "talk" and you will get added en-joyment from the hunt. We will give you clues to what he is saying as we go along.

The first sign that a fox is in a covert is a hound or hounds feathering a line; then a hound will open up with an authoritative ring to his voice which says to an experienced ear "this is fox" and the rest of the pack will soon honor him by joining in. The next few minutes are very important to the run as the fox will usually twist around the covert, perhaps crossing his own track several times in an effort to confuse the hounds and, if the pack does not push him he will elude them with one of his many tricks. However, a good pack with drive will keep on him and he will eventually break covert across the open fields. The whipper-in, or whoever views, will cry "tallyho" if he is not in sight of the hunts-man and then stand in the stirrups, remove his cap and point in the direction the fox took.

The fox has now gone away and, when the hounds are on the line, the huntsman will "double" his horn, that is, repeat several times one short note and then two very short notes. If the pack is at a loss (checks, stops tonguing because they cannot smell the scent) or does not seem to be hunting a line strongly, whoever viewed the fox will then ride up to the huntsman and give him details of where the fox went. After breaking covert, the fox will either pop down the nearest hole or go on to give a good run.

There will probably be some checks during a run depending on conditions. A good pack will immediately cast themselves, first forward, then to the sides in order to recover the line. If they are unsuccessful and their heads come up, the huntsman will then cast them by calling them and riding in the direction he thinks the fox took, or in one of several standard patterns, and cover the ground as quickly and efficiently as possible. Two of the most traditional casts are: "round the hat," which consists principally in making a large circle around the area where the hounds lost; the other is in the shape of a lazy S starting where the hounds lost, swinging backward and then across the front and backward on the other side and again forward across the front.

When the fox goes to ground, the huntsman will blow a long,

tremulous note on his horn and, dismounting, encourage and praise his hounds with such words as "dig him out." A good marking hound will dig enthusiastically and give tongue in a howling sort of way. The hunt may end in one of four ways: the fox eluding the hounds, the fox going to ground, the huntsman lifting the hounds, or the hounds killing their quarry. The first two have been discussed.

The huntsman lifts hounds when he calls them away from the line they are hunting. He never does this until they have checked. He lifts hounds because they are heading toward a dangerous area, because it is the end of a long day and the Master decides both fox and hounds have had enough, or because a view has been made ahead and he feels that the hounds are not doing well on the existing line so he takes them to the view, gambling that it is the hunted fox. Occasionally, hounds kill if the fox makes a mistake or is sick or injured. The fox is killed quickly by the lead hound who snaps his neck. The Master then awards the mask (head) to an appropriate person such as the first rider in at the kill or an honored visitor; the brush would be awarded perhaps to the first lady and the pads to the children.

THE HORSE

All horses, no matter how experienced they are in other fields, must be trained to hunt. A green or high-strung horse will take longer to learn than a horse that has been exposed to the excitement of the show ring and is thoroughly responsive to the aids. Some horses never learn.

One of the best methods to teach a horse how to hunt is to take him out on long hacks over the countryside through streams, ditches, trappy and thick places. Riding out with friends, galloping and jumping both in front and behind, is also invaluable. If your horse does not remain calm in these circumstances, he is not ready to hunt. Practice leaving the group and letting the group move away from you. A good hunter must not be tied by the apron strings to the crowd. He must be willing to walk through a dangerous place, even when the horses ahead have gone on, and he also must wait his turn at a fence as well as jog over it slowly if it is in a tight place.

If possible, introduce your horse to hunting slowly, especially if he is green. Start in the cubbing season in summer when he is (hopefully) lazy and relaxed and there are fewer people out. The first couple of times just take him to the meet to see the hounds and watch them move off. Then take him out for a hack so all seems part of an ordinary day. Keep a little away from all the excitement and do not walk up close to the pack where a hound may jump up and lick him on the nose, thus frightening him for months. The next step is to follow at the back of the Field (group of mounted riders) for an hour or so. If he shows extreme nervousness or hounds get running hard, take him home. The principle is to expose the horse to hounds as often, not for as long, as possible. If you have no alternative, you can try to get him to relax by keeping him out for the whole hunt when he is fit enough.

A word about fitness. To go foxhunting, a horse must be in physical condition to stay out three hours in the heat during cubbing and five hours, often including prolonged gallops, during the regular season. Obviously, a horse that is hacked once or twice a week will not be fit to do this. A horse in show condition would need some hill work and galloping. Exercise your horse as you would exercise yourself if you were getting ready for a ten- to twenty-mile cross-country run. Start with slow, hour-long works; build up to longer and faster exercises. Once the horse is hunting fit, you will ease up to a maintenance program such as: Saturday, hunt; Sunday, turn out; Monday, longe or hack; Tuesday, hack; Wednesday, hack including two one-mile strong gallops (or hunt); Thursday, hack including hill work; Friday, hack or longe. If your horse tires when out hunting, take him in as he is liable to make a dangerous mistake just when he needs all his wits about him. Signs of tiredness are stumbling, sloppy jumping, trouble getting his wind back after a gallop, and pulling at the bit.

Hilltopping is an excellent way to introduce a young horse to foxhunting. Some hunts frown on this practice, but others appoint an experienced person to lead this group of green fox hunters at some distance from the melee of the hunt. Inquire of the Master or hunt secretary if this is allowed. As your horse learns his lessons, you will move more toward the front of the Field. Do not expect him to act as he would at home. Most horses have a definite change of personality out hunting, and it is up to you that the change is for the better.

While out hunting, many horses start to kick from nervousness and/or being crowded by other horses. Prevention is the best cure. If he is kicking from nerves, walk around the checks whenever possible until he settles down. Jigging is another annoying habit which sometimes starts out hunting. See Chapter 7, Trail and Cross-country Riding, for suggestions on controlling bad habits.

Another change that may take place in your horse is that he becomes excited and rushes his fences. Keep in mind that horses are herd animals and this instinct becomes stronger during the group excitement of foxhunting. The hardest thing you can ask your horse to do is to stay within sight of the horses in front of him, but not allow him to go with them. Keep him within two or three lengths of the horse ahead or completely remove him from the group. As he gains self-confidence, you can teach him to be more independent.

This principle applies particularly to jumping. Rate your horse so that he approaches the fence at a steady pace, rather than getting there early and then making him stand and watch four or five horses jump before he is allowed to go. If this is impossible, turn his head so that he cannot see the fence, or walk in a small circle. Allow three to four lengths between your horse and the one in front in case the other horse refuses, jumps very slowly, or the rider falls. It is embarrassing enough to be flat on the ground, without being jumped on by the horse behind you! If you have a refusal, immediately go to the back of the Field before trying again. No foxhunter appreciates being held up by someone who cannot get his horse over a fence.

The tack you put on your hunting horse must fit perfectly and be in tip-top condition. What is safe and comfortable for an hour's hack may be dangerous and harmful to the horse during four and five hours out hunting. Check particularly those parts of the leather that rest on metal for thinness or deep cracking. Grasp the leather on either side of the suspicious spot and twist it firmly; if the cracks gape or the leather tears, throw it away. Be sure the jointures of the bits are smooth and close-fitting. Have your saddlemaker check the billets before the season starts. Never push the safety catch up on the stirrup bar. If your stirrup leather comes off the stirrup bar too easily, the saddle needs a trip to the harness shop.

Put as little tack on your horse as necessary, but make sure you have everything needed to control him. It is always wise to use a properly fitted martingale on a green horse until he has settled down. You may need to use a stronger bit, as many horses take hold out hunting. A breastplate will help keep the saddle from slipping back and a pad may ease the pressure on a horse's back. Sheepskin covers are available for girths that rub.

The hunting horse must always be shod with heels to give him added purchase. Borium, a hard steel melted onto the toes and heels of the shoe, will help give traction on slippery roads and ice, but also increases the concussive effects of the foot hitting the ground. Hence it should be applied smoothly in small amounts, rather than in large drops. The shoes should be on tight and all the clinches down. The horse should be thoroughly groomed and the tack polished and clean.

THE RIDER

In order to foxhunt safely and happily, the rider should be able to control his mount under all circumstances cross-country and be able to jump fences as high as the highest in the country in which he is going to hunt. Some countries have few fences and those are low; other countries require that you jump as high as five feet in order to stay with hounds.

Hunts have varying customs regarding visitors hunting, how many times they may cap, and the acceptance of new members and subscribers. If possible, ask a friend who is a member to introduce you to the secretary or Master beforehand and inquire if you may hunt on a certain day. If this is not feasible, call yourself and find out all the pertinent information, including the appropriate dress for the day.

Ratcatcher is traditional for the cub hunting season. A hard hat is always expected. Beginning with the regular season formal attire is worn, although some hunts wear ratcatcher on weekdays. The wearing of the colors and buttons, that is the collar of a specified color and buttons marked with the hunt insignia, and pink coats or the hunt's particular livery, is awarded by the Master to the members of the Field who have shown their knowledge and enthusiasm. If you are uncertain what to do or have a question, go to someone wearing the hunt livery.

Do not wear a pink coat or hunt livery or colors when visiting another hunt unless it is a Joint Meet or you are specifically requested to do so. Pink coats (named after Mr. Pink, a London tailor who started the fashion) or hunt livery of another color, such as buff, blue or green from an older tradition, are worn on Saturdays and holidays. Traditionally, hunting caps are only worn by the Staff, the Master, the hunt secretary, and children under eighteen. However, some hunts accept the wearing of them by all. The tails of the ribbons on the back of the cap should be sewn upwards if worn by a member, and should hang downwards if worn by a professional.

Riding clothes are designed for the practical purpose of protecting the wearer and must fit well. The finest hard hat available is worthless if it falls off. Buy the best you can afford and you will be repaid in comfort and durability. Ready-made attire can be very satisfactory if carefully selected. The leading suppliers have experienced people to help you. However, this is not always true of the smaller stores, so take along an experienced friend if you are unsure. Riding clothes are attractive when they fit well and are worn properly. Other adornments such as jewelry or scarves are inappropriate. Hats are worn squarely in the middle of the forehead, never on the back of the head or tilted at a rakish angle. Hair longer than collar length should be worn in a hair net or pinned up under the hat. Flowing tresses that are appealing in the ballroom look ridiculous on the top of a horse. Riding jackets should be of a discreet color and cut. They should be loose enough to allow freedom of movement and additional underclothing in the winter. Breeches should not be skintight, even if they are made of stretch material.

Wear your heaviest weight breeches when trying on boots. Boots should fit snugly at the top and be loose enough in the foot to allow for an extra pair of socks. They should be as tall as possible; when new, they should come right up to the bend of the knee, as they will sink at least one inch after wearing. Trees, either of plastic or wood, will prolong the life and looks of your boots.

Following are some of the basic attires to be worn in the basic riding situations. Of course, these do not cover all situations. For instance, the silk hat a lady or gentleman wears when riding a higher level dressage test is not the same silk hat that a lady wears sidesaddle or a gentleman wears with a pink coat. If you are investing in expensive clothes, put yourself in the hands of an experienced person.

The Master

RATCATCHER—Black velvet hunting cap, lightweight buff or tweed color jacket for cub hunting, tweed jacket for colder weather, informal riding shirt with colored stock or shirt and tie, buff, yellow or tattersall vest, rust, buff or gray breeches or jodhpurs, brown boots or leggings, yellow string or leather gloves, hunting whip.

FORMAL—Cap same as ratcatcher, pink or hunt livery frock coat, white, buff or rust breeches according to the livery of the hunt with three buttons at the knee, black boots with brown tops, white, buff or yellow vest, plain white hunting stock with gold safety pin worn horizontally, brown leather, white or yellow string gloves, hunting whip.

SHOWING—Informal shows same as ratcatcher. Recognized shows same as gentleman in a regulation hunting coat, except no hunting whip; appointment or corinthian classes, same as formal attire.

Gentleman Member

RATCATCHER—The same as Master except the headgear is a black hunting derby, always worn with a hat guard. (Note: hat guards are not worn now in England.)

Correct attire for a gentleman member, with pink coat and top hat. The armband denotes that this rider is a member of the hunt committee and is available to receive capping fees.

FORMAL—Regulation black hunting coat worn with plain black boots and black hunting derby, or pink, black or hunt livery coat of frock, shadbelly or weaselbelly cut, worn with silk top hat and guard and top boots; vest, stock, whip and gloves same as Master.

SHOWING—Informal shows same as ratcatcher. Recognized shows same as formal: no hunting whip, but crop if desired; appointment and corinthian classes, same as formal attire.

LADY MEMBER, Astride

RATCATCHER—Same as gentleman member.

FORMAL—Same as gentleman member, except the hunting coat may be dark blue, lady never wears a frock coat and only wears a pink coat or livery and top boots if she is a Master or a professional member of the Staff. Boots should be black leather and may have patent-leather tops. White breeches are worn only with the pink coat.

SHOWING—Informal shows same as ratcatcher; recognized shows same as formal.

CHILDREN

RATCATCHER—Same as adults except they may wear hunting caps and, until the child is well into his teens, jodhpurs are appropriate.

FORMAL—Same as ratcatcher, except that a blue, buff or green coat may be worn with jodhpurs, black or brown boots with breeches.

SHOWING—Same as adult.

GENERAL: Tabs at the top of boots should match the top, if there is one, and are sewn down only if the rider is a professional. Tops must be sewn onto the boot. Boot garters are part of formal wear; however, they should not be worn with breeches that do not have knee buttons. They should be positioned between the lowest two buttons with the buckle to the outside of the knee and the end of the leather pointing backward. The color of the garters should match the breeches if top boots are worn; otherwise they should match the boots, and be of patent leather with patent-leather tops. Spurs should be conservative and placed high on the heel; the end of the spur strap should point to the outside and should be cut off if it is of excessive length. Your clothes should be clean, your jacket always buttoned, your stock tied and pinned neatly and your boots polished. You are going to be a member of

The lady is correctly attired in a dark blue coat. The rubber ring on the bit of the horse prevents the bit from chafing the sides of his mouth. Saddle pads are not very elegant, but they save many a sore back.

the Field, and a well turned-out Field is a credit to the Master and a joy to the countryside.

On a hunting day, allow more than enough time to get to the meet at least ten minutes before the carded hour. Most hunts move off exactly at the time printed on the fixture card, even though it is called "the meet." Do not ride through any coverts on the way to the meet or on the way home if you leave early, as you may disturb just the fox who would provide good sport for the day. Greet the Staff and the Master and do not speak to them again until the end of the hunt, unless they address you. They are working all day to provide sport and do not wish to be distracted.

If you are a visitor, arrive early enough to introduce yourself to the Master and in turn be introduced to the members of the Field. Group spirit is one of the joys of foxhunting and an unknown face in the Field can produce awkwardness. You will also need time to find the secretary or Master to give them your capping fee; they should not have to seek you out. Have the exact amount of the capping fee ready as the hunt is not equipped to act as a cashier.

There is a traditional order in the Field. After the Field Master ride those members who have been invited to wear the colors, then those senior members who do not yet have their colors, then the juniors, then the professional horsemen and finally those on green or problem horses. Of course, you may always pass someone who has had a refusal or whose horse cannot keep up. If you cannot keep up, immediately wave on those behind so they do not miss the run.

Not only should you never pass the Field Master, but go to great lengths not to crowd him. The job of keeping the Field close to the hounds without over-running them or getting in the way of their cast at a check is difficult enough without the Master having three or four thrusters pushing at his horse's heels. Three or four lengths can make all the difference to his maneuverability.

Be constantly alert. You never know when you may view a fox. When you do view, note carefully what line he runs. Do not tally-ho if hounds are on the line; that would be stating the

George, Jr., is properly turned out in ratcatcher for hunting or showing. The pony has been clipped in one of several useful trace patterns.

obvious. Also note the condition of the fox; was he walking, trotting, or running? Is he healthy? A mangy fox will have a dull, ragged coat and may have little or no hair on his brush. Is he a fresh fox? Is he the hunted fox? If he has been running, he may be wet or muddy or his tongue may be hanging out if he is tired. If you see a fox, keep absolutely still until he is well on his way or else you may turn him.

When one of the Staff is in sight, then ride to the point where the line is, stand in your stirrups, point your hat in the correct direction. When no one is in sight, then tally-ho two or three times and carry out the above procedure when the huntsman appears. If hounds are not running and your tally-ho has had no response, then quickly go find the huntsman and tell him your story, including how long it has been since you viewed. When a farmer or car follower tells you he has viewed, get exact information before you gallop off.

A word of caution: be sure it is a fox that you have seen. It is amazing how much a cat can look like our Charles James, especially when you only get a quick glimpse. If you are unsure of your view, do not tally-ho, but ride up and tell the huntsman that you *think* a fox went such and such a place. He will then act appropriately on the information.

Constantly try to save your horse's strength, as the best run may come at the end of the day and it is too bad if you have to pull up because he is leg weary from needless gallops and quick starts and stops. Ride as if you are driving in heavy traffic. If you look well ahead, you will often see that hounds have checked, even though the horses directly ahead of you are still galloping. You can then ease your horse back. Especially try to slow down through boggy places and up hills. Always follow the Field Master. He knows what he is doing. For instance, he may go around the edge of a pasture even if hounds have gone across the middle, because he knows there are young calves in there. People who take their own line are the bane of a Master's existence. They turn and disturb foxes and often end up in the way of the hounds.

So do not follow another rider, even if he is wearing a pink coat and you think he is taking a better line than that of the Field

Master. He may be out of order, and added riders only compound the felony, or he may be doing a special job for the Master. When the Field or Staff inadvertently turn the fox, it is bad luck; when an individual riding his own line turns the fox, it is a serious sin.

Chatting while hounds are drawing or at a check is fine as long as it is done quietly. Remember that the Master is listening for hounds. However, if hounds are working within sound of your voice, stop talking as you may get their heads up. Sometimes hounds and Staff must come through the Field. When this happens, turn your horse's head toward them and give them as much room as possible. Nothing strikes fear into a huntsman's heart like a row of fidgety hindquarters aimed at him. And although the hounds may seem very much of a sameness to you, if your horse kicks one it is bound to be the best strike hound in the pack. Be careful of the hounds at all times. Never take the chance that they will get out of your way at the last minute; they probably will not. Remember most of them are overly trustful of horses as they spend a good deal of time during the years close to the huntsman's horse's legs.

Accidents do happen in the hunting field but, as in all accidents with horses, the vast majority can be avoided by care, forethought and observation. Tack, horse and rider should be in first-rate condition. Check the tightness of your girth two or three times during the day, especially on a "soft" horse who may lose several inches of fat, even on an easy day. Be conscious of the horses both in front and behind you. If you are on a strong-going horse, avoid getting behind a short-striding, pop-jumping animal, as frustration or worse is the result of this sort of situation. Conversely, if you are on a pony or a cob and someone is "riding in your pocket" wave him on. Keep a constant lookout for holes and wire. (See Chapter 7, Trail and Cross-country Riding.)

When you break a rail or cause any damage to a landowner's property, do what repairs you can on the spot and report it to the Master or secretary at the end of hunting. If there is any chance of animals getting loose through your temporary repairs, then report immediately. Always offer to pay for the cost.

If you suffer hunger pangs easily, carry a sandwich or cookies in a sandwich case or in your pocket if they are not too bulky. Avoid anything salty as it will make you thirsty, or anything like choco-late that will melt in the heat of the chase. If thirst is your prob-lem, carry something to drink in a flask held in a proper carrier. Some sort of hard candy such as lemon drops helps. Never put any hard object in your pockets; they can be very uncomfortable if fallen on. Of course, be sure that any wrappings are deposited back in your pocket, not on the ground.

At the end of the day thank the Master and the Staff and, if you are following the hounds home, do not ride too close to them. When you get to the stable, remember that the horse is more tired than you and take care of his needs (see Chapter 2, Grooming); then you will be able to put your feet up and relive the day's hunt.

12

The Fox Hunt
and Its Language

Unfortunately, many of the people who go foxhunting do not get full enjoyment from the sport because they do not throw their whole heart into it, or they do not know enough about the chase to get the most out of it. The adage "some ride to hunt and others hunt to ride" has much truth. However, the person who enjoys both the performance of his horse and that of the hounds and the fox is the one who comes home from a long day's hunt most satisfied. Make your hunting day something special. Cut yourself loose from workaday worries so that you may truly enjoy what nature has to offer as well as the thrill of a good horse moving at a fast pace cross-country. Too often someone says "I must leave early" because of some errand or appointment and they miss the best run of the day. Such a shame, especially when, if they had gotten out of bed an hour earlier, their duties would not have thrown a shadow over their sporting day.

Do not approach the sport faint-hearted, or you will miss the uplift of spirit that it can provide. Those who must wait for perfect weather and footing seldom get out foxhunting. Once you are out, worrying about the cold or the heat or the going will not improve the conditions. Of course, if it is slippery, exercise extra caution on the turns and at fences, but always heed the advice of the dressage world: "Ride your horse forward and ride him straight." The person who is constantly looking for ways around fences or is overly concerned about the conditions near them is missing the thrill of soaring boldly over an obstacle. Give your horse a chance to show you how good he is; most will rise to the occasion. With your head up and a nice feel of his mouth, ride him forward with a strong leg and a firm seat.

Read foxhunting books and stories (see the Bibliography) and get immersed in the spirit of the sport. Ask the old hands questions; most of them love to educate a newcomer. Most importantly, exercise your powers of observation and imagination. Notice how the huntsman draws various coverts. Some he will draw the same way time and again because he is sure of his fox and wants him to break out in a certain direction if possible. Other coverts he will draw in various patterns to make sure he does not miss a fox that is lying low.

"Coffee-housing" (talking) with friends is fine when you cannot hear huntsman or hounds or when you are trotting between coverts. But if you carry on a steady stream of conversation you will miss the most important "talk" of the day: that of the huntsman and hounds. In the beginning of the season you will recognize the voices of the puppies by their higher pitch and shorter note; the voice of a bitch at any age is usually higher than that of a dog. When you hear a hound speak and then hear the crack of a whip or the huntsman's rating voice or horn, you know the hound is babbling. Notice that when an older hound opens up, the huntsman is quiet about his encouragement as a pack will honor an older hound quickly. But, when a puppy opens up, the huntsman will usually give the rest of the pack a lot of encouragement as the older hounds are slow to honor the puppies; the puppies must earn the respect of the pack because the older hounds know them to be unreliable.

Get to know the pack, or at least learn to distinguish between those which are puppies and those which are the older hounds. Learn the best of the old hounds' names. Then, when you see a good old hound feathering a line, you feel the excitement of knowing, even before he speaks, that there is probably a fox up. Being able to recognize a few of the old hounds' voices will also add to your pleasure; when a hound opens up, look to see who it is, and put the name to the voice, or if he is not in sight, listen for the huntsman; he may call the other hounds on by crying "hark to Wilbur" and then you will know who spoke first. Even if you cannot put a name to the voice, just knowing which ones really mean business will keep you close to the hunt.

One way to learn more about the pack is to volunteer for hound-walking. This is one of several jobs (path-clearing, fence-mending) that must be carried out every year by the hunt. You will really enjoy your hunting more if you are truly an active member. Along the same line, pay your subscription promptly and contribute as much as you can when the call goes out for such things as a Christmas present for the Staff. Most hunts are financially hard-pressed and rely on the promptness and generosity of their members to keep the wolf from the door.

Scent is more mystery than fact. It is affected by so many variables that it is impossible to lay down any hard and fast rules about it. How strong it is at any given point on any given day depends on the fox, the weather and the ground conditions. The difference of a few degrees in the temperature can affect scent, and that is why hounds sometimes can run a fox in the morning well and yet have trouble in the afternoon, and vice versa. One thing is certain; a strong running fox, not too far ahead of the pack, lays down a good trail of scent almost anytime. So just because it is hot and dry or cold and windy, do not give up hope for a day's sport.

Some generalizations: scent should be good when the ground is wet but not soaking, when the barometer is rising, when the air is a little warmer than the ground, when it is cloudy, although a bright sun may help when the ground is frozen, and when the wind is from the west. Scent will not be good in rain, when the barometer is falling, when the ground is warmer than the air, when it is hot and dry, and when the wind comes from the south.

OVERLEAF

Contrary to the lay impression, the Field should never resemble a cavalry charge, whether hounds are running or the riders are simply moving to another covert.

Any condition for good or bad scent can be offset by any other condition for good or bad. The old fox hunters will tell you that scent will be bad if there are cobwebs on the bushes or if the hounds roll on the ground. Scent will be faint on plowed land and macadam roads and little better on sparsely covered ground such as close-cropped pasture and wheat fields. Dry leaves and cover that has a smell of its own, such as fresh pine needles, are also detrimental to scent. Therefore, you will understand why the hounds will fly across a grass-covered field but may be brought to their noses and pick along slowly in plowed fields. If Reynard runs a hard road, the hounds will probably be at a loss and will have to cast up and down until they find where he has left it for the grass.

Let us describe the course of a hypothetical run to help you know what to look and listen for during the hunt. The huntsman has thrown hounds into the first covert and is drawing it in large loops. As it is a large covert, the Field Master follows the huntsman, stopping here and there so as not to interfere with the cast. The huntsman is using his voice and horn just enough to let hounds know where he is. He wants the pack to cast with him as a unit, even though a widespread one, and yet he does not want to tell the fox any sooner than necessary that the hunt is on.

Hounds are hunting, noses to the ground, sterns waving, one not too far from the other. You hear a couple of high-pitched yips followed by a whir of feathers as a pheasant flies up. The huntsman rates the puppy who slinks off a few yards, quite ashamed of himself. The rest of the covert is drawn blank, without any luck.

As you come out into the open, you see the second whipper-in who had been posted to look for a fox. The huntsman now stops, blows his horn, and calls for his hounds that are still in the covert. The first whipper-in, who usually stays with the huntsman, is bringing hounds on. You hear his whip crack once or twice; that is to move hounds up that are not answering the horn. When the huntsman sees the whipper-in emerge from the covert, he knows he has all his hounds and off he trots to the next draw. The second whipper-in has already cantered on so that he will be quietly in position before the hounds start to draw.

The master greets a member of the Field while others wait for the time to move off.

The next covert is small, and the Field can stand on top of a hill and see three sides of it. Now is the time to be quiet and use your eyes and ears. Although the Field Master has positioned the Field where it is least likely to turn the fox, there is always a chance he may run in your direction. If you are absolutely quiet and still, most foxes will go right by with little deviation in their course. If there are only one or two of you, it also helps to stand by a tree or a bush so that you blend into the landscape.

Concentrate on looking in the direction that is ahead of the hound's cast as odds are that the fox will break out that way, but do keep glancing at the other visible areas in case he pops out behind them. A hound has started to speak in a strong, sonorous voice and then another honors him; it sounds good but it still may be an old line (cold trail) left by a fox a couple of hours before. But now the whole pack joins in, and you know this is a fresh line. Their voices are strong but they are moving slowly through the

213

A red fox pins his ears and flattens his body toward the ground when running full speed.

rather thick underbrush. This sly fox has twisted all around, knowing the briars and vines will slow his larger adversaries.

Your glance is now constantly circling the covert, for this fellow could pop out anyplace. There he is, cantering out behind the pack up the hill, not rushing as he hears that the hounds are still back in the covert working slowly. Watch carefully where he goes until he disappears over the hill. There is no "tally-ho," as the pack is working the line strongly around the last loop made by the fox. Here is the lead hound out of the covert and right behind her the rest of the pack. Their voices swell to a roar as they smell the strong scent lying well on the good grass. The second whipper-in is standing close to the line with his cap pointing in the direction the fox went. The huntsman now knows he viewed and therefore can calculate about how far ahead the fox is. As the hounds flee up the hill, the huntsman doubles his horn to cheer the pack on, for the fox has gone away and the hounds are after him.

And so is the Field. As you gallop along, listen to the cry of the pack. Its volume will tell you how strong the scent is. As you come over the rise there is a long sweep of country, completely open except for a patch of woods to the right and a hedgerow running horizontally across the far hill. You look quickly over all the open space but there is no fox to be seen. You then watch hounds as they swoop toward the woods, but you also keep an eye out beyond the woods in case Reynard has "waited" there. There go the hounds without pausing to the corner of the woods; scent is "screaming" and the fox is obviously ahead.

Staff and Field are tightly bunched and fairly close behind hounds so you take your horse back just a little in case they make a sudden check; you do not want to sail by the Master and Staff right into the hounds. Hounds stream down the valley and start up the far hill. Crows will often circle and scold a fox, so when you see some hard at it over the hedgerow you watch carefully, and there he is! Reynard bursts from the hedgerow, ears pinned back, body low, really running now as he hears the determination in the hounds' voices. The huntsman yells the cheery "whoop" as he views. When hounds arrive at the hedgerow, they are brought to their noses because the fox has run for a hundred yards or more inside it before breaking out.

The roar of the pack in full cry is now muted as some hounds work their way inside the hedgerow tonguing intermittently as scenting is difficult in this tight area. Other more adventurous hounds have pushed through the hedgerow and are silent as they cast on the far side. Which will prove the better hunter, the bold hounds or the sure hounds? A pack needs both types. If all the hounds would cast as soon as scent was weak, the pack would constantly be overrunning the line on a twisty fox or on a bad scenting day. On the other hand, if all hounds would run a fox only when they could smell his every step, the pack would be slow and lacking drive, and the fox would get too far ahead.

This time the bold ones have it as they strike the line where the fox broke out. The huntsman cheers the hounds in the hedge-row onto the lead hounds with a "hark to Nancy, hark to Driver," and the whole pack is off again. Over the hill across the meadow they race until they are at a loss on a hard road bordered by a woods. No hope of a view here so you watch the hounds work out their problem. Some cross the road immediately and check out the far side but the fox apparently was not pushed hard enough to cross straight over. Some hounds are now casting well up the road to the right, checking both sides but with no luck. They swarm back and start casting to the left but they are becoming discouraged; some of the puppies already have their heads up.

The huntsman decides to help them a little and "casts around the hat" backwards as the fox will often be turned by a road. He joins them and carries them down the road and then swings back left-handed, encouraging them softly with his voice and maybe a few short notes on the horn. There is old Wilbur feathering; then he opens up; the others race to him and they are off again, not quite as strongly as before as the line is a little old. Reynard must have run the road for a couple of hundred yards and then doubled back left-handed.

They run steadily for a couple of miles crossing a wide stream but picking the line up promptly on the far side. And then they swing through a small woods but the second whipper-in and Field Master circle the outside. You look ahead and learn why: two deer bound out at the far side. The whipper-in starts to ease forward but does nothing else and again you see why: behind the deer comes the fox. The deer bears off right-handed but Reynard, with a glance over his shoulder, decides hounds are too close for any twisting and races off straight ahead. Now the whipper-in gallops to stand on the line of the deer. The pack breaks out of the woods and keeps to the line of the fox except for a couple of puppies who start to bear right-handed. But the whip is there and straightens them out promptly.

The fox, with another glance over his shoulder, swings left-handed toward the spinney in the distance and you lose sight of him. But the pack is in full cry now and they race ahead and eventually disappear into the spinney. Suddenly there is silence. You sigh a bit because you know what that probably means; the fox has gone to ground. This is confirmed when a hound or two let out a sad sort of howl and the huntsman blows a long, tremulous note on the horn. By the time the Field arrives, the huntsman is off his horse and cheering his hounds with a few special words to his lead hounds. The run is over but not the day. A few minutes' rest for your horse and for hounds and you are off to draw another covert. Good luck and good hunting!

A mature red fox pauses for a moment and listens to hounds while making his decision of where to run.

GLOSSARY

Foxhunting has a special vocabulary of its own, as distinct from the ordinary horseman's vocabulary. To help you translate the key words at the beginning of your foxhunting career, a few of the most important definitions are given below:

BABBLE—a hound babbles when he gives tongue on a scent other than fox, or on no scent at all.

BACK—the fox doubles back in the direction from which he came; if a fox is viewed, the cry is "tally-ho back." Also: back hounds are hounds hunting the line that other hounds are hunting some distance ahead.

BLANK—to draw a covert blank is to be unable to find a fox in it; a blank day occurs when hounds fail to find a fox all day.

BREAST-HIGH—scent is breast-high when conditions allow the scent to rise high enough off the ground so that hounds do not have to keep their noses down low, and can therefore run faster.

BRUSH—the fox's tail is called a brush.

BURST—when hounds run very fast on a line without checking it is called a sharp burst.

BYE—a bye day is one on which hounds are taken hunting although it is not listed on the fixture card.

CAP—the cap is the headgear worn by the Master, Staff and children under eighteen. Also, a visitor is "capped" or pays a capping fee when he contributes a set amount of money to the hunt for his day's sport.

CAST—hounds cast or the huntsman casts the hounds when they search for the lost line of the fox.

CHECK—the hounds check when they temporarily lose the scent of the fox. The Field is at a check when they wait for the hounds to regain the line.

CHOP—hounds chop a fox when they kill it after a very short run.

COLD TRAIL—the line of scent made by a fox a good time before the hounds have found it.

COLORS—the distinctive color of the particular hunt, worn on the collar of the hunting coat and the collar and lapels of gentlemen's scarlet evening tails. It is a privilege to be awarded the colors of the hunt.

COUPLE—hounds are always counted by twos, i.e., couples. When the pack consists of twenty couple, it actually has forty hounds. Also: a couple (or coupling) is a leather or metal device by which one hound's collar can be attached to that of another hound's.

COVERT—pronounced cover—a small or large area of woods or brush where a fox might lie.

CROP—the stiff part of a hunting whip to which the thong, a long supple piece of leather, and the lash, a short piece of braided cotton or nylon, are attached.

CRY—the sound (music) given by the pack when running on a line.

CUBHUNTING—the early portion of the season before the regular season starts with the opening meet, also known as cubbing.

DRAW—hounds draw a covert when they spread out and search for the fox. Also: a draw is the same as a covert.

DRIVE—that urge in the hound to get to hunt hard and well forward on the line.

DROP—a fox is said to be dropped when he is released in a covert shortly before hounds are expected to draw. (Not considered the sporting thing to do.)

EARTH—any place where a fox goes to ground, but usually where he lives regularly; a fox's den.

ENTER—a hound is entered when he is first regularly used for hunting. The young entry is a group of hounds hunting their first season.

FEATHER—a hound feathers a line when he hunts hard with his nose close to the ground, waving his stern, but is not yet sure enough of the scent to give tongue.

FIELD—a group of mounted riders behind the Master.

FIELD MASTER—the person appointed by the Master to lead the Field.

FIXTURE CARD—the listing of the times and places of the meet, usually by the month.

FULL CRY—hounds are said to be in full cry when they are running well and tonguing strongly.

GONE AWAY—the fox is said to have gone away when he leaves the covert.

GONE TO GROUND—the fox is said to have gone to ground when he takes refuge in an earth or a similar place.

HEEL—hounds are said to be running heel when they run the line of the fox backwards.

HONOR—a hound honors another hound when he joins him and gives tongue on the line on which the first hound has opened up.

HUNTING WHIP—the crop, thong and lash together are known as the hunting whip.

HUNTSMAN—the person who hunts the hounds.

LARK—to gallop and jump fences unnecessarily, usually out hunting. This is not recommended.

LIFT—the huntsman lifts hounds when he takes them from a line they are hunting.

LINE—the trail of scent left by the fox.

MARK—a hound marks a fox to ground when he digs at an earth energetically and tongues in a different way than his hunting voice, usually similar to a howl.

MASK—the head of the fox.

MASTER—the person in charge of the hunt, also known as the M.F.H. (Master of Foxhounds).

MEET—the place where the hounds and Field assemble before hunting.

NOSE—a hound is said to have a good nose when he has the ability to hunt well by following the scent correctly with his nose.

OPEN—a hound is said to open when he is the first to give tongue on a line.

PAD—the foot of the fox; the center cushion of a hound's foot.

POINT—the farthest point of a run in a straight line from where the hounds picked up the scent.

RATCATCHER—informal hunting attire.

RATE—a warning call given by the huntsman or whippers-in to correct hounds.

RIDE—a lane cut through the woods.

RIOT—any animal that hounds might hunt other than a fox.

RUN—the period of time that the hounds are actually hunting the fox.

SCENT—the smell the fox left by the glands in his pads and his brush.

SPEAK—a single hound giving tongue.

STAFF—the huntsman and the whippers-in.

STERN—the tail of the hound.

STRIKE—a hound is said to strike a line when he first hunts it with certainty. A good strike hound is one that consistently finds the line of the fox first.

TAG—white tip on the fox's brush.

TAIL HOUNDS—hounds running some distance behind the pack.

TONGUE—the cry of the hound.

VIEW—to see a fox.

VIEW HOLLOA—the cry (usually "tally-ho") given on viewing a fox, and/or the raising of the cap.

VIXEN—a female fox.

WARE—the word used to caution another rider, e.g., "ware wire." (Short for "beware.")

WHELP—a bitch whelps when she bears puppies.

WHIPPER-IN—the member or members of the Staff who help the huntsman in controlling the hounds. Also called, in the colloquial, "whip."

13

Horse Shows and
Dressage Competitions

Sooner or later, most people who ride get the urge to compete in some sort of horse sport. The opportunities are numerous, and competitions for every taste, every level of skill, and every size of budget exist in most areas.

Horse shows of various kinds attract the largest number of competitors of any of the horse sports. The Fédération Equestre Internationale (FEI) is the international regulatory body whose rules govern all international horse events such as those held at the Olympic Games, the Pan American Games, the World Championships, and the international classes held at the National Horse Show, Madison Square Garden, New York.

The American Horse Shows Association, Inc. (AHSA) represents our country in the FEI and is our national regulatory body for horse shows, dressage shows and combined training events. The AHSA accepts members, recognizes and rates horse shows, judges, stewards and technical delegates. It also keeps records of winnings, and awards no less than thirty-nine "Horse of the Year" high-score trophies, ranging from one for the best half-Arabian horse to those for hunters, jumpers, ponies and gaited horses. It also offers special annual awards such as the AHSA Perpetual Dressage Trophy and the AHSA Combined Training Trophy. To be eligible for many of these awards the owner of the horse must be a member of the AHSA and the event(s) participated in recognized by the association.

Other organizations, both affiliated and non-affiliated with the AHSA, give year-end awards as part of their efforts in encouraging their particular horse-related endeavors. Three national organizations of particular interest to us are the United States Combined Training Association, The American Dressage Institute and the United States Dressage Federation. There are also many regional and local breed and activity organizations such as the Pennsylvania Horse Breeders' Association and the Delaware Valley Combined Training Association, and various dressage associations designed to educate and encourage those interested in their particular aspects of the sport. Names of these organizations are available from the national organization in the appropriate field.

The United States Pony Club, founded in 1953, is modeled after the British Pony Club. It is the regulatory body for pony clubs throughout the country. All the clubs have the same structure, program and standards. The object of the Pony Club is "to encourage young people to ride, and to learn to enjoy all kinds of sport connected with horses and riding; to provide instruction in riding horse-mastership, and to instill in the members the proper care of their animals; to promote the highest ideals of sportsmanship, citizenship and loyalty, thereby cultivating strength of character and self-discipline."

Those under the age of seventeen may become regular members and are rated, in declining order of experience and ability as A, B, C and D. Those seventeen through twenty years of age may become associated members and be rated as above. Despite the name, members may ride horses as well as ponies. To move from one rating to another, the member must pass standard written and riding tests. Each year regional rallies are held which lead up to a national rally. A rally is patterned on the combined training event in which the horse and rider are tested in dressage, in the test in the open and in stadium jumping. During a year's period, a Pony Club member may participate in one or all of the following: riding, games, jumping, foxhunting, shows, jousts, lectures and rallies.

PARTICIPATION

For a guideline to participation in any horse sport you need look no further than the sportsman's charter of the AHSA which asserts "that sport is something done for the fun of doing it and that it ceases to be a sport when it becomes a business only, something done for what there is in it; that amateurism is something of the heart and spirit—not a matter of exact technical qualifications; that the good manners of sport are fundamentally important; that the code must be strictly upheld; that the whole structure of sport is not only preserved from the absurdity of undue importance, but is justified by a kind of a romance which animates it, and by the positive virtues of courage, patience, good temper and unselfishness which are demanded by the code; that the exploitation of sport for profit alone kills the spirit and retains only the husk and semblance of the thing; that the qualities of frankness, courage, and sincerity which mark the good sportsman in private life shall mark discussions of his interest at a show."

When you decide to enter a competition, do so in the spirit of fun and winning—winning by your standards, which may or may not be the judge's standards. If your horse has put in a round that is "a winner," judged against his ability and training, then be satisfied. You are showing in order to receive the judge's opinion, whether it coincides with yours or not. If you do not know why a performance was not pinned and are honestly interested in the reasons, you may ask the steward or show committee to see the judge's card (which is not always available) or request to speak to the judge himself at a convenient time. (Note that under AHSA rule, you must get permission before questioning a judge about his decision.)

When you participate in a race or such that is judged against an arbitrary standard, then be willing to accept "racing luck," those many things that may occur during a competition that will go against your chances of winning. Of course, if a breach of the rules has occurred which affects you, then you should protest to the proper official. Approach the competition as a good sport.

How you tune up in the schooling ring has a lot to do with the quality of your performance before the judge. A parallel with some "air" under it helps to wake a horse up.

You are there to be judged or to outrun or to outjump the other competitors. Do not gripe about the courses or the lack of perfect conditions; they are the same for everyone. One day the luck will be with you and you will do better than perhaps you deserve; another day, the luck may be against you.

Be fair to yourself and the horse. Know the rules and conditions of the competitions in which you wish to compete. Become a member of the regulatory body and receive a rule book on the competition. First attend as a spectator, with a knowledgeable friend if possible, the type of event in which you wish to participate; familiarize yourself with all aspects of it from dress to the level of competition. Be sure your horse is prepared; if he is not going well at home, he will certainly do no better, and will probably do worse, under the stress of competition. If you do not know how your horse will react to excitement, take him to a couple of events without actually competing in order to orient him and to find out how long it takes him to settle down.

Allow double the time you think necessary to get ready and to drive to the show. Rushing usually results in the horse refusing to load on the trailer, forgotten equipment, or lack of preparation for the first class. A checklist of horse and rider equipment appropriate to the event and the amount of time you will spend away from your barn is the only way to be sure nothing is forgotten. A winner always looks organized because he is organized. The horse and rider are calm, clean, neat and polished. A good performance demands concentration and no one can give his full attention to the job at hand if he cannot find a spur, does not know what class is next or what the course is.

HORSE SHOWS

Horse shows may be roughly divided into three types: the highest level of competition is found in FEI and AHSA "A" shows and to a somewhat lesser degree in AHSA "B" and "C" shows. The next level of competition is found at shows recognized by state or local organizations. There is a good deal of overlap in these first groups. The owners of top horses select the shows they are going to attend on the basis of whether they offer points toward year-end awards in the desired divisions from organizations they are interested in,

Looking for the next fence as you land over the previous one, as Lornie is doing here, is essential to riding a good line in any course.

how that particular show fits in their overall schedule, the reputation of the show for good conditions and courses, and what classes are offered. The number of AHSA "A" shows a year throughout the country is not enormous, so those interested in AHSA year-end awards may also often compete in "B" and "C" shows, although they offer fewer points.

This involves extensive traveling. An owner of a top horse who does not wish to travel all over to recognized shows may concentrate on trying to win a year-end award from a state organization, such as the Pennsylvania Horse Breeders' Association. Therefore, you may run into very stiff competition in what would appear to be a small country show but is recognized by the PHBA.

There is also a third group of smaller shows and it is in these that the novice should start his career unless he is under the instruction of a trainer. Throughout the country there are many small gymkhanas, pony club shows of various kinds, schooling shows or just local shows that are not officially recognized by any organization. These shows are affectionately known as the "leaky roof circuit" and are a good place "to get your feet wet." You may have to ask around a bit until you find out when and where these small shows are being held, but once you get on a couple of mailing lists, you will be showered with prize lists, as most small shows trade their lists back and forth. You may also check local tack stores and riding establishments for prize lists and signs of upcoming events.

Become a member of the AHSA even if you are not ready to compete for year-end awards. Among other benefits, you will receive a rule book which will supply you with a wealth of information about all phases of showing. Attend several shows, with or without your horse, before you actually participate. Note how the ribbon winners dress, ride and handle their horses during the various tests. Braiding is not necessary at the small shows but the horse's mane and tail must be neat and clean. If his mane is unruly, then braid it.

There are styles and fads in the horse show world just as elsewhere. Keep away from the fads and observe the conservative styles used by most ribbon winners.

Some guidelines are: absolute neatness and cleanliness of horse, tack and rider; conservative clothes; braiding done with a color of thread or rubberbands that matches or blends with the horse's mane and tail; good sportsmanship at all times. You will need to plan ahead for the materials you will need for yours and the horse's comfort.

SHOW KIT

RIDER	HORSE
Coverall, especially if you are your own groom	Fly sheet, sheet or blanket
Jacket, other than riding	Fly spray
Boot pull and jockeys	Tail and leg bandages
Shoes	Grooming kit
Towel and washcloth	Saddle soap and sponge
Ice water, tea, etc.	Hay, grain (if a long day)
Cap, gloves, whip, spurs, boots	Bucket
Stock, tie, or choker	First-aid kit
Rain gear	All necessary tack
	Twelve-gallon container of water
	Extra shoes, if this could be a problem

Most horse shows have water available for the horses and food and drink for the exhibitors, but they often run out later in the afternoon and you can save yourself a good deal of walking if you bring your own.

Each type of class has its unwritten as well as written rules: a good showman observes both. For example, for a hunter over fences class the competitor should enter at a good trot, make a medium-size circle that will lead him nicely into the first fence and pick up a canter at an appropriate place on the circle. After he has completed the course, he should ease his horse smoothly into a trot and then walk just as he reaches the outgate. If the outgate is in an awkward position, he may execute a small circle before leaving. The overall effect of the performance should be one of promptness, calmness, smoothness, accuracy, alertness and, if possible, elegance. If you happen to catch the judge's eye on entering or leaving, give a small nod or a smile of acknowledgment. The performance will be marked down for any of the following: an incorrect lead on any part of the course, unevenness of pace, a pace that is too rapid or too slow, jumping and style faults, poor way of going, cross-cantering, or any show of bad manners.

Equitation classes over fences are judged on any of the above faults that are the result of incorrect riding as well as the rider's display of his horsemanship. In all equitation classes, the rider is the one principally being judged; the horse is only judged as a reflection of the rider's ability.

Hunter hack classes are judged on the correctness and elegance of the horse's carriage and way of going, manners, and the promptness and quality of his transitions. The horse is expected to go on light rein contact. The rider is not judged except in those ways that affect the horse's performance. (A tense rider does not show off a calm hack.) Martingales are prohibited in hack and equitation classes on the flat.

Classes on the flat are a true test of the good rider's intelligence and concentration. It is not an easy job to remain alert and show off yourself and your horse to your best advantage over a period of half an hour with possibly fifty horses in the ring. Remember that you are being judged from the minute you enter the ring until the ribbons are pinned.

Have your horse warmed up or worked down before all classes. It is amazing the number of riders who will sit on their horses for half an hour, never moving, waiting for their turn to be called and then expect their horses to put in a super performance over a course of fences. In classes on the flat, keep your horse placed where the judges can see him, but do not be a bully; a rider that is constantly cutting corners or pushing his way up on the inside does not endear himself to the judges, much less to the other competitors.

Subtlety is essential in the good horseman and top showman. If you need to wake your horse up, do not do it in front of the judges; carry your whip and use your leg on the side the judge cannot see. Keep away from fractious or bad-tempered horses at all times; even if they do not actually kick, they will upset your horse. When lined up in the middle of the ring, do not go to sleep; the horse may be on a loose rein but should stand squarely and quietly and yet be kept as alert as possible.

Open jumper and stadium jumping classes that are associated with combined training events are judged on the performance of the horse only; knockdowns and/or possibly ticks and time are the only things judged. In classes governed by FEI rules and in stadium jumping classes the rider is expected to enter the ring and salute the judge first, and, when a bell or whistle signal is given, he may then start the course. Refusals also count and, if you have a refusal at the second or third part of a combination, you must retake all elements of the combination. If a fence must be reset, the whistle blows and the horse is held up; the clock is then stopped. The rider is notified that he may start the course when the whistle blows again; the clock is then restarted. Flags at the start and finish must be observed.

We have discussed only some of the aspects of showing and given you a few hints to help you on the road to success. Your knowledge of the rules and constant observation is necessary to keep you up to date. Solicit the aid of a professional horseman, even if you can afford his help for only a couple of shows; it should bring you into the winner's circle sooner.

DRESSAGE COMPETITIONS

Dressage competitions are classified according to the degree of difficulty of the test (ride) that is required. They start with Training Level, and progress upward through First, Second, Third and Fourth levels to Prix St. Georges, which is the first of the international (FEI) levels. Next come the two FEI Intermédiare or Intermediate tests, and last of all, the Grand Prix, the summit of dressage achievement. The Grand Prix test is the level demanded in the Olympic Games, and it requires among other movements flying changes of lead *every stride,* the *passage* (a highly elevated, cadenced trot) and the *piaffer* (a collected trot in place). Obviously, the more advanced levels of dressage competition require years of specialized training for both horse and rider, but happily, Training Level through Third Level are attainable by anyone at all, and are well within the reach of the average field hunter or pleasure horse.

AMERICAN HORSE SHOWS ASSOCIATION
527 MADISON AVENUE
NEW YORK, N.Y. 10022

FIRST LEVEL, TEST 1

TIME ALLOWED: 5 MINUTES (SMALL ARENA)
6 MINUTES (LARGE ARENA)

_____

NAME OF COMPETITION

_____   _____

DATE   NO

_____

NAME OF HORSE

_____

NAME OF RIDER

_____ POINTS; _____ PER CENT
FINAL SCORE

MAXIMUM POINTS POSSIBLE   210

_____   _____

NAME OF JUDGE   SIGNATURE OF JUDGE

Guidelines and rules for dressage competition of all sorts up to Fifth Level are contained in the *Supplement to Rules on Dressage and Combined Training*. This handbook is available for a fee from the AHSA and is sent gratis to all members of the USCTA. It is a must if you are interested in dressage. In the AHSA publications you will discover that at the lower levels of dressage the horse may only be shown in a plain snaffle, with or without a dropped noseband. A figure-eight noseband may be used in Combined Training events but not in AHSA recognized dressage classes. The mouthpiece of a plain snaffle may be made of one piece or jointed, and of smooth metal, rubber or leather. It may or may not have cheekpieces. No martingales, whips or boots on the horse are allowed, although a breastplate is acceptable. The wearing of spurs is optional at the Training Level. No voice signals may be given.

In schooling or unrecognized competitions, ratcatcher attire is appropriate and the horse's mane and tail need not be braided. However, it is considered a compliment to the committee and the judge to be well turned out, all clothing and tack spotless, the horse groomed to a shine with its mane and tail pulled properly and lying flat. After all, elegance is essential to dressage.

The rider's general aspect will inevitably affect the marks throughout the test. The judge cannot help but be more generous in his markings as he watches for five to ten minutes someone who presents a calm, confident and happy demeanor. So always allow a few minutes to compose yourself before your ride, and enter the arena with an assured, pleasant expression even if you are on a green horse you expect to explode any minute. By the very fact that you have control of yourself, you will ride better and the horse will go better.

Know your test thoroughly, watch a couple of rides and mentally call the test ahead of them as a way of checking your memory. If you are at all unsure have the test read (called). Sometimes under the stress of competition a movement is forgotten. Ideally, the test is better not called.

You must present yourself at the arena at the time you have been given, under penalty of elimination. After the previous rider has left the arena, you may circle the outside of the arena until the

Major Beale and Another Folly at the canter. His formal attire is correct for higher-level tests.

bell rings. Do this as many times as possible in both directions at a walk and a trot in order to allow your horse to become accustomed to the judge's table, the markers, flowers and other things that might otherwise frighten him. When the bell rings, you have one minute to present yourself at the letter marker A. However, as a courtesy to the judge you should go to the entrance as quickly as you can. Make a circle outside in the pace at which the test starts, and approach the entrance in a straight line for several strides. Continue to X, where you halt and salute.

You are in the correct position to a side marker when your shoulder is parallel to it and to a center line marker when it is under the horse's girth. So the imaginary X should be under the horse and your shoulders should be parallel to B and E. This is perhaps the mot difficult transition of the test. The horse does not know what is expected of him, he does not have the side of the arena to help keep him straight, and the rhythm of the test has not been established. Practice a couple of halts shortly before you

232

FIRST LEVEL, TEST 1

		TEST	DIRECTIVE IDEAS	POINTS	CORRECTION	CO-EFFICIENT	TOTAL	REMARKS
1	A X	ENTER WORKING TROT (SITTING) HALT, SALUTE PROCEED WORKING TROT (SITTING)	ENTRY (STRAIGHTNESS) HALT (IMMOBILITY) AND TRANSITION FROM HALT	5				Not quite bright enough on center line. Must be more frank in trot
2	C M-X-K K	TRACK TO THE RIGHT CHANGE REIN, WORKING TROT (RISING) WORKING TROT (RISING)	CORRECTNESS, REGULARITY, THE FLEXION OF THE HORSE	5				Not quite positive enough!
3	A-C	SERPENTINE IN THREE LOOPS (WIDTH OF THE ARENA)	THE CORRECTNESS & REGULARITY OF THE LOOPS, THE CHANGE OF FLEXION AND POSTING DIAGONAL	6				Rider must take care not to come behind movement in 1 or 2 strides when chg. diag.
4	E B	TURN LEFT ACROSS CENTRELINE TRACK TO THE RIGHT	CORRECTNESS, REGULARITY, FLEXION OF THE HORSE	5				
5	A K-X-M M	MEDIUM WALK CHANGE REIN, FREE WALK ON A LONG REIN MEDIUM WALK	THE RELAXATION, THE LENGTHENING OF STRIDE AND FRAME OF HORSE	5				Lacking freedom & energy but is relaxed
6	C	WORKING TROT (SITTING) CIRCLE WIDTH OF THE ARENA	REGULARITY & SHAPE OF CIRCLE, THE FLEXION	5				
7	C	WORKING CANTER LEFT LEAD, CIRCLE WIDTH OF THE ARENA ONCE AROUND THEN STRAIGHT AHEAD	THE CALMNESS OF THE CANTER DEPART; REGULARITY & SHAPE OF CIRCLE, THE FLEXION OF THE HORSE	6				Not enough test Inner hand must not cross within - canter left
8	K F-X-H H	WORKING TROT (SITTING) CHANGE REIN, LENGTHEN STRIDE IN THE TROT (RISING) WORKING TROT (SITTING)	LENGTHENING OF STRIDE, MAINTENANCE OF RHYTHM THE BALANCE THE TRANSITIONS	6				
9	C	CIRCLE, WIDTH OF THE ARENA	THE REGULARITY, THE SHAPE OF THE CIRCLE, THE FLEXION OF THE HORSE	5				R hind leg must get more boldly under horse
10	C	WORKING CANTER RIGHT LEAD CIRCLE WIDTH OF THE ARENA, ONCE AROUND THEN STRAIGHT AHEAD	CALMNESS OF CANTER-DEPART, REGULARITY AND SHAPE OF CIRCLE AND THE FLEXION OF THE HORSE	6				Trans canter to trot ragged
11	F K-X-M M	WORKING TROT (SITTING) CHANGE REIN, LENGTHEN THE STRIDE IN THE TROT (RISING) WORKING TROT (RISING)	LENGTHENING OF STRIDE, MAINTENANCE OF RHYTHM THE BALANCE THE TRANSITIONS	5				Calm but lacking energy
12	H-X-F F	CHANGE REIN, WORKING TROT (RISING) WORKING TROT (SITTING)	THE REGULARITY OF WORKING TROT	6				
13	A G	DOWN CENTRELINE HALT, SALUTE, LEAVE ARENA, FREE WALK ON A LOOSE REIN	THE STRAIGHTNESS THE HALT (IMMOBILITY) THE RELAXATION IN THE FREE WALK	6				

COLLECTIVE MARKS:

	POINTS	CO-EFFICIENT	TOTAL
Gaits (freedom and regularity)	6	2	12
Impulsion (desire to move forward, elasticity of the steps, relaxation of the back)	5-	2	9
Submission (attention and confidence; harmony and lightness and ease of the movements; acceptance of the bit)	5	2	10
Position, seat of the rider, correct use of the aids	6+	2	13

TIME: _____ minutes _____ seconds

SUBTOTAL 115

ERRORS (-)

TIME FAULTS (-)

TOTAL POINTS 115

Example of a typical dressage test. You can learn a lot from judges' comments.

enter the arena. It is better to take a walking step and achieve a good, square halt than to stop right on X but abruptly.

A halt is considered "good" when the horse stands absolutely still and has made the transition to the halt in balance and without resistance. Forefeet and hind feet should form a square, the whole horse should be straight and he should remain on the bit (no glancing around) during the salute. Keeping the contact, quietly and smoothly transfer the reins to your left hand. A gentleman salutes by removing his cap with his right hand and dropping it down behind his knee, lining turned in toward the horse's side. A lady salutes by dropping her right hand down behind her knee and nodding her head. This should be accomplished slowly and gracefully while the rest of the upper body remains still. Pick up the reins, look ahead to the judge and proceed with the test.

Remember, not only do the marks for the General Impressions carry a lot of weight, but also that the judge has these General Impressions constantly in his mind as he marks each individual movement. So do not become flustered if one movement is done incorrectly. Maintain your poise at all times and correct any mistakes calmly. For example, a wrong lead will of course mark down a movement; however, if it is corrected promptly and smoothly, the movement will still earn some good marks and the horse will also maintain his poise. You should attempt to go well into the corners, but again, at this level fluency is more important than accuracy. Better to have a slightly too round corner or slightly too large circle than to lose the impulsion or rhythm of the movement. Any tense tail-switching, tongue-lolling, teeth-grinding, bucking, pinning of the ears or tossing of the head will cause a movement to be marked down, as it indicates a lack of acceptance and obedience on the part of the horse.

If your horse tends to lose his balance or rhythm in the corners, apply a half-halt a stride or so before. This will encourage him to gather himself and, if you then ask for an increase in impulsion, your problem will be solved. In order to accomplish good turns down the center line, think of them as half-circles. There is seldom room for a normal striding horse moving at ordinary paces to take a full straight stride on the short side before turning at A or C. For example, if the movement required is "K Working Trot (sitting); A Down Center Line," you will maintain a slight bend to the left through the corner and to the center line with your inside hand and, keeping your left leg at the girth, encourage the horse to bend around it with your right leg behind the girth to keep his quarters from shifting to the outside of the circle.

Canter departs are too often ragged in a test because the horse has not been prepared. The rider suddenly arrives at the marker, seems to remember that here is a canter, applies his aids in a hurry and the horse either rushes forward in the trot or throws himself into the canter. Again apply a half-halt as a warning a stride or two before the marker. Feel the horse's sides more strongly with both legs in order to gather him a little, steady him with your hands, and as you reach the marker, apply the canter aids. A good motto for riding a dressage test is: Prepare your horse; know your test; keep your composure, and ride with elegance.

14

Combined Training
and Hunter Trials

COMBINED TRAINING

Combined Training, also known as Eventing, is the horse sport which best tests the all-round skill of the horse and rider. At its simplest level, it may consist of only two tests, while at its highest level, the Three-Day Event, it consists of six tests and the overall Test in the Open may be as long as twenty miles. The origins of the sport are found in the days of the horse cavalry: the dressage was to show that the horse was calm, obedient and precise on the parade ground; the cross-country was to show that the horse and rider could travel with speed for long distances over varied terrain, jumping challenging obstacles on the way; the stadium jumping was to show that the horse was fit, sound, and supple enough to continue performing his duties. The sport, in the framework that now exists, first appeared in the Stockholm Olympics of 1912 and American teams, both military and civilian, have since seldom come home from the Olympic Games without a medal.

The Three-Day Event is the pinnacle of the sport and, because it is so strenuous a test of horse and rider, only a few are held in a year. The Horse Trial, being a much less severe test, is the base of the sport and provides the training-ground for competitors of even Olympic aspirations. Again, the *Supplement to Rules on Dressage and Combined Training* is essential to anyone interested in Eventing.

It contains all the rules and standards of the various phases encompassed in Combined Training Events held in the United States that are not of international caliber. The terminology is somewhat confusing, for several different kinds of competition come under the general heading of Combined Training, but we will try to clarify some of the terms. A *Combined Training Event* may consist of two or more tests from the following: dressage, roads and tracks, cross-country, steeplechase and stadium jumping. The same horse and rider must compete in all phases that are asked for in order to be eligible for a prize.

The *dressage test* consists of a series of prescribed movements on the flat, carried out in a standard arena, in which the horse is judged on his performance according to his level of training, and the rider is judged on his position and the use of his aids. The *roads and tracks phase* requires competitors to complete a marked course (without jumps) which may range from two to ten miles at a minimum stipulated rate of speed, usually a good trot. The *steeplechase course* of one to 2½ miles in length must be covered at a strong to racing gallop over eight to twelve fences, usually made of brush. The *cross-country course* ranges from one to 4½ miles, to be covered at a rate of speed ranging from a hand gallop to a strong gallop, over varied terrain and fences such as walls, coops, timber, gates, combinations, drops, ditches, water and any combination thereof. The *stadium jumping* is carried out over a relatively short course consisting of ten to twelve show-type fences.

All phases are judged on whether the competitor completed the course in the allowed time; penalties are given for such jumping faults as refusals on the cross-country, refusals and knockdowns in the stadium jumping, and for exceeding the time allowed on any of the courses. Style is only considered in the dressage test. The competitor is eliminated for such things as three falls of horse and/or rider at obstacles on the cross-country, three refusals at the same obstacle in any phase, or for any breach of rules such as failing to keep all red flags to the right and white flags to the left, jumping a fence out of order, failing to report to the starter at the prescribed time, etc.

The simplest combined training event is known as the *Com-*

bined Event; it is a two-phase event usually consisting of a dressage and a stadium jumping test but could be a combination of any two of the tests mentioned above. A *Horse Trial* is a three-phase event, usually held in one day, testing the competitor in dressage, cross-country and stadium jumping; sometimes a short roads and tracks phase is included. A full-scale *Three-Day Event,* which is also sometimes called a Horse Trials, takes place over a period of three days: the dressage test is held on the first day; the test in the open (which includes phase A, roads and tracks; phase B, steeplechase; phase C, roads and tracks; and phase D, cross-country) is held on the second day; the stadium jumping is held on the final day.

The levels of competition found in Combined Training, starting at the lowest, are Pre-training (novice), Training, Preliminary, Intermediate, Advanced (*open*). The Pre-training division is not recognized by the U.S. Combined Training Association, but most organizers of these events still follow the national rules closely. Guidelines for these events have been set up by the USCTA, but are not mandatory. From the training level upward, the owner of the horse must become a member of the USCTA. The member receives a rule book, periodic newsletters which contain interesting articles and photos, an omnibus schedule of approved USCTA events for the year, and becomes eligible for year-end awards. In order to get an idea of what standards to expect for the various levels, see the chart on pages 242–43.

PREPARING TO EVENT

A combined training event is quite different from any other horse sport. It is essential that you become thoroughly familiar with the regulations in the rule book, and that you attend a couple of horse trials at the lower levels as a spectator in order to become familiar with the proceedings.

Note the attire expected in each phase: formal dress (or proper ratcatcher at the Pre-training Level) for the dressage and stadium jumping tests; informal attire (chaps are not allowed) for the cross-country. The regulations for the dressage and stadium jumping tests are the same as those for all dressage and stadium jumping competitions. The cross-country is governed by its own body of regulations. All the information you need is contained in the *Supplement to Rules on Dressage and Combined Training*. We will not attempt to restate all the rules in this discussion as they are clearly stated in the pamphlet. If any of the rules are unclear to you, ask for an explanation from the organizer or the technical delegate of an event.

Study all phases of the competition. Watch a few dressage rides. Obtain a map and walk the cross-country course, carefully observing the types of obstacles. Spend a good deal of time watching the cross-country in progress. Note how the start and finish are conducted, then go and watch how the competitors handle some of the more difficult fences. Last, but certainly not least, observe some stadium jumping rounds. Now you can go home and school your horse in each of the three phases.

Unless you are an experienced competitor in other horse sports, you should start at the Pre-training Level. Although your horse is capable of jumping the 3′3″ maximum height of the Training Level fences, the courses are more difficult than this measurement may imply due to the type of obstacles and their placement. The qualifications for Pre-training are not rigid, but most state that the horse and/or rider must not have completed more than three events to be eligible. The Pre-training division may be divided into a novice horse and a novice rider section or into a junior pre-training and a senior pre-training in which either the horse or the rider must be a novice.

Having been to an event or two, you know exactly what to expect in the dressage and stadium jumping tests and have a fairly good idea of what to expect in the cross-country. The chart tells you the length, speeds and dimensions of the obstacles at the various levels, but the character of the course is dependent on what terrain and material are available to the course builder. One course may be laid out over hilly terrain providing banks and drops but possibly no water at all; another course may be on very flat terrain, not providing any drops but having several obstacles involving water or ditches. A good course provides a selection of all the basic obstacles, but this is not always possible, especially at the lower levels.

The fences should be "natural," that is of the type you would expect to find riding cross-country; walls, banks, steps, ditches, water, brush, fallen trees, gates, board and post and rails. However, the course builder may have rather innovative ideas about what is a "natural" fence: tires stacked in various patterns and aluminum drainpipes are popular. At the Pre-training and Training levels, the combinations should not be tricky, the striding should be easy, and the turns not too tight.

Accustom your horse to the basic variety of obstacles he may face before entering an event. Train him to jump strange obstacles promptly and willingly so that, when he is faced with something that is new to him, he will have the confidence to jump it willingly. School him over little ditches and banks to gain his confidence before tackling larger obstacles. If you do not have ditches or banks of the dimensions expected in the event, do not worry. A horse that will handle a four-foot ditch confidently will jump a six-foot ditch. The important thing is that a horse should recognize the type of obstacle and have the experience to handle it.

The rider can help the horse a good deal if he knows how he wants to approach the fences. The one constant to a good approach is impulsion, whether the pace be a trot or a gallop, the stride short or long. When a horse arrives at a fence with good impulsion, it is easier for him to keep going over it than it is to stop. If a horse hits a fence that he has jumped with good impulsion, he has a better chance of recovery when he lands. When determining what pace at which to tackle a difficult fence, the rider must take into consideration his horse's personality. Horses with a cautious nature need time to study an obstacle and, if hustled into a fence, may throw on the brakes at the last minute. However, most horses gain confidence from a strong, steady approach. But whatever the pace, impulsion, impulsion, impulsion!

You need not worry about getting to a precise point for takeoff on the cross-country course, particularly at the lower levels where the obstacles are low and/or relatively narrow. Make the basic decision on whether the situation calls for a short, bouncy stride or for a longer, freer stride and let the horse sort it out for him-

Schooling over little ditches is an essential part of the preparation of a combined-training horse.

self. Short combinations, obstacles followed by a sharp turn, downhill fences, drops, banks, steps up or down, and jumps into water should be approached on a short stride with the horse's hocks well under him; straightforward obstacles, ditches, and open water should be met on a lengthening stride. If your horse tends to jump big, you may wish to approach trappy situations from a trot; however, school your horse to come back into your hand and leg at the canter so that you will be able to establish a good rhythm throughout the course.

The pace for the Pre-training Level is a strong canter; for the Training, a hand gallop. Try to settle your horse into the rhythm of the pace right from the start; he should be willing to shorten his stride on turns and in trappy places and lengthen his stride in the open stretches while still maintaining a good rhythm. This will give both you and the horse confidence.

Certain types of fences always present the biggest problems and should be schooled at home, as it is unfair, and usually un-

STANDARDS FOR THE FIVE LEVELS OF HORSE TRIALS

	*Novice (Pre-training)	*Training	*Preliminary	*Intermediate	*Advanced
Those Eligible	Unrated horses four years or older. Riders any age.	Unrated horses four years or older. Riders any age.	Unrated or Grade III horses five years or older. Riders 14 years or older.	Grade II or Grade III horses five years or older. Riders 16 years or older.	Grade I or Grade II horses six years or older. Riders 18 years or older.
Dressage	1983 Training Level Test 1 or 2	1983 First Level Test 1 or Training Level Test 3	1983 First Level Test 2 or 3	1976 Three-Day Event Test, Intermediate Level	1975 FEI Three-Day Event Test
Roads & Tracks Phases A & C			Total distance shall be from 7,920 m. to 9,900 m. to be carried out at a speed of 220 m.p.m.	Total distance shall be from 9,900 m. to 13,860 m. to be carried out at a speed of 220 m.p.m.	Total distance shall be from 13,860 m. to 16,060 m. to be carried out at a speed of 220 m.p.m.
Steeplechase Distances and Speeds			Either 2,240 m. or 2,560 m. to be carried out at a speed of 640 m.p.m.	Shall be 2,640 m. to be carried out at a speed of 660 m.p.m.	Shall be 2,760 m. to be carried out at a speed of 690 m.p.m.
Height of solid part of obstacles shall not exceed			3'3"	3'3"	3'3"
Overall height of brush shall not exceed			4'7"	4'7"	4'7"
Cross-country	Approx. 2,000 m. carried out at a speed of 350 m.p.m.	Approx. 2,500 m. to be carried out at a speed of 400 to 450 m.p.m.	Approx. 3,000 m. to be carried out at a speed of 450 to 520 m.p.m.	Approx. 3,500 m. to be carried out at a speed of 520 to 550 m.p.m.	Approx. 4,000 m. to be carried out at a speed of 550 to 570 m.p.m.

Number of obstacles	12–18	16–20	18–22	20–24	22–26
Solid part shall not exceed the height of	2'11"	3'3"	3'7"	3'9"	3'11"
Spread at the highest point shall not exceed	3'0"	3'7"	4'7"	5'3"	5'11"
Spread at the base shall not exceed	4'6"	5'0"	6'7"	8'0"	9'2"

m. = meters
m.p.m. = meters per minute
1.00 m. = 3 ft. 3.37 in.
1.00 kilometer = ⅝ mile
1600 m. = 1 mile

m.p.h. = miles per hour
220 m.p.m. = 8½ m.p.h.
350 m.p.m. = 13 m.p.h.
450 m.p.m. = 16¾ m.p.h.
520 m.p.m. = 19⅜ m.p.h.

CLASSIFICATION OF HORSES

Grade 1: Horses that have accumulated 100 points or over. *Grade 2*: Horses that have accumulated 30 to 99 points, inclusive. *Grade 3*: Horses that have accumulated 10 to 29 points, inclusive. *Unrated*: horses with less than 10 points accumulated.

All other horses are classified as Unrated. Placings first through fifth at USCTA Approved Events are used in determining the classification of a horse. The above are some but not all of the standards required at the various levels as of 1984. Speeds and distances are somewhat more demanding at the Three-Day Event level.

Open Training, Open Preliminary and Open Intermediate are open to horses one grade above that stated for that level.
If cross-country-type obstacles, i.e. water, timber, are included in Steeplechase, they must conform to the cross-country standards of that level.
All fences involving height are measured from the horse's normal takeoff point; drops from the normal landing point.
The height and width of all stadium obstacles are regulated by the same standards as those of the cross-country for that level.
Only 50% of the obstacles with height on cross-country may be of maximum height.

243

successful, to ask even the boldest horse to tackle them in cold blood. The first of these are jumps into water. A horse is naturally suspicious of water because he cannot see what the footing is underneath him.

Practice walking him through narrow, then wide, shallow streams that have a good gravel bottom. When he does this exercise without hesitation, trot and canter him through so that he gets accustomed to the splashing water. Then find a stream or pond one and a half to two feet deep and work through that until he learns how to use his legs in the deeper water. Next, set a low fence on the edge of shallow water that is wide enough for the horse to jump into, rather than over; school this at a trot and canter. If possible, find a stream with a bank two or three feet high and jump down into the water. School your horse through any water you can find as long as the footing is good; if you are not sure of footing, go slow. Go back to the simplest exercises if your horse ever does get a scare in the water.

Ditches, with or without water, are probably the next biggest problem to the horse because he must look down to see what he is jumping. The very act of looking down tends to stop him. Start schooling over natural, shallow ditches. Continue until your horse recognizes a ditch some strides away by its appearance and by the way you are riding him (using a strong leg, keeping your eyes and his head up) and he tackles it willingly. Then school him over a manmade ditch that is a couple of feet deep and revetted (the banks held back by boards, railroad ties, etc.) as this will have a different "look" to him.

Combinations are also an important problem, although at the lower levels they should be relatively straightforward. They come in three basic types: a double or triple vertical in-and-out on the same level; a mixture of types, such as a drop followed by a ditch followed by a jump up a bank; and finally, an arrangement of elements involving a sharp turn in order to negotiate the "out." If the distance is long between the elements, meet them on a long stride; if short, meet them on a short stride, or even trot to the first element if you can maintain enough impulsion so that the horse will not stop.

You will also find fences where you will have a choice of jump-

ing in different ways. A simple example is the "brandy snifter."
Picture a brandy snifter lying on its side; the stem may be made
of two parallel logs, possibly measuring above the maximum
height for the level: the bowl of the glass will be formed by two
curved fences to be jumped as an in-and-out. Your choice will
be made on the knowledge of your horse's ability: if he is bold
and strong you would choose the "stem"; if he is cautious and
the striding suits him, you would choose the "bowl." When time
is important, you must give preference to the fastest way if it is
possible for your horse.

A precise approach is important to the success of handling a
combination or a choice fence so that the horse knows exactly
where you wish to jump the obstacle and so that he has the
maximum opportunity to turn if necessary. Check your rules on
refusals and combinations and be sure you thoroughly understand where the penalty zones are, particularly where they overlap, so that you do not inadvertently have a technical refusal by
crossing your track or leaving the penalty zone as you make a
turn into an element.

THE EVENT

On the day before the event there is usually an "official" course-
walking at some point in the afternoon. It is wise to go on this if
at all possible as there is usually an official of the event in charge
and you can then ask any questions about the course, penalty
zones, etc. Even if there is no official along, you will find more experienced "eventers" who will be willing to help you. After you
have done the official course-walking, go back and walk it by
yourself as you will not be able to remember all the details from
one walk, especially when you have been distracted by a group
of people. As you walk around, take notes that you can study that
evening on such factors as the landmarks that will help you keep
on course, where to watch out for going off course, and details
about the fences.

A helper is almost essential if you plan to compete in an event.
You do not wish to leave your horse unwatched while you make

a final check of the cross-country and walk the stadium course. You should also be able to relax for a while so that you are fresh for the stadium course.

Allow enough time before the dressage to work your horse to the point where he will perform at his best level. Some do better if worked early in the day, given time to relax, and then only worked a short period before the test. Others do better if they are worked just before the test.

Before you ride the cross-country, check any fences you are uncertain about or where the footing may have changed due to rain. Plan to be mounted fifteen minutes (more if the horse needs settling) before the start. Go out for a short gallop and school over a couple of fences, even if you do not think your horse needs it. You wish to tune him into the job ahead, which is very different from the dressage.

Know what speed is expected and what the time allowed is for the course. Even if time does not count, you will want to know what time you did the course in compared to the standard; this is one way to learn pace. Time yourself or ask the timer immediately after you have finished before he is busy with the next starter. If this is inconvenient, ask at the scoring center later in the day.

Ride the cross-country as you have planned it, but remain alert and flexible to conditions that may call for a change in your original plans. Do not underrate any fence, no matter how simple it may appear to you; it may look different to your horse or it may ride harder than you anticipated. Be wary of the first couple of fences, especially with a green horse; he does not wish to leave the security of the group and he has not yet had time to gather enthusiasm for the job.

The horse that is not having trouble with the course has the right-of-way over the horse with problems. If there is a horse in your way, call "'ware horse," and they should immediately clear the area. However, if there is a horse blocking an obstacle for whatever reason, pull up *outside the penalty zone.*

Actually, an official should stop you well in advance and start taking the hold-up time with a stopwatch. When it is all right for you to go, the official should then notify you that he will take your time as you pass the point where you were stopped. You

A typical Training Level splash would be a drop down into water, a couple of strides and a small jump out; be sure your horse is prepared for this kind of obstacle.

should then go well back from this point so that you have re-established the galloping rhythm and put your horse's mind back to the job by the moment you pass the timer.

Some officials say that they are going to give you a countdown of ten and then you are to start. They should not do this, but remember they are all volunteers and some are more knowledgeable than others. Simply ask them for a one-minute warning. Spend some of the time while you are waiting establishing with the timer how you are going to restart, and in the meanwhile keep your horse walking and alert.

After you have completed the last fence, do not make a mad dash for the finish. If you have not had any trouble on the course, you should not have any time penalties. If you have had a couple of refusals, you are probably out of the ribbons anyway, so save your horse's strength in order to make a good showing in the stadium jumping. The way to make time on the cross-country is to use *all* the good stretches to gallop on.

You are only allowed three refusals at any obstacle and then

247

you must retire or go on to the next obstacle, depending on the rules of the event. Even if the fence judge does not stop you, do not try the fence again as you may impede an oncoming competitor, damage the fence, and/or tear up the footing. The likelihood of your getting over the fence after three refusals is small and there always is another day. Be a good sport and treat others as you would wish them to treat you.

If you miss the finish flags, immediately turn around and go through them. You are not disqualified but have simply lost time. Dismount and take care of your horse the same way you would after any hard work. Offer him water and hay when he is cool.

Always walk the stadium on foot a couple of times. Note where the tight turns are and where the striding in a combination may be difficult for your horse. Watch how other horses similar to yours handle the combinations in order to get an idea whether you want two short strides or one long one. Remember to salute the judges and wait for the starting bell before going through the starting flags.

If you have a fall on either the cross-country or the stadium, you must remount at the point where you fell. The clock keeps running. When you knock down a fence that must be reset, the bell will sound and you must wait for the bell to sound again before restarting. This time is taken and subtracted from the total. The dressage tests are available after the scores have been totaled. Ribbon winners are expected to present themselves mounted and in proper attire.

Combined Training is one of the most demanding of the horse sports. It gives a small return in the way of prizes and ribbons but a very large return in the way of satisfaction.

HUNTER-RELATED EVENTS

With the growth in the number and quality of shows, the good field hunter (one that is regularly foxhunted) is less and less likely to be the good show hunter. The top or even good show hunter must be well above average in looks, form and way of going. He becomes too valuable to risk an injury or a change of temperament caused by taking him out hunting. In the lower-level shows, you are more likely to find the field hunter doubling as the show hunter. However, there are competitions designed specifically for the field hunter.

Hunter Trials are held over a course of one to two miles with a dozen or more fences typical of the country. The pace and style of the horse are judged on how he should perform out foxhunting. The pace should be a hand gallop, and fences in the open should be taken in stride. Trappy fences can be taken at trot and will be judged with an emphasis on handiness and manners. Small imperfections of style, rubs and ticks that would put the horse out of the ribbons at a show would not be considered. If a hack class is held, suitability as a field hunter is again emphasized while conformation and general appearance are deemphasized unless conformation is particularly specified.

Another competition growing in favor with fox hunters is the *Hunter Pace* event held over several miles of cross-country fences. This is judged only on time. The riders compete as pairs: the winners are those that finish in the fastest time or come in closest to an ideal time based on what a committee has decided is the pace at which this amount of country would be covered while out foxhunting.

For the more adventurous there are *Point-to-Points*, races of three to four miles held over suitable hunting country and open only to qualified hunters. Old-fashioned point-to-points usually demand a slower pace to win as they are longer and are not over a flagged course. Instead, the competitors must only go around three or four prescribed points and may choose any route in doing so. Therefore, not only the horse's speed and jumping ability are tested but so is the rider's judgment in choosing the fastest negotiable track between points.

Other point-to-point races are the Ladies', the Open and the Heavyweight. They may specify that they are only open to amateurs and are held over a flagged course. The fences are lower and the speed necessary to win not as fast as that demanded at the official *Hunt Races* held under the rules of the National Steeplechase and Hunt Association.

The Hunt Races usually offer a mixture of races on the flat, over brush and over timber. Hurdle races are held over brush fences approximately four feet in height. Steeplechase races are held over brush fences approximately five feet in height. The height of the timber fences averages about four feet except in the most famous of them all, the Maryland Hunt Cup, where the third and thirteenth fences are over five feet. Pony races on the flat are often held in conjunction with a point-to-point or hunt meeting.

V·Owning
Your Own Horse

15

How to Buy a Horse

Owning a horse is a serious responsibility, for the domesticated equine is a most dependent animal whose body demands a steady supply of food and water. (The following two chapters will provide a detailed review of his many needs.) Thus the first thing to consider before you purchase a horse is whether you can afford to keep him. After you have made the outlay of his initial cost, can you afford the board at a public stable or its equivalent, plus the additional charges for equipment, shoeing and veterinarian care? Even if a friend has volunteered to keep the horse at a nominal charge, can you afford the time for stall cleaning and whatever else is part of the agreement? And what will you do if the friend can no longer keep the horse?

When you plan to keep your horse at home you will need a stall or shed with storage facilities for feed, hay and straw, and a properly fenced paddock or pasture. If you only have space for a paddock, you will have to exercise your horse regularly, and provide hay and water all year round. Of course, if you have a lush pasture, grown in properly fertilized soil, with two acres or more per horse, a clear running stream or pond and a shed, your work and worry will be greatly reduced.

In the summer you will probably not need any extra feed unless your horse is in regular work, and he will be able to get out of the sun and away from the flies by retreating to the shed. In the winter he will need hay and grain in amounts commensurate with

his type, size and the amount of work expected of him. He will
be in better health, be more relaxed and will always retain some
sort of fitness while moving around a sizable pasture. The main
problem with a good pasture is that some horses will become
overweight on spring grass if they are not properly exercised or if
their turn-out time is not limited.

Keeping your horse at home involves such extra responsibilities
as nursing care and being available when the blacksmith arrives
as well as the normal chores of mucking out, cleaning, feeding,
watering, etc. If all the cares involved with owning a horse were
listed, anyone thinking of buying one might become discouraged.
Obviously the problems involved are more than balanced by the
satisfactions, but both should be carefully weighed before the big
step is taken.

BUYING A HORSE

Before you start looking for a horse, list your requirements under
two headings: Essential and Non-essential. For the novice horseman keeping his horse at home, the list would possibly read as
follows:

Essential
Good basic temperament and manners.
No riding vices.
No stable vices (cribbing acceptable if controlled by cribbing
   strap).
Gets along with other horses when turned out.
Does not jump out of paddock when alone.
Negative Coggins test.
Serviceably sound.
Suitable size.
Not more than $1500.

Non-essential
Good doer.
Good mover.
Good form over fences.

All shots up to date.
Gelding, under ten yers old.
Rides in van or trailer quietly.
Longes well.
Bay or brown in color.
Papers (if it is a Thoroughbred or a type of horse that has a
 registry).
Some show-ring experience.

Think through what you wish to do with your riding so that
you can define what sort of horse you wish. If you are a novice,
the horse you buy to suit your needs now may not fulfill them in
a couple of years. However, buy the horse that is suitable for you
now, as a good "school" type horse is always easy to sell when
you are ready to upgrade. The most common mistake made by
the novice horseman in buying a horse is selecting one that is too
much for him.

A green horse is not suitable for a green rider unless the pair
will be under the supervision of a trainer. A high-spirited Thoroughbred with a sensitive nature, no matter how well trained,
again is not suitable for a novice. A cold-blooded horse or pony
with experience under his girth and with a history of reliability
will not only prove more satisfactory but will usually demand less
care, less exercise to keep his temperament quiet and will probably cause less veterinarian calls. Remember the old saw, "a horse
does not go cross-country on his looks."

Do not be too rigid in your demands as to the horse's appearance, age or height. Most horses can be improved by good care,
exercise and training, so you may allow for improvement especially if the horse is not in condition. A big, plain head is not so
noticeable on a horse with a well-muscled neck; a common horse
carrying a lot of fat will be greatly improved when fit and sleek.

Many people wish a well-trained horse six to eight years of age
and, when this animal is available, he usually carries a high price
tag. It is well for the novice to consider the horse in the "aged"
(over nine years old) category. Around the age of eleven, a really
nice horse's price may be quite a bit lower than his true value
because of the supposedly fewer work years left to him. However,

his experience may more than overcome this disadvantage. If he is sound, he will probably remain so for several years as most lamenesses have made themselves evident by this age. The most common disease that shows itself in older horses is some form of arthritis and your veterinarian will tell you if your choice is predisposed to arthritic changes.

There is a preference for horses over sixteen hands as, in truth, they do tend to have more scope than smaller horses. However, if you do not need a horse that will stand out in the show ring or will jump five-foot fences, then definitely look into the smaller animal. Their price tends to be less and they are often easier to keep and easier to ride. Even if you are on the tall side, do not hesitate to try the 15.2 horse because, if he has a good front with a longish neck, good head carriage, and a good middle, he may ride as big as a sixteen-hand horse that lacks these qualities.

When you are ready to look at horses, you can certainly use the advice of a very experienced horseman. If you have a friend in this category who is willing to help you, you are in luck. If you are taking lessons with a professional, he or she will be helpful, although some may be too busy to go horse-hunting. The last alternative is to call a reputable professional in the area and ask him to look for you. The professional of course will expect a "commission" as financial remuneration for his time. The normal procedure is that he receives a percentage of the selling price from the seller of the horse. However, he must be involved in the purchase of the horse to make any money, and you may be a chronic window-shopper. Therefore, if he does not know you and how serious your intentions are, he may not spend time on your project. You can solve this problem by doing the footwork yourself and, when you find a horse, offer to pay the professional a flat fee for his time to come check you and the horse out.

You find suitable horses by reading the advertisements in the various horse magazines, by asking knowledgeable friends, or by visiting reputable dealers, professional stables or riding schools. Leave auction sales strictly to the professionals. When you have an appointment to see a horse, be on time. Nothing sours a seller more than standing around for an hour while his work piles up, wondering whether you are going to appear. When you arrive,

This is a nice type of 16.2-hand Thoroughbred gelding, except for his swayed back. It could indicate a weakness and presents problems in fitting the saddle, but it's never bothered Elderberry. When you are buying a horse, you must decide what imperfections you are willing to live with.

state clearly your experience, the prime things you are looking for in a horse and your price, i.e., in the $1,000 range. If you have a professional with you, let him do most of the talking.

The horse should then be led out for you to look at and be jogged in hand. If there is something about the horse that rules him out immediately, say so then and there. Do not waste your time and the seller's by having him ridden. A simple statement such as "he appears to be a very nice horse but I don't want anything that big" is sufficient. Never criticize a horse to the seller, no matter how glaring his faults. Once you have found a possible horse, ask to have it ridden at all paces and jumped by someone in the stable; never get up on it first yourself. If you still like the horse, ask to try it in the manner in which you wish to use it: i.e., hack cross-country if you are looking for a hack. A horse that goes well in a ring does not necessarily go well cross-country, and vice versa.

After you have ridden the horse a couple of times on separate days, you may decide that he seems to suit you. Now comes the hardest part of a horse deal. The buyer would usually like to take the horse for a trial period of a week or so in order to verify that the horse is what he appears, that is, that he has not been drugged in order to mask a temperament or soundness problem. The buyer also wishes to find out if he can live with his new horse, as it may have habits or vices which are unknown or just of no consequence to the seller but would make the horse unsatisfactory to the buyer. On the other hand, the seller does not wish to take the risk of damage from neglect or accident to his valuable property. The problem is largely one of establishing mutual faith. As no single procedure prevails in the horse world at this stage, we can only review some of the ways used to establish good faith; hopefully one of them will satisfy both the seller and the buyer.

If the seller knows the stable to which the horse is going, he will probably allow the horse to go on trial. He may or may not also require a down payment, and if so, it should be agreed in writing that it is returnable if the horse is not accepted. If the seller is hesitant about allowing a trial, the buyer could offer one or more of the following as evidence of good will: (1) a down payment (conditions above); (2) an insurance binder for full mortality on the horse during its stay; (3) a signed statement to the effect that the buyer will assume full responsibility for the horse and, if it is not accepted, will return it in the same condition in which it was received; (4) a check postdated to an agreed upon date.

If the seller is determined not to allow the horse on trial, he can show his good will by: (1) guaranteeing the horse suitable and agreeing to return the check if the horse proves unsuitable up to a certain date; (2) guaranteeing the horse as to certain specifics, e.g., a chestnut mare, six years old, sound of wind and limb, no vices, capable of jumping 3′6″ quietly, and the return of the check if the horse does not fulfill these specifics; (3) accepting a postdated check.

The last step in purchasing a horse is to have him thoroughly checked over by a veterinarian of the buyer's choice, and all purchase agreements should be conditional upon the horse passing the vet for the intended purpose. No matter how blemish-free the animal appears to you, only an expert can check his eyes, heart, etc. By all means be on hand when the veterinarian makes his soundness examination. Very few horses are free of blemishes or conformation faults that could possibly lead to unsoundness. Explain to the veterinarian what purposes you will be using the horse for so that he can more fairly evaluate the animal. If the horse has not been on trial and there is any possibility that he may have been tranquilized, ask the vet to also take a urine sample.

If the horse is absolutely "clean" and gives no clinical evidence of unsoundness, then he can be simply passed as sound. However, if the horse has blemishes, defects or conformation faults, the veterinarian will point these out. If he knows what kind of work will be expected of the horse, he can then give you a fair estimate of its suitability for this use. However, do not expect him to assume the powers of the Almighty and project the future. For example, if the horse has had a bowed tendon, even though it is now healed and he moves soundly on it, the veterinarian cannot pass him as sound. However, if you have stated that you wish to hack and show the horse lightly, he may say that in his opinion the horse is a good risk for this kind of work. On the other hand, if you are looking for a horse to event or hunt hard, the veterinarian will probably say that, in his opinion, the horse is a bad risk. So ask questions, but do not ask the impossible.

While conducting his examination, the veterinarian may see some clinical evidence of a possible unsoundness in the way the horse moves or in obvious calcium formations, etc. He may then suggest radiographs (X rays) of a certain area(s). Even with the radiographs, he may not be able to say absolutely that the horse will be sound or unsound for a certain length of time, but he will be able to present you with the facts and risk factors. It is then up to you to make the decision. The radiographs will be a help in warning you of future problems and will be useful as a comparison if, at a later date, other radiographs are taken of the same area. When the veterinarian examination is finished and it appears that you will buy the horse, ask him if the horse needs any change of shoeing, feeding, etc.

Hopefully you are now ready to buy your horse. Ask the owner details of his regime: how fit is he; what is he being fed; what tack is used on him and why; is he accustomed to being turned

259

out and for how long; does he have any peculiarities around the barn, while being ridden, or while vanning or trailering; what shots he has had, and when was he last wormed and with what; is he prone to colic, tieing up or thrush? Last, but essential, do not purchase a horse without a negative Coggins test, which indicates that the animal is free of equine infectious anemia, taken within three weeks of purchase.

BOARDING YOUR HORSE

Boarding rates are traditionally divided into full, rough, and turn-out. Exactly what you receive for each board depends on the individual stable. Visit all the boarding stables in your area and write down what they offer for what amount of board. Investigate the facilities thoroughly. Are the stalls, water and feed buckets clean and well constructed? Are the horses clean, healthy and happy? Is the barn well ventilated and well cared for? Are normal safety precautions observed? Are the workers kind and quiet around the horses? Is the feed of good quality?

Be suspicious if a stable offers an unusually low rate. Feed and good horse care are expensive. A way to save money is not to patronize a cheap stable but to do some of the work yourself. In these days of expensive labor, even a first-class stable may be glad to give you a lower rate if you clean your own horse and tack.

When you have selected a stable, write down what you will receive for your rate so that there will be no misunderstandings with the owner. Veterinarian care, shoeing and clipping are always extra charges. If your horse requires special feed or vitamins, these will probably be extra as well. Find out the stable schedule. Nothing is more annoying to the stable manager than to have someone come to ride just as the horses are being fed. Be considerate at all times. Running a stable well is hard work. You can make it easier by always coming on time and, if you have a change of plans, letting the manager know well in advance. No one likes to discover at 4:00 P.M. that there is another horse to be worked.

16

Keeping Your
Horse at Home

Some aspects of basic horse care are discussed in detail elsewhere in this book (particularly in the Grooming and Veterinary chapters), so this chapter will concentrate on the basic daily or periodic routines, starting with the most essential of all: feeding and watering.

FEEDING

A mature horse needs a minimum of twelve gallons of water daily, the amount varying with the weather and the type of work he is in, to remain healthy. Many horses are quite choosy, and will not drink enough if the water is not fresh; be sure to keep buckets and water bowls clean. If your horse does not have a constant supply, such as a stream or an automatic waterer, and his supply cannot be refreshed during the day, then make available two twelve-gallon buckets of water. He also needs some salt every day and this can be supplied by putting a large salt lick in the field or a small one in his stall, or by adding one-half teaspoon of salt to his feed. It is a good idea to purchase salt bricks that also contain trace minerals.

Feeding your horse is an art in that it requires a "skill in performance acquired by experience, study and observation." We must know which feedstuffs contain what proportions of proteins, carbohydrates, minerals and vitamins. Then, by observation and experience, we decide what proportions of these feedstuffs a horse needs at any particular time.

When planning how to feed a horse we must consider (1) the mechanics of his digestion, (2) how food affects his weight and temperament, (3) how much and what kind of nutrition he needs for his age and use.

Digestion

Food passes down the horse's esophagus into his stomach, which is small and only able to contain between eight and sixteen quarts. Food remains in the stomach about one hour and the enzymes that make digestion possible are added here. From these facts, we can observe that a horse should not be fed large quantities at one time because the food will not remain long enough in the stomach to be properly prepared for digestion. If your horse tends to gobble his grain and then his hay, the hay should be fed at separate times. When hay is offered free choice, then the problem does not arise.

Horses should not be allowed to drink large quantities of water at one time and, if water is available at all times as it should be, this problem will not arise except after exercise. A horse should not be exercised until one hour after feeding, and if the exercise is to be strenuous, food and water should be withheld for several hours to allow the food to be processed through the extensive digestive tract.

From the stomach, the food passes to the small intestine, which is twisted in several spirals, where it is further mixed with the digestive enzymes. It then passes into the caecum, a large, unevenly corrugated portion of the intestines where the main digestive process starts. The food then passes through a narrow neck into the unevenly corrugated large intestine and colon where the bulk of digestion occurs. Food is assimilated through the intestinal wall and the residue is passed out as manure. Bacteria in the intestines live on and break down the fiber and cellulose in the horse's food. If there is not a regular supply of food, the bacteria die; if there is an oversupply, the bacteria cannot handle it and the impaction form of colic occurs.

Therefore, we see that the horse's digestion is a delicate mechanism and should not be loaded with coarse grains such as unprocessed barley and overly mature hay with woody stems. On the other hand, the intestines need a regular supply of bulk and have trouble handling fine, wiry hay or too much fines (powdery substances such as soybean meal). Pasture or free-choice hay will keep the digestive tract happy. If the horse is on a rationed diet, then give small amounts at regular intervals rather than lumping his food for the day into a couple of feeds. When the pasture is sparse or frozen, and the horse is turned out all day, he should be given some hay to pick at.

Weight and Temperament

An attempt to duplicate the horse's natural grazing pattern by having hay or grass constantly available not only will help your horse's digestion but will keep him in a contented frame of mind so that he is less likely to form such bad habits as weaving, cribbing, wood-chewing and bolting his grain. A couple of smooth rocks, a couple of ears of corn, or a few handfuls of chopped hay mixed with the grain will slow down a horse that eats too fast.

Mature horses need some energy just to exist; growing animals and broodmares more energy; horses in regular work need more than the preceding, and horses subject to stress need as much as thirty times the energy a horse needs for maintenance. Horses derive energy from the carbohydrates, best supplied by grain. Corn contains the highest percentage of carbohydrate per pound followed closely by barley, then oats, and wheat bran. If more carbohydrate is consumed than the horse needs to supply the amount of energy expended, then the excess is stored as fat and the horse by the intake of carbohydrate, then his body will use the energy stored as fat and he will lose weight.

In theory, if a horse consumes more carbohydrate than he needs, the excess is stored as fat but it appears that this kind of diet also makes some horses "high" (fractious), especially if the main source of carbohydrate is oats and the horse is stabled much of the time. This problem can be solved by longer turn-out periods, more exercise, and, with some horses, feeding more barley or bran and less oats.

Therefore, it is simple to know if your horse is getting enough energy food by his weight. You want your horse sleek not fat. Overweight horses suffer the same problems as overweight people plus they are more susceptible to founder and have more strain on their legs.

Kinds of Nutrition

Grass, and a little lower on the scale, hay, also supply carbohydrate but at a significantly lower rate per pound than grain. So if your horse is overweight, lower the amount of grain before you lower the amount of hay.

Protein is essential for tissue building so the greatest amount of protein is needed by pregnant and lactating mares, and during the first two years of life. Horses cannot digest or assimilate all the crude protein supplied, so find out the digestible protein of whatever feedstuffs you are using. Ten of the amino acids found in protein are essential to horses and of these ten lysine appears to be the most important.

Foodstuffs are then evaluated on the percentage of digestible protein and the percentage of the essential amino acids, particularly lysine, that they contain. Legume (alfalfa and clover) hay comes out on top in this category, followed by timothy hay and young growing pasture followed by barley and then corn and oats. Among the supplements, soybean meal is very high in good quality protein (higher even than the legumes) followed by linseed meal and dried skim milk.

We start with the rule of thumb that a mature horse weighing a thousand pounds, working two hours a day needs a minimum of one pound of digestible protein a day. He can get this from approximately ten pounds of legume hay, twenty-five pounds of grass hay or young grass (one acre of very well maintained pasture yields approximately forty pounds of grass per day during the growing season) or twelve pounds of barley, bran, corn or oats. One pound of soybean meal or dried skim milk supplies one-third the daily need for protein; one pound of linseed meal supplies one-fourth the protein needed; one pound of molasses supplies one-tenth the protein needed.

Just as protein is important for the building of tissue, calcium and phosphorus are important to the building of bone and should be present in the diet in a ratio of one and a half to one. Again, these minerals are most important to the broodmare and the young. Excessive calcium intake has not yet been proven to be detrimental, but an excess of phosphorus withdraws calcium from the bones.

Legume hay and pasture are high in calcium, followed by timothy hay and other pasture grasses. Grains are lower in minerals than hay and pasture and all contain more phosphorus than calcium. Wheat bran is high in phosphorus but not all of it is assimilated. Steamed bone meal supplies calcium and phosphorus at a ratio of two to one. Monosodium phosphate supplies phosphorus. Ground limestone supplies calcium. A mature horse that is not subject to stress receives sufficient vitamins and minerals if he is turned out on properly fertilized pasture in the summer and receives a balanced ration of good hay and grain in the winter. For broodmares, horses under three years of age, and horses under stress, consult your veterinarian, and explain what feed the animal is getting before adding supplements and/or vitamins. Some vitamins, notably vitamin D, can be quite harmful if overfed.

Commercial Feeds

There are many commercial feeds on the market designed to be used with the basic hay-grain diet or even to replace it totally. There are also supplements that can be added to the hay-grain diet that can insure that your horse is receiving the necessary vitamins and minerals.

One of the most useful commercial feeds for the average horse is "sweet feed," which is a mixture of grains and some combination of protein, vitamin and mineral supplements such as soybean meal, linseed meal and alfalfa pellets, all bound together with molasses. Some companies have different grades; those costing more contain higher quality feedstuffs. The advantages of a good quality sweet feed are: (1) it provides a somewhat balanced diet; (2) convenience, the horseman does not have to buy and mix the various grains and supplements; (3) it whets the appetite of some horses. The disadvantages are: (1) it is difficult to judge the quality of its components; (2) it should not be stored for long periods of time, particularly in the summer, as it tends to ferment; (3) some horses do not like it. A good quality sweet feed should consist mostly of grains, should smell fresh and should not contain lumps of sticky feed. If you get the top of the line sweet feed from a reputable dealer, you can be well assured of good quality.

Pellets are another form of commercial horse feed and come in three types: pure alfalfa pellets, grain pellets with supplements, and hay-grain pellets with or without supplements. It is impossible to determine the quality of the pellets by examination, so you must rely on the reputation of the manufacturer. However, they are a very clean feed and are easy to store. Alfalfa pellets make a good supplement when you do not wish to feed alfalfa hay. Grain pellets are an expensive way to feed. Hay-grain pellets may be a solution for the horse owner who does not have access to good pasture or hay; however, the horse should still receive some roughage on the side if only to satisfy his need to chew.

Another source of roughage is beet pulp, which must be soaked in water for several hours. It is then easily digested and, although low on nutrients, quite appealing to some horses, and fattening. It can be mixed with grain to tempt the picky eater.

Grain

You should know how much grain you are feeding by the pound, not by dry measure, as grains vary greatly in volume. (See the Weight-Volume Chart on page 269. All the grains should be free of extraneous materials, be fresh, and have the best possible test weight. Cheap grain is a waste of money; you will have to feed more to keep your horse in the proper condition and it will always be lower in vitamins, minerals and digestibility.

Oats, corn and barley have a much higher ratio of carbohydrate to protein, and you can satisfactorily substitute one for another if it is of better quality and/or cheaper in your area. Wheat bran has a higher ratio of protein to carbohydrate. It also has a much higher phosphorus content and it has a very fine texture. For these reasons it is not used as the basic grain in the diet but it makes an excellent supplement.

Consider the following facts before deciding what mixture of grains is best for your horse: Oats suitable for horses should have a test weight of forty pounds or more per bushel. They should be plump and light in color. Oats and corn may be fed whole or processed. Processing of grain makes it more digestible but also more expensive. Unless your horse has a dental or digestive problem, there is no need to feed processed oats or corn. Crimped or crushed oats are those in which the hull has been split but the kernel remains in the hull. Steamed-rolled oats are those in which the grain has been completely flattened.

Corn has a higher carbohydrate and lower protein content than oats. Its carbohydrate metabolizes easily into heat. If you wish to put weight on your horse and help him keep warm in the winter, then increase the proportion of corn in his feed. If he is overweight or working hard in the heat, decrease or eliminate the portion of corn. Good quality corn is bright yellow, smooth-kerneled and plump. Corn is available on the cob, as shelled whole kernels, and as cracked (chopped) kernels.

Barley stands between oats and corn in its carbohydrate and protein content. It has a hard, indigestible hull so it must be cooked or processed before feeding to horses. Barley is available flaked (the same process as rolling is to oats) from the manufacturer. It is difficult to judge the quality of flaked barley.

Bran is a by-product of whole wheat. It has a higher protein than carbohydrate content. Fed dry, it is slightly constipating; fed wet, as in a hot mash, it is a laxative. If it is fed with other grains, these effects are somewhat nullified. A bran mash is made by adding very hot or preferably boiling water to the bran until it is moist but still fluffy; cover and let steam until cool enough to eat. A wetter bran mash would be indicated if a more laxative effect is desired.

Other grains, or sweet feed, may be added to the mash; the steaming effect will increase their digestibility. One or two fluffy bran mashes a week, with or without other grains, will benefit most horses. Toss the mash a couple of times before feeding so that it is evenly cooled. Some horses dislike a bran mash and it can be made more palatable for them by the addition of molasses and/or grain.

Hay

A horse is a forager by nature and needs bulk in his diet. This can be supplied by grass and/or hay. Good pasture should be as weed free as possible and contain a mixture of grasses and legumes that are suitable for horses and grow well in your area. Consult your state agriculture service or your local agricultural supply firm for advice. The soil should be tested yearly and the necessary fertilizers, preferably organic, should be applied. The pasture should be mowed often to encourage your tender grass which is more nutritional and palatable.

The younger the hay, the more nutrition it contains. Unfortunately, it is uneconomical for the farmer to cut it at the stage the horseman would like it. However, you should still try to find the youngest hay available. The most common types of hay are grass hays, such as timothy and orchard grass, and legume hays such as alfalfa and clover. Mixed hay is also available which usually contains a mixture of one grass hay and one legume hay.

Grass hays supply less protein per pound than the legume hays, but are sufficient for the average riding horse that is also receiving some grain. The legumes are higher in protein and more fattening but are also more expensive, harder to handle, and can have some undesirable side effects. Clover tends to be dusty and may cause respiratory problems in some horses. Alfalfa, fed to horses that do not need the extra protein, is suspected in some cases of causing the tieing-up syndrome. Alfalfa is available in pellet form and may be used as a supplement; one pound of pellets is equal to two pounds of hay.

Unless it has been barn dried, hay should be stored six weeks after cutting before it is fed to horses. Fresh hay should have a good green color. After hay has been stored several months it will lose much of its color, but this does not necessarily mean that it is not nutritional; hay loses most of the nutrition it is going to lose in the first month of storage. Therefore, if you are going to judge hay by its color, you should see it within a few weeks of cutting. Alfalfa suitable for horses should be from the second or third cutting as the first cutting contains a higher percentage of stems to leaves and these stems are woody.

Small, tight seed heads, flowers or leaves and tender stalks indicate young hay. All hay should be weed-free (weeds are unpalatable and those with wide leaves tend to go moldy even in properly cured hay because they hold so much moisture), be low in dust and absolutely free of mold. Mold exhibits itself as a fine gray powder which adheres to the hay and smells "moldy." The affected hay tends to stick together in a lump. Never use moldy hay as bedding or toss it where your horse can get hold of it. He does not know it is bad for him and he will eat it; it may cause serious respiratory problems resulting in heaves.

Feeding your horse is not difficult if you understand the kind and amount of nutrition he should receive. Once you are sure he is receiving the necessary vitamins and minerals, you can judge whether he is receiving enough grain by his weight and energy level. If your horse is in poor condition or if you are going to ask him to perform under stress, then you should consult with your veterinarian.

Usually, feeding a balanced mixture of high-quality forage and grains will guarantee that the horse is receiving the proper nutrition. Feeding at regular intervals during the day will satisfy his digestion. Some rules of thumb: introduce new feed slowly; feed each horse according to his condition and amount of work; be quick to adjust his feed if he starts to gain or lose weight; remove oats from his feed if he is sick or injured.

WEIGHT-VOLUME CHART

	One Quart Weighs	*One Pound Measures*
Barley	1.5 lbs.	.7 quart
Corn	1.7 lbs.	.6 quart
Linseed meal	.9 lb.	1.1 quarts
Sweet feed	.8 lb.	1.3 quarts
Oats	1.0 lb.	1.0 quart
Bran	.5 lb.	2.0 quarts

SAMPLE FEEDS

Medium to large Pony (*not in work*)	Ten lbs. good hay or pasture—if poor quality, supplement with one to two lbs. commercial "complete" horse feed, or one-half lb. alfalfa pellets, or one-fourth lb. bran and one-half lb. barley.
Medium to large Pony (*in regular work— ridden every day, foxhunting, showing, eventing*) *Grain divided in two feedings.*	Ten lbs. good hay or pasture and one to four lbs. oats and barley mix 50%/50%—if forage is poor quality, supplement above with one to two lbs. commercial "complete" feed, or one-half lb. alfalfa pellets, or one to two lbs. sweet feed, or one-half lb. bran and one-half lb. barley.
Horse (*16 hands*) (*not in work*) *Grain may be given in one feed.*	Twenty lbs. good hay or pasture and one to four lbs. corn, oats or barley—if forage is poor quality, supplement with two to four lbs. commercial "complete" feed or one lb. alfalfa pellets and one-half lb. bran.
Horse (*16 hands*) (*in light regular work*) *Grain given in two feeds.*	Twenty-five lbs. good hay or pasture and two to four lbs. corn, oats or barley—if forage is poor quality, supplement with four to six lbs. "complete" feed or one lb. alfalfa pellets and one-half lb. bran.
Horse (*16 hands*) *medium work* (*light hunting, showing, etc.*) *Grain given prefer- ably in three feeds but acceptable in two.*	Twenty-five lbs. hay or pasture plus four to eight lbs. corn, oats, or barley or a mixture of these—if hay is poor quality, supplement the above with one to two lbs. of alfalfa pellets and one lb. bran or one-half lb. calf manna.

To figure out the weight of the hay you are feeding, count the number of bales in a ton, divide into two thousand pounds, and you will come up with the weight of each bale. If the average bale weighs forty-four pounds, one-fourth of a bale will contain approximately eleven pounds. The weight of the hay per bale will vary with the type of hay and the adjustments on the baler, so you must check each load if you are concerned with the exact amount of hay you are feeding each horse. Your supplier can probably give you these figures.

All these amounts are based on the feeding of a horse that is a "good doer." A Thoroughbred horse may need more grain to keep him good flesh. Calf manna, mentioned in the last grouping, a supplement put out by Carnation (Albers) Company, is a good all-around supplement. It is suitable for horses in light work and heavy work, in the amounts of one-half to one pound. Remember that the above feeds are just samples; every horse must be fed as an individual. Quartered apples or carrots are always welcome and are useful in enticing the picky eater. The grain ration may be made up of one-half sweet feed and one-half oats, ignoring other supplements if the hay is good.

BEDDING

Almost as basic as your horse's dietary requirements are his stabling and bedding requisites. Your choice of bedding should be based on your storage facilities, your horse's particular needs, and quality and price. Bedding is cheaper by the ton; straw bales can be stacked but loose bedding, such as sawdust, must have its own specially designed facilities on the same level as the stalls to be practical. Good quality bedding, though more expensive, saves money in the long run in ease of handling, cleanliness and durability. Straw is usually cheaper in the summer and can be bought right out of the field if properly cured, as it does not have to "sweat"; the prices of other beddings vary with the market. Baled wood shavings are somewhat more expensive than loose shavings; sawdust is often available free at the sawmill. Horses that eat straw or have respiratory problems are better off bedded on wood shavings or Stazdry, a commercial product made from sugarcane pulp.

Straw makes the most attractive bed for your horse, although not the most absorbent or easiest to handle. Its low cost and availability made it the national bedding for horses up until recently. Now the rising cost of the product and of labor has brought straw into about the same price range as wood shavings and Stazdry. Straw manure will be removed free of charge by truckers supplying mushroom houses, or it can be spread on fields not used as pasture.

Good straw should be bright in color, long, hard and free of dust or weeds. A gray color indicates that it has been rained on; it will then be dusty and soft. Open a bale and shake it out; if it is soft and contains a lot of chaff, it will be dusty and will not make a durable bed. Wheat and rye provide the best straw if combined and cured properly. Barley can provide good straw if cut just at the right time; however, it tends to be short and soft. Oat straw is not considered suitable for horses and they will eat it.

Wood shavings sold commercially either by the bale or loose are dust-free, absorbent and make a good bed. Once the stall is made up it takes little time to remove the droppings and wet spots and put in new shavings. The whole stall should only need to be cleaned out occasionally if it is well looked after on a daily basis.

Shavings are available from furniture and fence companies or lumber mills at little or no cost. Of course, you must pick them up and the supply may be erratic. These shavings are not as uniform as those available commercially and may contain a high percentage of sawdust. If the shavings come from green lumber, they will contain a certain amount of moisture. This quality does not affect their usability as bedding but it opens up the possibility of combustion. These shavings should be stored outside under a tarpaulin or plastic sheeting, or in a building that allows for maximum air circulation. Dig into the center of the pile regularly to check for heat buildup. On the other hand, if the shavings are very dry and contain a high percentage of sawdust, they can make a dusty bed. This can be remedied by sprinkling the bed lightly with water as necessary. A bed made with a bottom layer of shavings or sawdust and topped by straw has proved satisfactory for some horsemen.

Sawdust is available for the asking at sawmills. It has the same moisture-dryness qualities as non-commercial shavings only accentuated. Handle as stated above. Sawdust and shavings draw more moisture from the horse's hooves than other beddings. Take the necessary precautions.

Stazdry, although initially expensive, makes an excellent, dust-free bed, and may be the best bedding for the horse owner with a storage and manure-removal problem, or a horse with respiratory problems. When using shavings, sawdust and Stazdry, you remove substantially less bulk from the stall and have a smaller manure pile. However, this manure is useless to the mushroom grower, so its removal must be considered. It can be spread on fields not used for pasture. Shavings and sawdust are acid, so the pH of these fields will have to be watched and lime applied accordingly. The manure can be used to make a longeing ring or galloping track, or it can be composted. If you have too much for your own use, a nursery may be interested.

CLEANING THE STALL ("Mucking-out")

To clean the stall efficiently you need a four-pronged fork for straw and a ten- to twelve-pronged fork for shavings or sawdust. For all types of bedding, you need a manure basket or tub for quick pick-ups, and a spring (grass) rake, large shovel, stiff broom and wheelbarrow or cart for thorough cleanings.

The stall should be thoroughly cleaned once a day and picked up as often as possible. Remove the horse if at all possible or tie him to the side. Start by going around the edges with the pitchfork, piling the clean straw against the wall and the dirty straw in the center or directly into a wheelbarrow. After you have removed the dirty straw, rake up the dirty areas, sweep the residue into a large shovel, and sprinkle all bare areas with lime or Lysol or Creolin solution in order to keep down odors and bacteria. At least once a week (and every day if possible), shift the dry straw from side to side, sweeping clean the corners and sides of the stall. Leave the stall open to air if it is not needed immediately.

To make up the stall, place clean straw in the heavily used places as it is more absorbent than the old straw. Shaking out fresh straw with a pitchfork causes more dust than pulling it apart by hand. Mix the new with the old straw until the bed is level in the center and banked slightly to the sides. The bedding should be thick enough to provide a good cushion. If the horse spends a lot of time in the stall, he needs a deeper cushion to ease the strain on his feet.

To finish off, sprinkle the aisles with water to keep down the dust and sweep clean. Store all cleaning tools where they will not be a hazard to horses or humans.

OCCASIONAL CHORES

In addition to daily grooming, feeding and mucking-out, there are also a couple of more occasional chores involved in caring for your own horse—clipping, mane pulling and braiding. They are tricky and take some practice to do well, but they are not really difficult, and some people come to rather enjoy doing them. Before you start doing it yourself, it is very helpful for you to watch someone who is truly proficient, and, if possible, make your first attempt under his or her supervision. Some skills that are very difficult to describe precisely in print (especially tail-braiding) are very easily demonstrated.

Mane Pulling

Some people roach or clip off manes entirely, and polo ponies and three-gaited saddle horses are customarily shown and used with no mane. On a hunter, however, it usually looks terrible, quite aside from the fact that it gives you nothing to grab on to in emergencies!

In this country, the mane traditionally is made to lie on the off (right) side. If it is pulled and thinned about once a month, it should never get out of control and will stay easy to braid. Unless it is very thin, the mane is normally thinned and shortened in the same operation. The only tool that is required is a mane comb— *never* scissors or clippers.

To begin, take the mane comb in your right hand and hold a

274

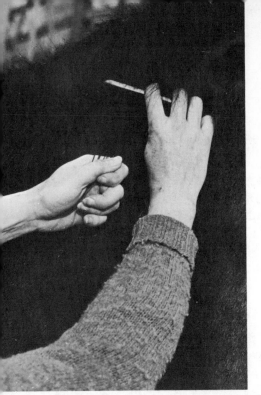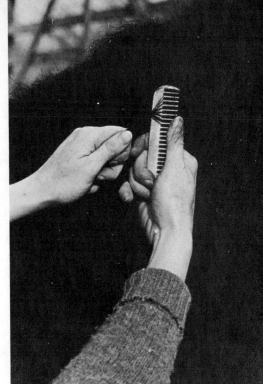

The trick to pulling a mane is not to take too much hair at a time; then wrap the hair around the comb and pull, mostly with the hand that is holding the comb.

small section of hair by its ends between the thumb and forefinger of your left hand. Lift the bulk of the hair off the top with the comb. When a very small section of hair remains in your left hand, wrap that section around the mane comb with the comb well up toward the roots of the hair. Then pull gently and firmly on the comb and the hair will come out by the roots. Move systematically up and down the mane until it is the length and thickness you wish. If the mane is already as thin as desired but you wish to shorten it, then use either of the following methods: a mane knife is available for just this purpose, or you can just snap the ends off by pulling in a jerky motion with your thumb and forefinger.

Some tails are quite bushy at the top or so thick overall that they are unattractive. The tail can be thinned in much the same way as the mane. However, do not pull the hair at the very sides if you ever wish to braid the tail. Most horses look their best with their tails hanging about six inches below the hock. If you wish a natural-looking tail, you can then pull the lower hairs out until you reach this length or, if you prefer, you can simply square it off ("bang" it) with scissors.

A braided mane and tail give a neat, finished appearance to a horse. All the hunter-type horses will be braided at the larger shows except for the Welsh ponies, whose mane and tails must be natural, and perhaps the jumpers. A braided mane is sufficient at the smaller shows although a well-braided tail will enhance your horse's appearance. He should be fully braided for conformation classes. Many small, thin braids will give a short neck a longer look; fewer thick braids will give a thin neck a more substantial look.

The end of the tail may be wrapped into a mud knot and neatly incorporated into a braided tail if the going is muddy at a show. A mud knot can be quickly made from an unbraided tail for exercise or for hunting. It is a courtesy to the Master to braid the horse's mane for the important meets such as Opening Day, but you need not braid the tail to have your horse looking smart out hunting. A braided tail can actually be a hardship on him as it will catch in briars and branches. Braiding and making a good mud knot in the tail are best learned by watching someone who knows what he is doing, and from lots of practice. Some tips: have the mane and tail in good condition and the proper length; keep your hands close to the horse's body; wet thoroughly; make the braids small; make each section the same size by measuring with the comb, i.e., half or three-fourths its length. In the winter, wash the mane, tail and sheath of geldings with a good animal shampoo or mild soap, rinsing thoroughly, as often as needed.

With a scissors or a small hand clippers, you may trim a couple of inches of mane out from where the bridle lies behind the poll, and also trim the long hair on the jaws, whiskers and fetlock hair. If your horse has good hooves, then don't upset the balance that nature has achieved by constantly covering them with hoof dressing. However, for special occasions when you want him to look his best, and for those spells of very dry or very wet weather, have available a good quality dressing made only from natural oils. (Never use old motor oil, as it contains harmful chemicals.) Some dry, brittle hooves can be helped by some preparations. They should be applied well into the coronet, the wall and the sole. As the hooves' condition improves, apply only to the coronet as hooves that are too soft are as much a problem as those that are too dry. Observation and the advice of the blacksmith will dictate how often it should be applied.

Clipping

To achieve a successful job of clipping, the horse should be clean and the clippers sharp. Clean the blades often with kerosene mixed with a little light oil or a commercial preparation. If your clipper becomes hot, stop clipping. Allow plenty of time. Large horses are better off clipped in two sessions, i.e., the head one day and the body the next. If your horse is tense or ticklish, get an assistant, and make your sessions brief. A small ear clipper is invaluable around the head as it is handy, quiet and has less vibration than the large clippers.

Apply a twitch to your horse's upper lip if necessary to do his head and other tender places. Better the distraction of a twitch on his lip than the danger caused by a frightened, nervous horse. A twitch is made of rope or chain threaded through a hole made in a two-inch, round pole about two feet long. Slipping your hand through the loop, grasp the end of the horse's upper lip just below the nostrils. Slide the loop over his lip and twist the pole until the loop is just tight enough to stay on. If the horse acts up, give a half-twist to the pole to tighten the loop; when he relaxes, return to the original hold. A twitch adjusted too lightly causes unnecessary discomfort and will eventually numb the lip and lose its effectiveness.

Naturally, horses resent the use of a twitch. Stand well to the side when applying it, in case the horse strikes. Unless you know your horse, you should have the help of an assistant. If the horse raises his head out of reach, the assistant can run the end of a chain around the noseband of the halter and hold his head down. The chain end of a shank can be used as an effective twitch by running it through the side ring of the halter, under the upper lip, and fastening to the far side. Make sure the chain lies flat so that it does not cut the gum.

Use the clippers in short, even strokes and hold any loose skin taut with your free hand. Leave a saddle mark of unclipped hair on thin-skinned horses, but clip the back, for the first time or two, on horses with thick coats.

Do not attempt to clip your horse too often as it will be a frustrating, uneven job. The coat should be dense enough to peel off in a ribbon in front of the clippers. At the most, two strokes in the same place should achieve a finished appearance. If you are not sure, try a test patch under the belly.

When you are finished clipping, brush the horse with a soft brush (his skin is sensitive now) and rub him off with a damp and then a dry towel. It takes several days for the horse's coat to look well after clipping so make allowances if you wish him to look his best on a particular day. No unevenness will show if you trim places you have missed within the first three days.

There are several different clipping patterns. A horse is fully clipped in order to allow rapid evaporation of sweat when at work and to facilitate cleaning. The legs of field hunters are not clipped, as they need their coat to protect them against the cold and briars. However, those who grow excessive hair may have one clippers' width of hair removed from the fetlock to the elbows and hocks. Some Thoroughbred horses grow so little coat that they never need to be clipped. Others grow so much coat by the first of October that they need to be clipped in order to remain comfortable even during an ordinary hack. A horse or pony with a heavy coat that is clipped early in the season will grow enough hair by the cold weather to protect him even outdoors without a blanket. A compromise to a full clip is some type of a "hunting" or trace clip (the top line is left unclipped), which is very useful on horses that are not worked hard or are not going to be used throughout the winter.

Blankets and Sheets

Remember, if you remove the horse's natural protection against the elements, you must replace it in some manner. A great variety of blankets and sheets is available. Buy the best quality you can afford, as they will last the longest. In normal winter weather and in a well-insulated stable, a sheet and heavy blanket should be sufficient for the clipped horse. In extreme cold, a blanket liner of some type should be added. If the horse is to be turned out, a coverall made of such durable material as canvas or specially treated duck will add an extra layer of warmth while protecting the good blankets from mud and other horses' teeth. A turn-out blanket should have leg straps and these should be adjusted tight enough so that a hoof cannot become entangled while the horse is rolling.

A great deal of attention should be paid to the fit of the blanket. One that is too large will not stay in place and one that is too small will rub and not provide proper warmth. Some horses have a genius for twisting blankets, and the addition of a roller (padded surcingle) or leg or tail straps will help. Others, especially those turned out in blankets, develop rub marks, usually at the point of the shoulder. This can be prevented by sewing pieces of synthetic sheepskin, available at your saddlery store in sheets, at the appropriate places. Another solution to the problem is foam rubber held in place with a patch.

Horses that are not clipped should not need blankets unless they have an unusually fine coat or are being cleaned regularly. Thorough brushing and vacuuming removes not only the surface dirt but the deep dandruff and sebaceous material that help keep a horse warm. If you don't wish to clip or blanket your horse, do not clean him down to the skin. By all means knock off (clean the surface of) any mud, and wash the mane and tail occasionally. However, before and after you ride you must still always clean the back, girth and bridle areas thoroughly.

The domesticated horse is more or less dependent on human beings for his well-being. The more sensible attention you give your horse, the friendlier, happier, healthier and handsomer he will be.

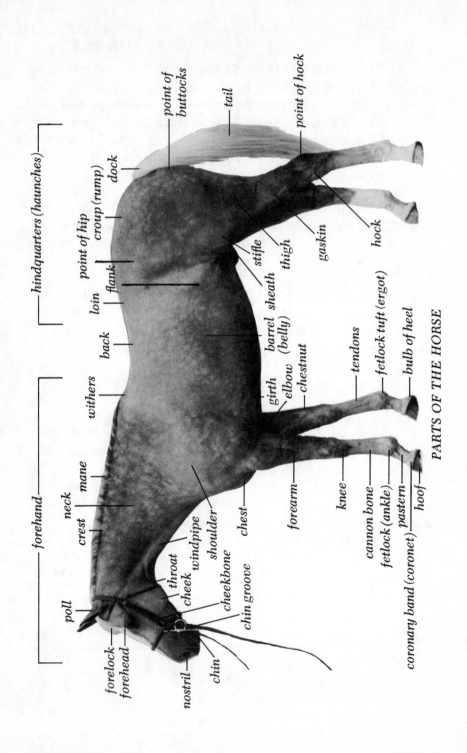

PARTS OF THE HORSE

hindquarters (haunches)

point of buttocks
tail
point of hock

dock
point of hip
croup (rump)

hock
gaskin
thigh
stifle
sheath
barrel
flank
loin
back
withers

forehand
crest
mane
neck

poll

forelock
forehead

nostril
chin
throat
cheek
windpipe
cheekbone
shoulder
chin groove
chest

girth
elbow
(belly)
chestnut

forearm

knee

cannon bone
fetlock (ankle)
pastern
coronary band (coronet)
hoof

tendons
fetlock tuft (ergot)
bulb of heel

17

Routine Health Care

The purpose of this chapter and the next is not to make you your own veterinarian, but rather to help you to avoid certain problems and recognize others whenever possible. These notes should help you to realize when professional help is needed and what to do until it arrives.

Know your horse. Be aware of his general appearance and attitude toward life. If he is normally alert and full of life, but one morning is sluggish around the stable or at exercise, look for trouble. Do the same if he is usually very quiet and relaxed, but suddenly appears nervous or irritable. If there is no apparent lameness, check his temperature. In a horse at rest, it should be within one degree more or less of 99° on a regular clinical thermometer. Veterinary thermometers are also available and make the job a little easier. When you use a regular thermometer, tape a piece of string firmly to the end so that it cannot be lost inside the horse and will be easier to find if it is ejected into the bedding.

Be familiar with the appearance and feel of your horse's normal legs and feet as well as his old injuries. If you feel a little heat or swelling (filling) where it should not be, then some sort of trouble is brewing. The same goes for an old injury. Enlargement or heat in an old splint, curb, sidebone, etc., is a warning that a change is taking place although the horse may not yet show any lameness. Many a serious illness or lameness could have been prevented if only the horse had been rested and nursed for a few days when indicated.

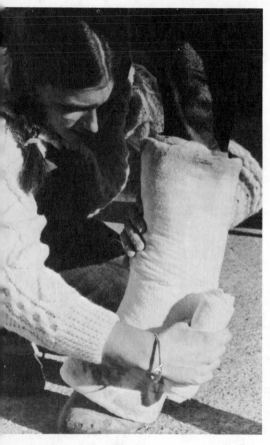

You should learn how to apply a proper standing bandage if you own your own horse. Three sheets of specially prepared cotton, available at your saddlery store, will provide the proper thickness.

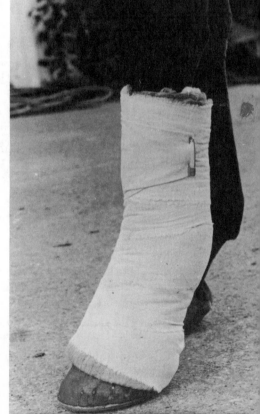

Shipping bandages must come down over the bulbs of the heel to provide the proper protection. The pin may be covered with tape for an added guarantee of safety.

When should you call the veterinarian? Severe accidents or lameness speak for themselves, but it is harder to decide what to do about more minor problems. In the next chapter, the discussion of symptoms and treatment for many common problems also contains advice as to when you are likely to need professional help. Generally, it can be said: if you do not know exactly what you are doing or the problem does not improve in three days with your care, then call the veterinarian. Even a minor cut can be serious, and it gives evidence that it is serious by not healing quickly.

Be ready to state clearly the pertinent facts regarding the horse's condition before you make the phone call. Describe what the horse's problem is, how it occurred, how long it has existed, whether the horse has a fever or not, and how serious you think it is. Ask the veterinarian what, if any, measures you should take until he can come. If you do not understand his instructions or do not have the medicines at hand, say so.

After the veterinarian has taken care of your horse, make sure you understand the nature of the problem and the follow-up instructions. If you do not know how to do something, do not be shy but say so. When you are told to change a horse's routine because of disease or lameness, make sure you know what to feed during the recuperation period and how to start up the old routine. Vets are busy people and often forget to volunteer this information.

The horse owner is ultimately responsible for the kind of veterinary care received. Veterinarians spend many years in study and, particularly those who have a totally equine practice, give up most of their lives to their practices. However, it is impossible for them to remember the extent of each owner's knowledge and the various problems of each individual horse.

The nursing care surrounding the basic sicknesses and lamenesses has become automatic to the veterinarian and he may take for granted that the owner has the same knowledge. For example, your horse has had a gravel and the vet has cut it out, put on a poultice and given an anti-tetanus booster; his only instructions are to replace the poultice in a couple of days. He has taken for granted that you know what kind of poultice to apply and how to do so, how long to keep reapplying it, when to start working the horse and what to feed him in the meantime. If you do not know any or all of these things, then ask.

When your horse has chronic diseases or lamenesses, always remind the veterinarian about them even if they seem unrelated to the problem at hand. They may have some effect that you would not realize and they probably will determine the type of nursing care. To use the horse with a gravel again as an example: if he is subject to tieing up, founder, or lymphangitis, he should not be allowed to stand in the stall for several days; he should be handwalked two or three times a day (the poultice protected by a burlap bag or such), and his feed perhaps drastically restricted.

You are also responsible for the kind of farrier care you receive. You must call the horseshoer as often as your horse needs shoeing, allowing him enough time to fit you into the schedule. Do not wait until the horse's shoes are clanking and expect the blacksmith to come the next day. After he has shod your horse a couple of times, ask him if he thinks your horse should be done more or less often; some horses need attention every three weeks and others go along happily for six weeks.

The farrier should see your horse move before he shoes him for the first time and he should check him periodically for any change in his way of going. He must know if your horse has any problems relating to his feet and way of going and he must know the horse's primary use. A show horse is shod differently from a hunter, who is shod differently from a hack.

ROUTINE HOOF CARE

A routine of daily cleaning and regular shoeing is the only road to sound and healthy hooves, and you should keep a shoeing record for every horse you own. A horse's feet need trimming or shoeing every three to six weeks, depending on his age, the amount and kind of work he is doing, and the weather. For instance, a horse will grow more foot when the going has been consistently soft than when it has been consistently hard. Routine application of good hoof dressing is necessary for most stabled

"No foot, no horse." Learn as much as you can from your blacksmith about the care of your horse's feet.

animals as the bedding draws a lot of the natural oils from the foot. The same goes for a pastured animal in dry weather. Hoof dressing applied to the coronary band (coronet), walls and the soles of the foot twice a week should be sufficient for the normal horse. If the hoof has a dry, brittle appearance, sometimes accompanied by fine cracks, then the dressing should be applied more often. However, under normal circumstances, do not apply hoof dressing on a daily basis just because it looks nice. The hoof needs to breathe and constant application of hoof dressing will clog the pores.

IMMUNIZATIONS

All horses should receive a permanent tetanus vaccination and booster shot and a booster once a year thereafter. They also may need a booster shot if they receive a wound of any depth. Keep a record of when boosters are received so the veterinarian will know whether the horse is protected.

Immunization against influenza, Eastern and Western encephalitis and Venezuelan equine encephalitis should be carried out on a regular basis. (Consult the chart on pages 290–91 for more information.) Broodmares and foals must be immunized against certain other diseases as well as the above. Discuss an appropriate immunization program for your horse with your veterinarian, and keep a record of all shots and vaccinations administered.

DENTAL CARE

A horse's teeth should be checked and generally floated (the sharp points filed off) once a year. This is particularly important in the five-year-old and under and the twelve-year-old and over groups. Young horses' teeth are constantly changing. Sometimes they do not shed a milk or wolf tooth and it becomes infected. The teeth of older horses soften and therefore have more tendency to develop sharp points due to wear. A horse with sharp teeth will not chew his food properly and therefore will not receive full benefit from it. He will also show resistance to the bit as it will hurt various parts of the mouth as they are pushed against the sharp edges of the teeth.

PARASITE CONTROL

Another essential part of routine horse care is a semiannual (at least) worming. All horses are infected with worms. It is up to the horse owner to keep the number of worms infecting the horse below the level where they affect his condition. To achieve this, it must be first determined what sort of worms are infecting the horse.

The life a horse leads determines what kinds of worms he has. For example, if a horse is not turned out to pasture in the summer he will not be susceptible to bots. The botfly lays its yellow eggs on the coat of the horse, mostly on his forelegs, from July until a killing frost. These eggs are then carried into the horse's system through his mouth when he rubs against them, where they later hatch as larvae. Regular removal of the eggs by clipping or scraping with a dull razor, bot egg knife, or trimming comb keeps down infestation.

The first step then in worm prevention is to take a fecal sample to the veterinarian, who will run tests to determine the kinds and quantities of worms your horse has. He will then recommend either of two methods for killing the worms. The usual method used when a variety of worms are present is tubing, in which the vet passes a pliable tube through the horse's nostril down the esophagus directly into the stomach. The various worm medicines are mixed with water and pumped directly into the horse's stomach.

The advantages of tubing over simply feeding worm powders are twofold. First, effective worm killers that are unsafe to be eaten can be used. Secondly, the exact quantity of worm medicine given is received while medicines applied to feed can be tossed and blown out of the manger. Often a worm powder will be prescribed for feeding seven to ten days after tubing to catch maturing eggs that were not touched by the earlier medicine.

The other method of worming is to simply feed worm medicines appropriate to the types of worms the horse has. This is particularly suitable for foals and young horses that are constantly turned out to pasture. They must be wormed regularly, as often as every two months, because their systems are more susceptible to certain worm damage than those of older, healthier horses. One way to make sure your horse eats a worm powder is to mix it with syrup and put it in a small amount of grain. Remove all other feed until it is consumed.

A combination of the two methods is usually satisfactory for most horses. Have a fecal count made twice a year, in late fall and late spring, tell your vet your horse's daily and seasonal routine, and have him suggest a regular program for your horse. The importance of regular worming is often underrated because many horses do not show any external signs until a heavy infestation makes them actually sick. But worms are parasites which, by definition, means that they nourish themselves at the expense of the host (although not normally destroying it). So whenever worms are present they are causing damage. As their numbers increase, the damage increases. Signs that a horse is suffering from worms are colic, general poor condition, a staring coat, tail rubbing and diarrhea.

Aside from a regular worming routine, hygienic care of the stall and pasture will do much to keep down heavy infestation. Clean the horse's stall daily and pick up droppings as often as possible. Sprinkle lime or a Creolin or Lysol solution on the exposed floor after cleaning. Scrub the water and feed buckets with a Creolin solution (follow directions on bottle) weekly, and floors of stall when possible. Many horsemen prefer to place the hay on the floor instead of in hay racks as this is the natural position from which a horse would feed. If you follow this practice, then put the hay in the corner that the horse uses least to make manure. When you place the hay near the feed box, and always in the same place, you will find he will seldom make manure at that end of the stall.

Ideally, permanent horse pasture should be rotated with cattle as horse worms do not affect them and cattle eat grasses that horses ignore. If this is not possible, leave pasture free of horses for one year. If this practice too is not possible, then keep pastures well mowed and clean by picking up or at least spreading the droppings. Exposure to sunlight kills some types of worm eggs. Small paddocks should be picked up regularly. Every effort should be made to keep pastures from maintaining too many horses. When you bring a new horse in, do not turn him out until he has been wormed as he may introduce a new genus or species of worms to the property. Do not spread horse manure on the property unless it has been stacked for at least three months. Sources of water should be kept fresh.

Flies are another problem common to horses. Cleanliness will help keep down large numbers in the stable. The manure pile should be located as far away as possible and there are several commercial fogs and timed-release sprays available for use in the stable. Repellents which can be applied directly to the animal are also helpful. Whenever possible, stagnant water and marshes should be drained from the pasture.

Ticks will also attack horses, usually in the mane and tail regions. Small ticks can be pulled off gently and dropped into a can of kerosene or burned. When they are larger and gray with blood, it is better to drop a little turpentine (use a medicine dropper) on the head which makes it release its hold and fall off. Horses seem quite susceptible to tick bites and develop nasty sores where large ticks have remained or been pulled off. It is helpful to rub some antiseptic cream into the spot where the tick was.

FIRST-AID LIST

Essential

mild antiseptic wash
antiseptic soap
sterile gauze pads
roll of sterile gauze
roll of sterile cotton
oral dose syringe for liquid
  medicine
balling gun for pills
colic medicine
antibiotic cream

antiseptic powder
roll of sheet cotton for bandages
four-inch-wide, eight-foot-long
  bandages
large safety pins
adhesive tape
thermometer
liniment
rubbing alcohol
cough medicine

FIRST-AID LIST, continued

Non-Essential

Vaseline
hoof dressing
masking tape
saline solution
white lotion tablets

Reducine
thrush medicine
poultice powder
electrolytes

The above list contains only suggestions of what you might need in your medicine cabinet. What is essential to you depends on your horse's particular problems, the area in which you live, how quickly a veterinarian can reach you and how close you are to a pharmacy.

HEALTH RECORD

Name of horse .... Height .... Sex .... Year foaled ....
Normal temperature .... Special Problems ....
Vitamins and/or other supplements—Type .... Dates ....
Coggins test run—Date .... (attach copy)

Immunizations
Tetanus Toxoid

First Permanent	Second Permanent (in one month)	Yearly Boosters	Other Boosters

Influenza Vaccine (just prior to cold weather)

First Permanent	Second Permanent (in one to three months)	Yearly Boosters

HEALTH RECORD (continued)

Eastern and Western Encephalitis (just prior to insect season)

First Annual	Second Annual (in one week to ten days)	First Annual	Second Annual (in one week to ten days)

Venezuelan Equine Encephalitis (one vaccination is sufficient, as of current information)

Others

Parasite Control—Fecal Report

Type of Worms	Dates	Type of Worms	Dates	Type of Worms	Dates

Worming Medicine Administered

Type	Follow-up	Dates	Type	Follow-up	Dates	Type	Follow-up	Dates

Dental Record

Examined	Procedure	Dates	Examined	Procedure	Dates

Ailments

Dates	Nature	Treatment	Comments

18

Veterinary Notes

As we have already mentioned, this book is not a veterinary text but as even a novice horse owner you need a basic familiarity with the more common problems you may encounter, their typical symptoms and usual treatment. This chapter will provide at least the bare essentials. It is organized in five sections: first, problems involving feet or legs, starting from the ground and moving up; second, internal diseases; third, respiratory problems and chronic conditions; fourth, skin conditions; and finally, wounds and bruises.

DISEASES AND LAMENESSES OF THE FEET AND LEGS

THRUSH: an inflammation of the sensitive frog caused usually by the constant presence of moist, decomposing organic matter (manure) and sometimes by the lack of frog pressure. The frog receives insufficient pressure or action when it is prevented from coming in contact with the ground by improper shoeing, or over-trimming or contracted heels. Thrush is recognized by a characteristic foul odor and the rotting away of the frog starting in the clefts. As the disease progresses, the cleft(s) deepen, the whole frog becomes ragged and spongy, and eventually the horse will go lame.

Prevention: pick the hoof out daily of any stabled horse. This should be done thoroughly but without undue digging at the clefts, which would leave them open to bacteria. In a horse known to be prone to thrush, the feet should be picked out every day even if he is turned out at pasture, as wet ground can set off an attack of the disease.

Treatment: clean and scrub the hoof with hot water and soap. Trim away any flaps and ragged pieces of frog. In mild cases, apply six percent tincture of iodine or a commercial thrush medicine to the affected parts for a few days. If clefts are deep enough to hold packing, insert a piece of oakum or cotton soaked in the medicine. Remove after forty-eight hours and replace with dry packing or more medicine if necessary. If the deterioration is extensive or the horse is lame, call the vet. Thrush medicines can blister heels, so grease heels first with Vaseline and apply carefully.

CORN: a severe bruise under the heel of the shoe. It is usually caused by the shifting or the improper placement of the shoe slightly to the inside of the wall. When a corn becomes deep-seated, it is usually chronic; therefore, when lameness indicates a possible corn, immediately stop work and have the shoe removed.

Prevention: proper shoeing and daily inspection of shoes to see if the heels have shifted in toward the sole.

Treatment: remove the shoe, pare out the corn, poultice until sound. If the corn is minor and the shoe can be placed without touching it, the horse is reshod normally. If the corn is severe, the horse must be shod with a suitable corrective shoe.

NAIL PRICK: damage to the sensitive laminae of the hoof caused by a misplaced nail. If the nail penetrates the sensitive tissue, the horse shows pain and goes lame immediately. If the nail has been merely placed too close to the sensitive tissue and the friction over a period of days causes lameness, it is harder to diagnose. Horses with shelly feet are prone to nail prick as the blacksmith often has difficulty placing the nails exactly where he wishes.

Prevention: keep the horse quiet during shoeing and maintain a healthy hoof.

Treatment: in a nail prick which causes immediate lameness, the nail will be removed, as well as the shoe, iodine poured into the hole and the foot poulticed until sound. Do not try to reshoe the horse as he probably will not go sound. If a nail prick is suspected because the horse goes lame two to five days after shoeing, the same procedure should be followed.

CONTRACTED HEELS: the walls of the hoof are contracted in one or more places, on one or both sides of the foot in the region of the quarters and heels. It is usually caused by bad conformation of the hoof, aggravated by improper shoeing.

Prevention: proper shoeing with attention to frog pressure and as widely spread heels as possible.

Treatment: mild cases that do not cause lameness can be worked on by the blacksmith. Various types of shoes will help, such as a bar shoe or a beveled shoe. If lameness occurs or the contraction increases, the vet may have to groove the walls to encourage growth to the outside.

BRITTLE FEET: feet with dry walls that chip or crack easily. They are caused by constant wetting by nature and/or man and drying by the sun and straw, etc. Also may be caused by an inherited tendency to the condition or by poor diet.

Prevention: keep hooves as dry as possible during baths, etc. Apply a good hoof dressing more often than to a normal horse.

Treatment: apply Reducine blister around the coronet for ten days, stop for ten days, then apply again for ten days, to encourage healthy growth. Dress horn with castor or mineral oil twice a day for a couple of weeks, gradually reducing applications thereafter.

SAND CRACK: a crack in the wall of the hoof running downward from the coronet to the ground. It is often not visible near the coronet, but rather from the ground up. The vast majority are minor and surface if corrected in the early stages.

Prevention and Treatment: groove the hoof just above the crack with a rasp, then treat the same as for brittle feet. However, if there is any sign of lameness, call the vet.

QUITTOR: a fistulous sore on the coronet. It is usually caused by the horse stepping on himself.

Prevention: never ignore even minor sores on blows to the coronet.

Treatment: apply Furacin or a similar type healing ointment and bandage. Reapply and keep bandage until healed. If lameness does not disappear in a few days, call in professional help as this soreness can be caused by a variety of things, i.e., gravel, infected sand crack, etc.

LAMINITIS (founder): is a disease of the sensitive laminae under the horn (wall) of the hoof. The disease is always painful and serious. The definitive causes of this disease are not yet known, but it is often associated with any of the following: overweight, a bad attack of colic, foaling, undue weight placed on one leg because of an injury to another, the horse not put on a laxative diet when kept confined in the stall. Other common causes are extreme exertion in relation to the fitness of the horse; too much high-protein, carbohydrate containing foods, i.e., oats, corn, and not enough exercise; too much rich grass when the horse has not become accustomed to it; and eating large quantities of oats, apples, etc. Ponies are particularly prone for the latter two reasons. The results of founder will be seen in a dropped sole varying from flat to convex, horizontal ridges in the wall caused by uneven horn growth, and a dished shape to the toe.

Prevention: see *causes* and do not allow them to occur.

Symptoms: leg or legs (usually the front) will swell and contain considerable heat. The horse will exhibit great pain and will not wish to move at all. When it is forced to move, it will put the weight on the heel of the hoof. As the disease progresses the horse will sweat profusely and run a high temperature.

Treatment: call the veterinarian. Stand the horse in cold running water or ice water. Follow-up treatment will involve corrective shoeing and particular care in prevention as the disease tends to become chronic, especially in ponies.

NAVICULAR DISEASE: a corrosive ulceration of the navicular bone caused by inflammation, possibly with a congenital predisposition. It is found usually in the forefeet. Sometimes the bone is so weakened by the ulcer that a fracture occurs. The original cause is some sort of trauma or concussion, either a severe blow or hard or fast work over a long period of time, especially too soon after rest. Lameness occurs and it may be intermittent at the onset of the disease.

Prevention: correct contracted heels and maintain frog pressure at all times. Avoid high heels in the horse and on the horse's shoes and fast work on hard surfaces.

Treatment: consult the veterinarian. There is no cure, but corrective shoes may be helpful. In advanced cases, blocking the heel nerves (digital neurectomy) may prolong the horse's useful life.

RINGBONE: a bony enlargement in the pastern area. It is called high ringbone when it occurs just around the pastern bones and low ringbone when it occurs just above the coronary band. The causes are many. Among them are: (1) heredity, (2) straight pasterns; (3) a blow in the area; (4) heels too long on the horse or on the shoe; (5) a sprain.

Symptoms: in the early stages the lameness will come and go and the source will be hard to pinpoint. As the disease progresses, the bony enlargements will be felt around the pastern or the top of the coronary. Lameness will be constant.

Treatment: call the veterinarian. The placement and size of the ringbone regulate the chances of getting the horse sound. If there is high ringbone, the chances are better and firing or blistering of the area may be suggested.

SIDEBONE: a hardening (ossification) and enlargement of one or both of the lateral cartilages of the foot. The causes are approximately the same as ringbone. However, permanent lameness is seldom caused by sidebone alone.

Symptoms: at the onset, heat and possibly a hard lump(s) which can be felt on either side of the heel.

Treatment: if not lame, stop work and turn out or handwalk. Hosing, icing, or standing a horse in a stream three or four times a day will help cool out the heat if it is present. Resume exercise when horse is sound. If lameness appears, call the veterinarian.

WINDPUFF (wind gall): semisoft enlargements slightly above the ankles on the inside or the outside, in front or behind. These "puffs" are caused by wear and hard work and are found in many older horses. In their normal size, they seldom cause lameness. However, if they become large or hard as the result of a strain or a blow, lameness may occur.

Treatment: if of moderate size, they are best left alone. However, if they are noticed in their early stages or they have a tendency to enlarge, their size can be kept down by rubbing with liniment after work and applying bandages. If lameness occurs, call the vet, who will possibly blister or fire them.

FILLED TENDONS (stocking up): occurs more often in the hind legs than in the front. The condition is caused by poor elimination, strain, or concussion. It often becomes chronic with a particular horse. The filling is more pronounced if the horse is kept inactive.

Symptoms: The leg or legs swell from the ankle up and occasionally the fetlock up but do not contain heat.

Treatment: if slight filling exists, treat the same as for windpuffs and keep the horse exercised or turned out daily. If poor elimination is suspected, regulate the horse's feed accordingly. If the filling appears suddenly or contains heat, call the vet as this is not ordinary stocking up but could be one of many things, such as lymphangitis.

BOWED TENDON: a sprain of the tendon(s) that run down the cannon bone, or the sheath that covers them; often connected with suspensory ligament problems. Note: Often gives advance warning in the form of heat and filling along the tendons. If the horse is worked in this condition, the tendon or tendon sheath lets go under the strain. Therefore, stop work and call the vet if you see an unexplained change in the condition of your horse's front legs. There are many causes for bowed tendons, such as:

(1) Sudden stops on hard going.
(2) A blow, such as an overreach, or being hit by a loose rail in jumping.
(3) Too much work on hard going, or too soft or uneven going.
(4) Galloping and jumping out of very heavy going, especially if the horse is not fit or overtired. (Fox hunters, beware! If a horse seems unwilling at the end of a long day, consider this possibility.)
(5) Long toes and low heels; long sloping pasterns; legs that are tied in below the knee also make the horse more subject to this condition.

Symptoms: lameness, pain, swelling and heat varying from mild to extreme depending on the amount of damage.

Treatment: hose leg and apply cold-water bandages. If severe, stand in ice if possible. Call the veterinarian immediately.

SPLINT: a bony enlargement on the cannon or splint bone, usually on the front legs. Splints are caused by too much work on hard ground, especially in young horses, sharp turns on the forehand, or a blow.

Symptoms: a hard enlargement can be felt or seen. Heat may or may not be present, the horse may be lame.

Treatment: if the horse is sound and the splint does not appear to interfere with tendons or ligaments and is not too close to the knee, continue with very light work and apply cooling lotion or hose fre-

A pair of bowed tendons, the right more pronounced and lower than the left. The right foot has been allowed to grow a longer heel to relieve some of the pressure on the tendon; the left should have been allowed to do the same so that the feet match.

quently. Slowly resume normal work. If the horse is lame and/or heat is present or the splint is badly placed, apply cooling lotion or hose and rest. If the horse does not regain complete soundness after the heat has left and the splint "sets," call the vet, as it may have to be blistered or fired. (In these treatments a severe counter-irritant action is created through the use of a strong caustic ointment or a heated firing iron. They act through the increased blood supply to the affected area as well as the enforced idleness of the patient.) When an old splint acts up, call the vet as there may be a fracture which should be cared for by an expert.

GRAVEL: a small object that works its way into the sole or the wall of the hoof from the ground up. The surrounding tissue then festers and the horse becomes quite lame. It is found most often in barefoot horses whose feet are not picked out daily.

Treatment: if suspected, call the blacksmith or vet immediately, as the gravel will work its way toward the coronet. In a matter of a few days it will be lodged so deeply that it cannot be cut out and then you must let nature take its course. It could be a matter of months before the gravel works its way out at the coronary band. Cut out the object, flush the area with strong iodine, then poultice until the horse is sound.

THOROUGHPIN: distension of the tendon sheath above and on either side of the point of the hock; usually more prominent on the outside. It is caused by strain, or by faulty conformation.

SYMPTOMS: enlargement comparable to windpuff on ankles. In usual cases horses do not go lame.

Treatment: none if horse is sound and thoroughpin is small. If signs of enlargement occur or if thoroughpin appears as the result of a sprain and the horse is lame, call the vet.

CURB: thickening of the tendon or ligament about three-fourths of an inch below the point of the hock. Usually it is caused by a sudden strain on the hocks, especially when the horse is tired. A horse with weak hind legs is susceptible to this ailment.

Symptoms: a bowed type of swelling will appear and the horse will usually go lame temporarily.

Treatment: if the horse remains sound, treat as you would a splint. If he becomes lame, call the veterinarian. Proper treatment can keep down the size of a curb. In some cases it will actually disappear over a long period of time. A curb that is set will seldom bother a horse.

Not the best hind legs: there is a thoroughpin just in front of the point of the hock, and a pair of curbs below the point of the hock. Also note the windpuffs just above the ankle.

Bog Spavin: a puffy swelling on the inside and to the front of the hock.

Symptoms: a small, soft bulge appears on the front of the hock. The horse is seldom lame. It is caused by strain or faulty conformation. Occasionally a horse is born with a bog.

Treatment: treat as for thoroughpin.

Bone Spavin: a bony growth inside and just below the hock joint. It is sometimes inherited but is usually caused by strain and faulty conformation.

Symptoms: a hard projection appears in the area inside the hock joint. The horse may go lame. A bone spavin between the two bones of the hock is not visible, but the horse will go lame when it is large enough to interfere with the normal actions of the joint.

Treatment: Call the veterinarian as soon as a change in the appearance of the hock is noticed, whether the horse is lame or not.

Stringhalt: a nervous disease of one or usually both hind legs. Its causes are unknown.

Symptoms: the hind leg(s) will move in a jerky, high-stepping movement which is particularly noticeable after the horse has been at rest. It is most noticeable at a walk, less at a trot, and not at all except in extreme cases at a canter. The condition tends to improve as the horse is worked. A mild case in a horse that is just used to hack would not interfere with his usefulness. However, a rather severe case should be discussed with the veterinarian as to whether it is rendering the horse unsafe to jump, gallop over rough terrain, etc. There is no treatment at the moment for this except an operation which is not always satisfactory.

Capped Elbows: the point of the elbow becomes swollen. It is caused by bruising of the elbow by the heel of the shoe when the horse is lying down, or by lack of sufficient bedding or rough, uneven flooring to the stall.

Treatment: massage with iodine ointment or bathe constantly with lead lotion. If an abscess forms, call the vet, as it must be lanced. A thick leather ring strapped around the pastern can prevent recurrence if the capped elbow is caused by the way the horse lies down. Another solution, if suitable, is a three-quarter shoe.

CAPPED HOCK: swelling over the point of the hock. It is caused by shortage of bedding in the stall and by the horse leaning on his hocks or kicking when in the stall or while being shipped.

Treatment: if recent, the area should be poulticed. If the injury is old, ask the advice of the vet as it is usually better to leave the situation alone. Protect the hock or hocks with a hock boot at appropriate times to prevent re-injury unless their presence makes the horse kick more; in such cases, pad the van or stall instead.

STIFLE LAMENESS: strain or dislocation of the stifle. This will occur especially when the horse is overtired or perhaps saving a sore leg by throwing his weight on the other.

Symptoms: mild to severe lameness.

Treatment: call the veterinarian and move the horse as little as possible. The veterinarian may apply an internal blister.

LYMPHANGITIS: an inflammation of the lymphatic vessels, usually occurring in the hind legs. The leg or legs may sometimes swell considerably, and feel hot to the hand. The temperature may rise as high as 105°. Lameness eventually becomes acute and is shown by a jerky movement of the hind legs. Its causes are similar to those of azoturia (see below), such as too much grain coupled with lack of or irregularity of exercise, but it also can be caused by the introduction of infection after a break in the skin.

Treatment: stop all grain and give wet bran mashes. Bandage the legs with cotton, and call the veterinarian as a series of antibiotics will be part of the cure. Prompt treatment and analysis of the cause is important as this disease tends to be recurring.

INTERNAL DISEASES

AZOTURIA: also known as "tieing-up," usually occurs when a fit animal is kept on his full grain ration but is not exercised for twenty-four hours or more. There is some argument that these are two separate diseases, but for practical purposes the symptoms and treatment are almost the same; the term "tieing-up" is applied to the milder symptoms, while that of "azoturia" is applied to the more severe. The first sign of this disease usually occurs within ten to fifteen minutes after leaving the stable or when the horse is being cooled out. The horse takes smaller and smaller steps with his hind legs and does not seem to want to increase his pace. An aware rider will realize he is shortening his stride. If riding continues, the horse will break out into a profuse sweat and possibly start blowing out of proportion to the amount of work he is getting. If allowed to stop, he will be unwilling to move forward again. The muscles over the loins and quarters become hard and very sensitive. In a full-blown case of azoturia the urine is coffee-colored, the horse will be unable to move, will try to lie down, and will show severe signs of stress.

Prevention: if a horse must remain in the stall for twenty-four hours or more, thus missing his daily exercise or turn-out time, stop all grain. A wet bran mash is acceptable to feed. If the horse's regular exercise has been interrupted in this way, turn him out in the paddock or longe lightly before resuming full exercise. Once your horse has tied-up or had azoturia he probably will be prone to another attack at least for some time. Be particularly careful about thorough cooling out periods, regular feed and consistent amounts of grain. Cut down on his grain ration for a time, if possible. Out hunting, keep the horse moving at checks. When the weather is wet and/or cold and windy, exercise the horse with a suitable blanket covering his loins and quarters.

Treatment: immediately return the horse to the stall and cover him with warm blankets, paying particular attention to the loins. When the case appears to be mild, the horse may be led back to the stable as long as the symptoms do not increase and the horse is not distressed. When possible, some sort of transport should be arranged and the horse not asked to move at all. Call your vet immediately, as prompt treatment will effect a prompt cure and prevent possible damage to the horse's kidneys. The more severe the case, the more likely the horse will be susceptible to the disease in the future. If you have a tranquilizer or antihistamine, ask the vet about administering it.

TETANUS: is caused by an organism found in many soils around horses. It enters the horse's body by means of an open wound and the symptoms will be evident anytime between five and twenty days from the time of contact. The first symptom will be some sort of stiffness, slow feeding and quick breathing. The earliest reliable clue will be in the eye. If the horse's head is raised, the small membrane in the corner of the eye, commonly called the haw, will cover up to three-fourths of the eyeball. To obtain a cure for this dread disease, it is essential that it be detected in the early stages. More advanced symptoms are sweating, difficulty in swallowing, the tail held high, dilated nostrils, the lips drawn back and the teeth exposed

Prevention: this disease can be prevented. All horses should be given a shot of tetanus toxoid followed by a booster shot one month later. Yearly shots of serum will keep the anti-tetanus toxin level high and protect the horse under circumstances where a cut may not be noticed. If a deep cut occurs, the veterinarian will usually give a booster shot if it has been more than three months since the last booster shot.

Treatment: call the vet immediately.

COLIC: the term applied to severe or violent abdominal pain resulting from digestive disturbances or obstructions which irritate or block the stomach and/or intestine. The horse owner can manage mild cases of certain kinds of colic by himself. However, all cases of colic must be watched closely as at any point complications such as a twisted or ruptured intestine can occur. Every horse owner should own a syringe and a bottle of colic medicine. No matter what kind of colic is developing, a dose of colic medicine will not hurt. If caught in time, the colic medicine and walking may relieve enough of the causes of the horse's pain to eventually relieve the problem.

The causes of colic are many and certainly some of them are not always known. However, thought should be given to those causes known so that colic can be prevented. It is very common in horses, more so than in any other animal, mostly because of the following: (a) the horse has a small stomach in relation to his size: (b) the puckering nature of the large intestine which allows food to lodge there; (c) the amount of room allowed to the intestines within the abdomen; (d) the frequency with which horses are infected with intestinal worms.

Some other causes of colic are:
(1) Insufficient supply of water.
(2) Irregular feeding.
(3) Long spells where the stomach goes without food and then is allowed extra large amounts, especially of hard feed.
(4) Sharp teeth which do not grind the food properly.
(5) Sudden changes in diet.
(6) Unhealthy foods such as "green" oats, moldy or improperly cured hay, etc.
(7) Cribbing and wind-sucking.
(8) Strangulated hernia.
(9) Defective secretion of digestive juices.

Symptoms: colic is commonly divided into three types: spastic, flatulent and impaction (constipation). The symptoms of all colics can be somewhat interchangeable, although each type has some specific peculiarities. However, the exact cause of the colic is not always so important. The important thing is to remove the cause of the pain. Some of the following symptoms will be found in every attack of colic: (a) the horse shows that he is becoming uncomfortable by stall walking, lying down and getting up, stamping his feet, nipping, nuzzling or looking at his belly, breaking out in a patchy or full sweat, rolling; (b) a mild to serious fever; (c) signs of violent pain, such as attempting to lie down even while being handwalked; (d) the horse is unusually quiet, dull, lying down but not staying down very long, glancing at his sides.

Treatment: administer colic medicines in all cases. Follow directions for the amount and times to repeat. Bed the stall down thoroughly and bank the walls to prevent the horse from being cast and bruised. Handwalk the horse until he appears to be comfortable, then return him to the stall. If he remains quiet and is able to urinate or pass feces, then he may be left alone for a while. Check constantly for several hours as some colics come and go. If the horse is still in pain, he must be kept walking. A horse lying down, rolling and thrashing around, not only endangers himself externally, but is possibly encouraging the twisting of an intestine. If it is recommended and available, a wet bran mash or one to two quarts of mineral oil in sweet feed, possibly in conjunction with the proper dose of a tranquilizer, may be sufficient in the milder cases to take care of it. If signs of colic do not improve and/or disappear in a couple of hours, every effort must be made to get professional help.

Coughs, Colds, Influenza, Pneumonia, Bronchitis, Pleurisy: often afflict horses and are similar to the same human diseases. The horse owner will not go far wrong if he treats them in the same manner.

Prevention: keep the horse on high quality feeds and in a well-ventilated stable. Allow him as much fresh air as possible all year around, but avoid drafts. Cool out properly after exercise. Administer yearly flu shots. Although these vaccines are not effective against all types of viruses, they do help immunize the horse against the common flus carried around horse shows, etc.

Symptoms: any one or a combination of the following: coughing, thin to dense discharge from the nostrils, rise in temperature, lack of appetite. If more serious symptoms, such as trouble breathing, staggering, temperature above 104°, head held extended, difficulty swallowing, swelling in the jaw area appear, call the vet immediately as one of the more serious diseases such as pneumonia, bronchitis, pleurisy or strangles is present.

Treatment: isolate the animal, keep him warm, give him laxative feeds, and stop any strenuous exercise. If there is a rise in temperature, stop all exercise except walking. Administer cough medicine if called for. Check temperature for four to five days as it can fluctuate greatly. If after this period the temperature is still above normal and/or the symptoms are not greatly improved, call the vet because a secondary infection is probably present and antibiotics would be recommended. Never ignore "cough" symptoms as permanent damage to the horse's respiratory system can occur. Many a case of "heaves" and chronic cough could have been prevented by a few days of rest.

ROARING AND WHISTLING ("Windy"): abnormal sounds ranging from low (roaring) to high (whistling) produced only during the inspiration of air and due to some paralysis of the larynx. These conditions can be inherited, but more often follow an attack of the more serious respiratory diseases, especially in large horses. They are usually found in horses with long necks and narrow throats and often do not appear until the age of four or five.

Symptoms: an unusual sound is made by the horse, most often at the trot or canter. As early cases can be difficult to detect, the horse should always be checked by an experienced person. Roaring and whistling are chronic and the importance of their effects on the general constitution of the horse range from minor to serious. Some cases remain the same for the life of the horse and others become progressively worse.

Treatment: in mild cases, general fitness and lack of excess weight will keep the noise under control. In more serious cases, the only treatment is surgery.

BROKEN WIND (Heaves): emphysema of the lungs due to chronic coughing, eating dusty and/or moldy food or consistently exercising soon after feeding.

Symptoms: (1) a deep, long cough sometimes in spasms; (2) double expiration, i.e., the normal contraction of the abdominal muscles during expiration is quickly followed by a longer contraction. In advanced cases, the symptoms can be seen while the horse is at rest; otherwise they are brought on by exercise.

Treatment: although there is no cure, mild cases can often be kept under control by exposing the horse to as little dust as possible; dampen all feed and replace hay with pellets, replace straw with a dust-free bedding such as wood shavings. Keep the horse fit and free of excess weight; turn out at pasture as much as possible. A suitable cough medicine should be used as necessary.

SKIN DISEASES

GALLS: tender or raw spots on the skin caused by friction or pressure from the saddlery. They appear either in the form of small lumps under the skin or in the form of raw skin. The lumpy type gall behind the elbow is usually caused by failure to pull the skin out from under the girth by pulling the front legs forward after tacking up. Other causes of both types of galls are: unnaturally sensitive skin or tender, loose skin found in an unfit horse; improper cleansing or cooling of the skin after riding; dirty or badly fitted girths and saddles.

Prevention: loosen the girth for the last ten minutes of a ride, leave the saddlery on the horse until ready to wash, scrub the back and girth areas with warm water to which some antiseptic has been added, then bathe the areas in cold water or lead lotion. Do not splash the cold water over the horse's kidneys. Another method for toughening the horse's skin is the use of salt water or alcohol, although constant use of alcohol is drying. Have your saddle checked once a year by your saddler and keep your leather clean and soft. Make sure all your tack fits your horse comfortably.

Treatment: if the area is raw, wash thoroughly with soap and water and dry and treat with a healing agent. If the area is swollen, bathe often with white lotion and massage gently. If it does not improve rapidly or becomes hard and hot, call the veterinarian. If the area is behind the elbow, the horse can still be ridden by attaching the girth to the back two billet straps and using a shaped girth or a string girth. Ride the horse for a few minutes and if the area is not being rubbed you can proceed. If the area is rubbed, riding must be stopped until it is completely healed and the hair is growing in. If the gall is on the back, the horse can sometimes be maintained in work by using a rubber pad with a hole cut out over the sore place or using a doubly thick pad which will distribute the pressure more evenly over the horse's back.

MUD FEVER (sometimes known as weed poisoning): a condition found on the lower legs caused by irritation from mud or possibly certain weeds. The legs, particularly the front of the cannon bones, are swollen and hot. If allowed to go untreated, swelling increases, circulation is hindered, serum oozes out of the skin and collects on it. Eventually cracks form in the skin and infection gains access. Lymphangitis may occur as a secondary effect of the disease.

Prevention: keep the horse's legs clean of mud. However, when the horse has had a "hard day," do not clean immediately. If you do so, you may rub irritants and bacteria into the open pores of the skin. Rather let him rest in comfortable warmth. If the day is cold, then bandage the legs with cotton until dry. Proceed to clean as usual.

Treatment: if the disease is noticed in its early stage as shown by a scabby thickening of the skin, then scrub thoroughly with an antiseptic soap. Clip the hair if it is thick and dress the area with Vaseline. If this treatment does not effect a cure in a few days, then further steps are necessary. Dress the legs with an ointment containing Ichthyol, cover with cotton and bandage, leaving on for two or three days depending on how seriously the leg is swollen. Stop all grain and give small bran mashes. This is important, as grain will slow the healing process. When the legs are clean of scabs and serum, dress with a healing agent. Start to work if the horse is sound, but after work dry the legs, keep applying ointment and dress with cotton bandages. When all irritation is gone, continue for at least a couple of weeks with dry cotton bandages as this will help the circulation and prevent a recurrence.

RINGWORM: a skin disease which is highly contagious. Circular areas of hair become raised, eventually leaving a bald spot. If allowed to go untreated, the area which started out the size of a dime extends outward, but always in a circular shape, and other spots appear.

Prevention: there are several kinds of ringworm and there are many sources. The only prevention is utmost cleanliness if the horse is exposed to the disease.

Treatment: scrub the area thoroughly with antiseptic soap, removing any dry scales to get at the fungus. Dry and then apply an iodine ointment or bluing. Isolate the horse and anything that touches him. Disinfect his sheets, etc., frequently. Continue these procedures until all areas show new hair growing. If the horse appears to have contracted a bad case of ringworm, call the vet, as a new internal medicine is having some good effects.

CRACKED HEEL (scratches): horizontal cracks or scratches in the back of the pastern of one or more legs. These occur when the horse is constantly exposed to mud, water or deep sand and white legs are more susceptible. In the early stages the skin is red and small scabs appear. If these symptoms are not treated, the "cracks" deepen and extend, the area swells and the horse becomes lame.

Prevention: horses, and more often ponies, who grow long fetlock hair down to the heel should not have this hair trimmed as it effectively sheds the water and mud. However, horses with light or moderate fetlock hair should have it trimmed as this tuft of hair is just the length to drip accumulated water and trap mud into the hollow formed by the pastern and the heel. Keep the area dry and clean. A piece of burlap bag is excellent for this purpose. Greasing the heels and pasterns with Vaseline, lanolin or kaolin before exposure will protect sensitive horses.

Treatment: cut or clip hair from the area and the ankle above. However, do not use a fine-blade clipper. The purpose is to remove all extra hair that prevents the area from drying while at the same time leaving the horse some natural protection. In the earlier stages, faithful application of zinc ointment or Desenex and use of preventive measures will effect a cure. This disease has a strong tendency to recur, so good hygiene is essential. If the pastern is swollen and sore, apply Furacin or a sulfa ointment and bandage. Keep the horse out of water and mud until he is well on the way to recovery. If the disease has progressed to the point where the horse is lame and the swelling intense, do the above and call the vet as a course of antibiotics will attain the quickest cure.

WARBLE: a nodule under the skin of the back or sides of the horse formed by the larvae of the warble fly. The warble fly lays her eggs on the horse's skin during the summer. When the eggs hatch, sometimes the larvae find their way under the skin where they lie dormant all winter. In early spring a hard nodule appears and swells over a period of a couple of weeks.

Prevention: routine hygienic care, such as weekly scrubbing the back with alcohol.

Treatment: when a small hole is seen at the head of the swelling, the time has come to attempt forcing the larvae out by gently pressing around the swelling. If successful, you need only scrub the area clean and it will heal in a few days. If not successful, repeat on successive days. Application of hot towels will speed the process. Do not squeeze until the hole appears, and always be gentle. If the larvae is killed under the skin, infection and a large swelling will occur. For this reason, if a warble appears under the saddle or girth, riding must stop until it is expelled. Not all lumps on the back or sides are warbles, but if suspected, stop riding until sure.

WOUNDS

Horses acquire wounds in so many and varied ways, of so many and varied kinds, that it is impossible to cover the subject thoroughly short of writing a small book. So here we will only discuss some of the basic types of wounds that horses acquire accidentally during a normal lifetime. Some principles of wound care are:

(1) Apply no medicines to a wound that is serious enough to call the veterinarian. Wash all wounds thoroughly with mild soap, or a mild antiseptic, and water. If the wound is more than superficial, use only antiseptic material to scrub with, i.e., sterile gauze squares.

(2) Do not use strong antiseptics such as alcohol or hydrogen peroxide as the damage they do to tissues is severe in proportion to the amount of bacteria they kill.

(3) Do not use gall medicine (bluing) on any but the most superficial wounds as it encourages a scab to form too quickly, often trapping infection under it.

(4) Do not use medicines with a mineral oil base on areas where excess granulation (proud flesh) may form. Use only those with a vegetable oil base. For our purposes we will divide wounds into four types:

    a. Simple surface wounds.
    b. Deeper wounds through the top layers of the skin.
    c. Puncture wounds.
    d. Contusions (bruises).

SURFACE WOUNDS: the wound is shallow enough that the whole of its area moves when you move the surrounding skin. It can then be considered a surface wound. If it is not gapping, and if there is no reason to suspect that it will leave a scar, then a cure will be affected by plain good nursing. First, thoroughly cleanse the area with a mild soap or antiseptic and water. By thoroughly clean we mean scrub gently but firmly to remove all chances of infection. If it is on a part of the horse's body that is impossible to bandage, apply a wound spray or powder. In other places dress with Furacin, cover with sterile gauze and bandage. Scabs should not be disturbed unless there is suspicion of infection underneath or excessive granulation (proud flesh) developing. If so, scrub with mild soap and water and repeat above procedures.

PENETRATING WOUNDS: wounds that penetrate through more than the top layers of the skin and wounds inflicted with force over a bone should be seen by a veterinarian as they may need suturing (stitches) or may contain foreign particles. A tetanus shot may be in order and antibiotics may be necessary. However, sometimes none of the above procedures are indicated because the wound is not long enough or wide enough to necessitate stitching, the horse has just had a tetanus shot, and the wound is fresh; with proper care it should not need antibiotics to keep out infection. Such wounds are often found in the area of the coronet or the heel caused by a grab or blow from another foot.

Start first with energetic cleansing. Flaps of skin or ragged edges which are obviously going to die back should be trimmed and the hair around the wound clipped. Then an antibiotic type ointment should be generously applied, covered with sterile gauze and bandaged firmly. Whenever bandaging, make sure the pressure is even. If bleeding in this or any other type of wound does not stop in a reasonable amount of time, efforts must be made to stanch it.

There are two kinds of bleeding: arterial and venous. Arterial bleeding will not stop of itself and it is recognized by its spurting appearance. Venous bleeding, if not massive, should stop by itself. To stop bleeding on head wounds, application of ice or ice water is useful. The most effective way to stop arterial bleeding is to apply a tourniquet above the wounded area. However, except in the case where professional help will be a long time in coming, a tourniquet should not be applied except by a knowledgeable person. If the bleeding cannot be stopped by pressure bandages, then apply a tourniquet using a piece of rubber tubing approximately six inches above the wound. Losen every five minutes. Remove as soon as the bleeding has stopped. Bleeding can sometimes be stopped by simply pressing firmly and holding the artery with your thumb for several minutes. A safer method for the inexperienced is to bandage firmly where possible. If possible, cover wounds with sterile gauze, apply a pad of material over that and then bandage all firmly. Add two, three bandages if necessary, each bandage being a little tighter than the last. If the wound is gaping or on an unbandageable part of the body, pack with gauze, sterile towels, etc., and apply pressure. When bleeding stops, the wound should be cleansed and cared for in the usual manner.

PUNCTURE WOUNDS: those caused by an object whose length exceeds its width, such as a stick or nail. Although in most wounds the idea is to stop the bleeding and close the openings as quickly as possible, the opposite is true of a puncture wound. The most important aspect in the cure of a puncture wound is that it drains freely. Unless absolutely sure of the depth of the wound and that all of the foreign body that punctured it has been removed, it is best to call in the veterinarian, because tendons, etc., may have been damaged. If it seems relatively minor, cleanse very thoroughly, flushing with a stream of water such as from a garden hose. Care for these types of wounds as you would a penetration wound with daily checks to make sure that it is healing from the inside out and infection is not being sealed in by a scab or premature closing.

CONTUSION (bruise): that type of wound inflicted by a blunt object so that the skin is not broken. If swelling is noticed within twelve hours, hosing or some sort of constant application of cold water twenty minutes out of every hour will be very beneficial. Overnight, apply a poultice or a wet bandage made with lead lotion. If swelling is under control and the horse is not lame, then it should be gradually absorbed. However, if tendons, ligaments or muscles have been involved and swelling increases, hematoma or abscess forms, or lameness occurs, it is imperative that professional help be called. Agents can be given to keep the swelling down, and, in the case of an abscess, it possibly should be drained. If the swelling is known to be old, i.e., more than twenty-four hours old, then bathing or steaming with hot water to which some liniment has been added for twenty minutes is recommended. Dry the area and then rub with liniment and bandage if possible. Repeat twice daily.

Some signs to watch for if a wound is not healing: the horse is not eating well, increasing lameness or swelling, a rise in temperature. If any or a combination of these symptoms occurs, it would be prudent to call the vet for further examination of the wound and/or administration of an antibiotic.

List of Sources

Major National Horse Organizations

American Horse Shows Assn.
598 Madison Ave.
New York, N.Y. 10022

Masters of Foxhounds Assn. of
   America
112 Water Street
Boston, Mass. 02109

U.S. Combined Training Assn.
292 Bridge Street
South Hamilton, Mass. 01982

U.S. Dressage Foundation
P.O. Box 80668
Lincoln, Neb. 68501

U.S. Equestrian Team, Inc.
292 Bridge Street
South Hamilton, Mass. 01982

U.S. Pony Club, Inc.
303 South High Street
West Chester, Pa. 19380

NOTE: In addition to the above, there are of course many regional and breed organizations. Almost all have official newsletters or magazines which are sent to members; of special importance on the above list are the AHSA's *Horse Show*, which is essential for keeping up to date on rule changes; the *U.S.C.T.A. News*, a very readable magazine about eventing; and the *U.S.E.T. News*, which covers the activities of our international riding teams.

Horse Magazines

The Chronicle of the Horse. Middleburg, Va., 22117
A weekly, covering horse shows, combined training, foxhunting, Pony

Club activities, racing and hunt racing as well as presenting articles of general interest. An important classified advertising medium; also publishes annually the official U.S. roster of organized hunts.

Dressage and Combined Training. P.O. Box 2460, Cleveland, Ohio 44112
A monthly magazine dealing exclusively with dressage, including both excellent instructional articles and detailed coverage of major national and international competitions.

The Field. 8 Stratton Street, London, W.1, England
A fine English weekly covering all field sports as well as horticulture. Frequent articles on racing, showing and foxhunting. (Inquire about their air-freight service if you care about getting the news while it's current.)

Horse and Hound. 189 High Holborn, London, WC1V 7BA, England
Another English weekly, this one the basic news medium for English foxhunters, show jumpers, eventers and point-to-pointers. There is also extensive coverage of racing and steeplechasing and lots of advertising.

Practical Horseman. 19 Wilmont Mews, West Chester, Pa. 19380
A truly practical monthly, stressing instructive articles on training, showing, racing, breeding and general horse care.

The Spur. Berryville, Va. 22611
Bi-monthly from the heart of the Virginia horse country, dealing mostly with foxhunting, hunt racing, Thoroughbred breeding and eventing.

Major Mail Order Houses

There are innumerable tack shops, and there is no substitute for personal examination for many of the items that you will need to buy. However, nobody can stock everything, and the firms listed below, all of which publish comprehensive catalogs, also play a very useful role.

DeLuxe Saddlery
1817 Whitehead Road
Baltimore, Md. 21207

Eiser's, Inc.
1304 North Broad Street
Hillside, N.J. 07205

H. Kauffman and Sons Saddlery
   Co., Inc.
138–141 East 24th Street
New York, N.Y. 10010

Miller Harness Co., Inc.
131 Varick Street
New York, N.Y. 10010

Libertyville Saddle Shop
309 Peterson Road, P.O. Box M
Libertyville, Ill. 60048

Schneider's
3777 Green Road
Cleveland, Ohio 44122

Meyer's, Inc.
175 E. Main Street
Lexington, Ky. 40507

Dealers in Horse Books

Most of the larger saddlery dealers list an extensive selection of current
horse books in their catalogs. The dealers listed below specialize in
equestrian literature both new and out-of-print, and are more likely
to be able to provide older books and foreign publications.

J. A. Allen & Co., Ltd.
1 Lower Grosvenor Place
London, SW1W OEL, England

Sydney R. Smith
Canaan, New York 12029

R. E. Way
Brettons, Burrough Green
Newmarket, Suffolk, England

El Zar Book Bar
P.O. Box 1904
Cedar Rapids, Iowa 52406

Horse Books, Ltd.
1 Tahoma Lodge
Lubbock Road
Chiselhurst, Kent BR7 5JS, England

Bibliography

The following list is far from complete, but shows the books that I have personally found most helpful. The titles marked with an asterisk (*) are out of print, but not especially difficult to find through one of the specialist horse book dealers.

Aldin, Cecil, *Ratcatcher to Scarlet* (also a sequel, *Scarlet to M.F.H.*) London: Eyre & Spottiswoode Ltd., 1926.
A bit dated, but still sound advice from an experienced English fox-hunter to his protégé, and charmingly illustrated.

Baily's Hunting Directory. London: J. A. Allen, various dates.
Issued annually since 1897, Baily's contains a listing of all the recognized packs of hounds both in the British Isles and "overseas," including addresses of Masters and Hunt Secretaries and a brief description of the countries.

Bloodgood, Lida F., *The Saddle of Queens*. London: J. A. Allen, 1959.
An interesting illustrated history of the sidesaddle and feminine equitation by a noted horsewoman.

Chamberlin, Harry D., *Training Hunters, Jumpers and Hacks*. New York: Arco, 1972.
Current edition of a book originally written in the 1930s by the famous Army Olympic rider, and probably still the best basic book on training the hunter-type horse.

Codrington, Lt.-Col. W. S., *Know Your Horse*. London, J. A. Allen, 1974.
Another established book, invaluable to the novice rider or new owner.

Bibliography

Discusses not only injuries and diseases, but also general horse care and stable management.

d'Endrody, A. L., *Give Your Horse a Chance*. London: J. A. Allen, 1971.
An all-encompassing modern classic dealing with all phases of eventing.

Hanauer, Elsie, *The Science of Equine Feeding*. New York: A. S. Barnes, 1973.
A thorough discussion of equine nutrition, that oft-neglected science.

Henry, Samuel J., *°Foxhunting Is Different*. New York: Derrydale Press, 1938.
Stories about American foxhunting, including some tales about our first president and his friends, with charming illustrations by Paul Brown.

Jackson, Noel, *Effective Horsemanship*. New York: Arco, 1974.
A serious study of how the principles of classical equitation can be applied to jumping, eventing, even polo.

Littauer, V. S., *Commonsense Horsemanship*. New York: Arco, 1972.
One of the classics of American equestrian literature; provides the novice with a good background for general riding.

Lyon, Lt.-Col. W. E., *First-Aid Hints for the Horse Owner*. London: Collins, 1965.
Compact and easy to understand.

Mackay-Smith, Alexander, *°American Foxhunting*. Millwood, Va.: American Foxhound Club, 1970.
Handsomely illustrated collection of the classic American foxhunting stories and poems.

Miller, William C., and West, Geoffrey P., *Black's Veterinary Dictionary*. London: A. & C. Black, 1972.
A comprehensive reference work, listing all diseases alphabetically. Now in its tenth edition.

Morris, George, *Hunter Seat Equitation*. Garden City: Doubleday, 1971.
The basics of hunter-seat equitation as practiced in U.S. show rings today, simply and clearly explained and well illustrated.

Museler, Wilhelm, *Riding Logic*. New York: Scribner, 1968.
A concise presentation of the basic German approach to riding and jumping. An established classic of the literature.

Podhajsky, Alois, *The Complete Training of Horse and Rider*. Garden City: Doubleday, 1967. (Paperback by Wilshire Book Co., 1973.)
The principles of the Spanish Riding School of Vienna, as summarized by its famous director. A must for dressage enthusiasts.

Seunig, Waldemar, *Horsemanship*. Garden City: Doubleday, 1971.
A classic for the serious student of dressage, containing excellent specific solutions for various training problems. Not such easy reading, but worth it.

Smith, Peter C., *Design and Construction of Stables*. London: J. A. Allen, 1967.
A very helpful book for anyone planning to build his own stable, by an architect-horseman.

Somerville, E. Œ., and Ross, Martin (pseudonyms), *Some Experiences of an Irish R. M.* London: Longmans, Green & Co., 1907 (and many later editions).
Delightful stories concerned with hunting in Ireland before World War I—the most famous of the sporting novels by this celebrated collaboration, and nothing conveys the feeling of the sport any better.

Stanier, Sylvia, *The Art of Long Reining*. London: J. A. Allen, 1972.
Invaluable pamphlet on longeing and the use of long reins.

Steinkraus, William. *Riding and Jumping*. Garden City: Doubleday, 1969.
An over-view in general, illustrated with photographs of many show-ring greats; fascinating for anyone interested in horses.

Stoneridge, M. A., *A Horse of Your Own*. Garden City: Doubleday, 1963.
An extremely readable general survey of the whole range of Eastern-style horse interests, horse care and activities.

Tuke, Diana R., *Bit by Bit*. London: J. A. Allen, 1972.
A useful review of the various kinds of bits and their uses; a sequel, *Stitch by Stitch*, deals with saddlery.

Bibliography

Willcox, Sheila, *The Event Horse*. Philadelphia: J. B. Lippincott, 1973.
The author, the only three-time Badminton winner, assumes the reader has a basic knowledge of riding, but then takes him all the way from buying an event horse prospect to the full-scale three-day event itself.

Wynmalen, Henry, *Dressage*. New York: Arco, 1971. (Paperback by Wilshire Book Co., 1973.)
A very good basic book.

Index

Abscesses, 311
Accepting, 144, 146
Aged horses, 255–56
AHSA. See American Horse Shows
    Association.
Aids, 72, 137–43. See also Signals.
    accepting (holding), 144, 146
    diagonal, 92–93
    forward movement and, 146–47
    hand, 139–41. See also Hands;
        Reins.
    lateral, 93
    leg, 139. See also Legs, rider's.
    reinforcement of, 137–38
    repetition of, 148
    seat, 138–39
    timing and, 147
    voice, 138, 168
    weight, 141–43. See also Weight,
        rider's.
    yielding motion and, 145
Alfalfa, 268, 269, 270
American Dressage Institute, 313
American Horse Shows Association
        (AHSA), 17, 221
    gaits defined by, 132
    levels of shows, 225–26
    tests, 130–31, 231
American hound, 189, 190
Anatomy of horse, 280
Anemia, equine infectious, 260
Antiseptics, 309
Apparel. See Attire, riding.

Arenas, dressage, 155–56
Arteries, bleeding from, 310
Attire, riding, 18–21
    buying, 20–21
    for combined training, 238
    for dressage competitions, 231,
        232
    for foxhunting, 196–200
    sidesaddle, 173
Awards, AHSA, 221–22
Azoturia, 301–2

Back
    bracing of, 141
    in foxhunting, 217
Backward movement, 80–81
Bacteria, 262
    washing and, 31
Balance. See also Weight, rider's.
    impulsion and, 150
Bandaging, 282
    for cracked heel, 308
    for mud fever, 307
    of wounds, 310, 311
Banged tail, 276
Bareback riding, 105
Barley, 267, 269, 270
Bathing of horse, 31
Bedding, 271–73, 274
Beet pulp, 266
Beginners, 18
Bending, 87–88
    around corner, 79
    forward. See Leaning forward.

Index

Bits, 33–37
  bridoon and, 40, 57
  direction changes and, 145
  dressage training and, 131
  for foxhunting, 196, 201
  longeing and, 165–66
  placement of, 55, 56–57
Blacksmith, 254, 284
Blankets, 278–79
Bleeding, 310–11
Bluing (gall medicine), 307, 309
Boarding a horse, 260
Bog spavin, 300
Bolting, 97
Bones
  diseases of, 295–96, 297, 300
  nutrition and, 265
Book dealers, 315
Boots, 20
  for foxhunting, 198, 200
  longeing, 167
Botfly eggs, 287
Bowed tendons, 297, 298
Bracing the back, 141
Bradoon, see Bridoon.
Braiding, 226, 276
Bran, 265, 267–68, 269, 270
  diseases and, 301, 302, 307
Breastplates, 43–44
Breathing problems of horse, 304–5
Breeches for foxhunting, 197, 198
Bridles, 33–44
  adjustment of, 56
  bridoon, 40, 57
  curb chains, 34, 39, 40, 41, 56
  double, 38, 40, 65
  for dressage competition, 231
  Kimberwicke, 34, 37–38, 57
  for longeing, 165, 166
  nosebands, 44
  pelham, 39–40, 43, 57, 65
  removal of, 69
  snaffle, 35–37
Bridoon, 40, 57
Brittle feet, 294

Broken wind, 305–6
Bronchitis, 304–5
Bruises, 311
Brushes, 26
  care of, 29
Brushing, 23, 26–30
Bucking, 97
Burrs, 28
Buying a horse, 253–60
  advice, seeking, 256
  age of horse and, 255–56
  good faith and, 258
  guarantees and, 258
  list of requirements for, 254–55
  regime of horse and, 259–60
  size of horse and, 256
  trial procedures, 257–58
  veterinary check and, 258–59

Calcium, 265
Calf manna, 270, 271
Cannon bone, 280
  injuries to, 297
Canter, 89–94
  beats of, 89
  jumping and, 111–12, 123
  longeing and, 169, 170, 172
  timing of aids and, 148–49
  working, 152
Cantle, 44, 45
Capped elbows and hocks, 300–301
Caps for foxhunting, 198
Carbohydrates, 263, 266, 267
Casts, in foxhunting, 192
Catching a horse, 26
Cavalletti, 112–13, 154
  longeing and, 169, 170
Cavessons, 44
  longeing, 164, 165
Chains
  curb, 34, 39, 40, 41, 56
  lead shanks, 24–25
Chaps, 20

Cheekpieces, of bits, 35, 37, 38, 39, 57
Chin straps (of cap), 19–20
Chores, stable, 273–79
Circling, 144, 159
  in longeing, 168–70
Cleaning. *See also* Grooming.
  of stall, 273–74, 288
  of tack, 51–54
  of wounds, 309–10, 311
Clipping, 277–78
  cracked heel and, 308
  of mane, 276
  patterns of, 278
Clothing. *See* Attire.
Coat, horse's. *See also* Grooming.
  clipping of, 277–78
Coats for foxhunting, 197–200
Coggins test, 260
Colds, 304–5
Colic, 303–4
Collection, 40, 132
Combined training, 236–48
  attire for, 238
  chart of standards for five levels, 242–43
  courses, 239–40, 245
  cross-country in, 236, 237, 240–241, 242, 244, 246–48
  eligibility for, 242
  jumping in, 239, 240–48
  levels in, 238, 239, 242–43
  preparation for, 238–45
  Pre-training Level, 239
  rules and standards, 237, 239, 242–43
  speed in, 237, 241, 243, 246
  warming up for, 246
Combing, 26–27, 28
Commands, voice, 138
  for longeing, 168
Competitions, 221–50. *See also* Combined training; Dressage; Hunter trials; Shows, horse.

Constipation, 267, 303
Contact, dressage and, 144–45, 146, 153
Contracted heels, 294
Controls, 72. *See also* Aids; Signals.
Contusions, 311
Cooling out, 99
Corn (food), 263, 267, 269, 270
Corns (of feet), 293
Coronary band (coronet), 280, 286
  sores on, 294
Costs
  boarding, 260
  commissions, 256
  for instruction, 17–18
Coughs, 304–5
Counter-canter, 92
Courses, 239–40
  walking of, 245
Covert, 218
Cracked heel, 308
Crop. *See* Whip.
Cross-country, 99–105
  in combined training, 236, 237, 240–41, 242, 244, 246–48
  preparation for, 246
  requirements of, 246–48
Cross-ties, 25
Cubbing season, 190–91, 194
Curb chains, 34, 39, 40, 41, 56
Curb rein, 39, 40, 65
Curbs (unsoundness), 299
Currying, 26–27

Dandy brush, 27, 28
Defenses, natural, of horse, 25
Dental care, 286–87
Diagonal
  aids, 92–93
  posting and, 83–84
Diet. *See* Feeding.
Digestion, 262–63
Direct reins, 87, 88
Diseases. *See* Health care.

Dismounting, 69–70
Ditches, schooling over, 240, 241, 244
Drag hunting, 10, 180
Dressage, 129–63
  acceptance in, 144, 146
  AHSA and, 231
  aids, 138–43
    hands, 139–41
    legs, 139
    reinforcement of, 137–38
    seat, 138–39
    weight, 141–43
  arenas, 155–56
  associations, 222, 313
  attire for, 231, 232
  basic principles, 143–49
  in combined training, 236, 237, 242
  competitions, 229–35
  contact and relaxation, 144–45, 146, 153
  definition of, 129–30
  exercises for horse, 153–54
  exercises for rider, 154–56
  impulsion, 149–50
  leg-yielding, 158–61
  levels of, 229, 230
  obedience, lightness and supple-ness of horse, 153
  paces, 150–52
    ordinary walk, 151
    working canter, 152
    working trot, 152
  points awarded in, 132
  position and seat of rider in, 134–37
  presentation at, 231–32
  shoulder-in, 159, 161, 162–63
  tests, 130–31, 155, 229, 230, 231, 233
  turn on forehand, 156–58, 161
  willingness to move forward, 149–50

Dressing
  hoof, 276, 284–86
  leg, 307
  of wounds, 310
D-ring, 34, 37, 45
Drinking (by horse), 103, 227, 261
Driving the horse, 139

Eating by horse. *See* Feeding.
Eggs
  warble fly, 308
  worm, 287, 289
Elbow, 280
  capped, 300
  galls of, 306
Emphysema, 305–6
Encephalitis, immunization against, 286
English hound, 189, 190
Equipment. *See also* Tack.
  for cleaning, 52
  for grooming, 26, 28
Equitation classes, 228
Ergot, 280
Eventing, 236–48
Exercise(s), 153–56
  azoturia and, 301–2
  in dressage, 153–56
  foxhunting and, 194
  for horse, 153–54
  jumping, 111–12
  longeing, 164–72
  for rider, 154–56

Farrier, 254, 284
Fecal counts, 288
Fédération Equestre Internationale (FEI), 221
  levels of shows, 225
Feeding, 253–54, 261–71
  boarding and, 260
  bulk and, 263, 266, 268
  colic and, 304
  commercial feeds, 265–66

Feeding (*Cont.*)
  digestion and, 262–63
  grain, 264, 265, 266–68
  hay, 264, 265, 268–71
  "high" horses and, 263
  kinds of nutrition, 264–65
  lymphangitis and, 301
  overweight and, 264–65
  pellets, 266, 268
  salt and, 261
  supplements in, 265, 266, 270, 271
  sweet feed, 265–66, 269
  of tired horse, 32
  water requirements and, 261
  weight and, 263–65
Feet, horse's
  brittle, 294
  care of, 29–30, 284–86
  diseases of, 292–301
Feet, rider's. *See also* Legs, rider's.
  trot and, 83
FEI. *See* Fédération Equestre Internationale.
Fences. *See also* Jumping.
  in combined training, 242–43, 244–45
  hair, cracked heel and, 308
  longeing and, 170
  types of, 120–21
Field Master, 182
Filling (in legs), 296–97
First-aid supplies, 289–90
First Level, 132, 230
Fitness, 150. *See also* Exercise.
  foxhunting and, 194
Fitzwilliam girth, 49
Flat, working on, 93
Flat classes, 228
Flies, 102–3, 289
  warble, 308
Flu, 304–5
Food. *See* Feeding.
Footfalls, feeling the horse's, 147
Footing, gallop and, 96

Forage, 268, 269, 270
Forehand, turn on, 156–58, 161
Forward movement, 146–47
  willingness for, 149–50
Founder (laminitis), 294–95
Foxes, 184–88, 213
  cubbing and, 190–91
  eating habits of, 185–86
  mating of, 186
  scent of, 188
  stratagems of, 188
Foxhound. *See* Hounds.
Foxhunting, 10, 179–220
  arrival for, 202
  attire for, 196–200
  casts in, 192
  children and, 200
  damages caused in, 205
  drag hunting, 10, 180
  in England and Ireland, 181
  gentleman member, 198–200
  glossary, 217–20
  horse and, 193–96
  hounds and, 189–93. *See also* Hounds.
  huntsman, 182, 191, 192, 208, 212, 215–16
  jumping in, 195, 196
  kicking and, 195, 205
  language of, 191–92
  Master, 182, 183–84, 198, 213
  organization of, 181–84
  safety measures in, 205
  scent and, 188, 209, 212, 217
  shoeing for, 196
  tack and, 195–96
  training for, 193–96
  viewing the fox, 192, 202–4, 214
  whippers-in, 182, 212, 216
"Frame" for jumping, 122
Frog (of hoof), 30
  inflammation of, 292
Full-seat, 110
Fulmer snaffle, 34, 35
Furacin, 294, 308, 310

Gaits
canter, 132, 152
trot, 132, 152
walk, 132, 151
Gallop, 94–96
full, 95–96
hand, 94–95
Galls, 62, 306
Garters, boot, 200
Geldings, sheath washing for, 31
General Impressions, dressage, 132, 234
Getting started in riding, 15–21
Girths, 48–49
checking of, 61–62, 100
galls and, 306
placement of, 54
Gloucester Foxhunting Club, 180
Grain, 264, 265, 266–68
diseases and, 301, 302
mixtures, 267, 269
pellets, 266
Grand Prix test, 229
Granulation, 309, 310
Grass, 264, 268
Gravel, 283, 284, 298
Grid jumping, 117
Grooming, 22–32
after ride, 31–32
clipping, 277–78
daily, 26–30
mane pulling, 274–76
safety measures in, 22–23
strapping, 32
tail, 275–76
tools for, 26, 28
of unclipped horse, 279
Guarantees, 258

Habit, sidesaddle, 173
Hacking, 93
Hair. *See also* Brushing; Grooming.
clipping of, 277–78
fetlock, cracked heel and, 308

Half-halt, 146, 234, 235
Half-seat, 94, 110
Halt, 76–80
in competition, 234, 235
square, 135, 234
Halters, 23–24, 25
longeing and, 164
Hand gallop, 94
Hands, rider's. *See also* Reins.
basic position for, 66, 67
circling and, 144
dressage and, 139–41, 143–46
jumping and, 113, 114, 118, 124–25, 128
trot and, 82, 83
turning and, 87–88, 144, 156
Hats, 18–20
for foxhunting, 197
for sidesaddle riding, 173
Hay, 264, 265, 268–71
judging quality of, 268–69
pellets, 266
weight to feed, 270–71
Health care, 281–311
dental, 286–87
first-aid list, 289–90
foot and leg diseases, 292–301
hooves in, 284–86
immunizations, 286, 303, 304
internal diseases, 301–6
parasite control, 287–89
record, 290–91
skin diseases, 306–9
wounds, 309–11
Heat in legs, 281
Heaves, 305–6
Heels
cleaning of, 27, 31
contracted, 294
cracked, 308
Hematoma, 311
Hilltopping, 194
Hocks, 280
swelling of, 300, 301

Home care for horse, 254, 261–80
  bedding, 271–73, 274
  blankets and sheets, 278–79
  chores, 274–79
  cleaning of stall, 273–74
  clipping, 277–78
  feeding, 261–71. *See also* Feed-
    ing.
  mane pulling, 274–76
Hooves, 30, 284–86
  contracted heels, 294
  dressing for, 276, 284–86
  laminitis (founder) of, 294–95
  nail pricks of, 293
  sand crack in, 294
  thrush and, 292–93
Horse, parts of, 280
Horseshoes. *See* Shoes, horse.
Horse shows. *See* Shows, horse.
Horse trial, 238
Hounds, 189–93
  breeds of, 189, 190
  characteristics of, 189, 191
  huntsman and, 208, 215
  killing by, 181, 193
  language of, 191–92
  learning about, 208–9
  lifting of, 193, 219
  scent and, 209
  training of, 190–91
  walking of, 209
  whippers-in and, 182
Hunter class, 227
Hunter hack classes, 228
Hunter pace event, 249
Hunter Seat riding, 10
Hunter trials, 248–50
Hunting, fox. *See* Foxhunting.
Hunt Races, 249–50
Huntsman, 182, 191, 192, 208,
  212, 215–16

Immunizations, 286, 303, 304
Impulsion, 149–50
  jumping and, 240

Influenza, 304–5
Information sources, 17, 313–15
Institutions, teaching, 16–17
Instruction, search for, 16–18
Intestines, horse's, 262, 263
  pains in, 303–4

Jeans, 20
Jigging, 103
Jodhpurs, 20
Judging, 223, 227–28, 229
  in combined training, 237
  dressage, 231
Jumping, 109–28
  advanced, 118–20
  cavalletti for, 112–13
  of combinations, 244–45
  in combined training, 239, 240–
    248
  contact and, 124–25, 128
  cross-country, 237, 240–41, 244,
    246–48
  distances (spacing) for, 121–22
  foxhunting and, 195, 196
  in hunter trials, 249
  impulsion and, 240
  intermediate, 116–18
  left behind in, 115
  longeing and, 170
  preparation for, 110–13
  saddles for, 44, 45, 46
  seeing the distance in, 123
  setting up jumps for, 121–22
  in shows, 227–29
  sidesaddle, 174
  stadium, 236, 237, 248
  style over fence, 122–28
  timing and, 117, 123–24
  types of jumps for, 120–21
  into water, 244, 247

Keeping horse at home. *See* Feeding; Home care of horse.
Kennelman, 182

Index

Kicking, 25, 30, 103
  foxhunting and, 195, 205
  safety from, 22–23
Kimberwicke (Kimblewicke), 34,
  37–38, 57
Knife, mane, 275

Lameness, 284, 292–301, 311
Laminitis, 294–95
Larvae, 287, 308–9
Larynx, paralysis of, 305
Lateral movement, 158–63
Lead
  canter and, 89, 91, 92–93
  signals for, 92–93
Leading of horse, 23–25
Leaning forward, 76
  emergencies and, 96
  jumping and, 114
  trot and, 83
Leather
  care of, 51–54
  girths, 48–49
  for halters and shanks, 24
  quality of, 51
  stretching of, 86
Left behind, 115
Legs, horse's
  cleaning of, 27
  diseases of, 292–301
  feeling movement of, 147
  feeling of, for unsoundness, 281
  jumping and, 109–10
  mud fever of, 307
  picking up, 29–30
  scratches of, 308
Legs, rider's
  backward movement and, 80
  canter and, 92–93
  dressage and, 135, 137, 139,
    146, 158–61
  footfalls and, 147–48
  forward movement and, 146–47
  gallop and, 94
  halt and, 76

jumping and, 113–14, 116, 118,
  124–25
  sidesaddle riding and, 175–76
  sideways movement and, 160
  sitting trot and, 85–86
  turning and, 87–88, 144, 156
Legume hay, 264, 265, 268
Leg-up, 64–65
Leg-yielding, 158–61
Lessons, riding, search for, 16–18
Lines, longe, 164–65, 168, 171
Linseed meal, 264, 269
Longeing, 154, 164–72
  assistant for, 171–72
  canter in, 169, 170, 172
  cavalletti in, 169, 170
  cavesson, 164, 165
  commands, 168
  jumping and, 170
  lines for, 164–65, 168, 171
  safety measures for, 171
  side reins in, 165, 166, 167
  surcingle, 166
  trot in, 169, 170, 172
  whip in, 164, 168, 171, 172
Lonsdale girth, 48
Lumps (warbles), 308–9
Lung disease, 304–5
Lymphangitis, 301, 307

Magazines, 313–14
Mail order houses, 314–15
Mane
  braiding of, 226
  grooming of, 28–29, 32
  jumping and, 113, 115
  pulling, 274–76
  trimming of, 276
Mange, 181
Manna, calf, 270, 271
Manure, 288
  removal of, 272, 273
Martingales, 41–44, 196
Maryland Hunt Cup, 250

Mash, 267–68
  diseases and, 301, 302, 307
Master of Foxhounds, 182, 183–84,
    198, 213
Masters of Foxhounds Association
    of America, 181, 313
Meal, 264, 269
Medication
  for brittle feet, 294
  for colic, 303, 304
  for cracked heel, 308
  first-aid, 289–90
  for ringworm, 307
  for thrush, 293
  worm, 287–88
  wounds and, 309
Milk, dried skim, 264
Minerals, 265
Mounting, 62–65
  sidesaddle, 175
Mouth, problems of, 34–35
Mouthpieces. *See* Bits; Bridles.
Mucking-out, 273–74
Mud fever, 307
Mud knot, 276
Mullen mouthpiece, 35
Muscle soreness, 82

Nail pricks, 293
Nail puncture wounds, 311
Navicular disease, 295
Neat's-foot oil, 54
Nodules (warbles), 308
Nosebands, 44, 56, 231
Novices, 239
  buying a horse and, 255
  shows and, 226
Nursing care, 283–84. *See also*
    Health care.
Nutrition, 264–65

Oats, 266, 267, 269, 270
Obstacles. *See* Jumping.
Oils for tack care, 53–54
Opposition, rein of, 87, 140–41

Organizations, 17, 313
  foxhunting, 181–84
  show, 221–22
Outfits, riding. *See* Attire.
Overweight horses, 264–65
Owning a horse, 251–311
  buying, 253–60
  health care, 281–91
  keeping at home, 261–80
  veterinary notes, 292–311

Pace
  combined training, 241
  hunter, 249
  slowing and increasing, 142
Paces, basic, 150–52. *See also* Can-
    ter; Trot; Walk.
Pads, saddle, 50
Pain, 303–4
Parasites, 287–89
Parts of horse, 280
Pastern, 280
  cleaning of, 27
  cracks in, 308
Pasture, 264, 265, 268, 270, 288–
    289
Pasturing, 26
Pelham, 39–40, 43, 57, 65
Pellets, feed, 266, 268
Penetrating wounds, 310–11
Penn-Marydel hound, 190
Phosphorus, 265, 267
Pink coats, 197
Pivoting. *See* Turning.
Pleurisy, 304–5
Pneumonia, 304–5
Points, dressage, 132
Point-to-points, 249
Pole. *See also* Cavalletti.
  longeing, 169, 170
Pommel, 47
  cantering and, 90–91
  pad, 50
  sidesaddle, 173, 176
Pony clubs, 17, 222, 313

Index

Port (of bit), 40
Position
  basic, 66–69
  for canter, 89–91
  checking of, 68
  for dressage, 134–37
  emergencies and, 96
  for gallop, 94, 95
  halt and, 76–80
  for jumping, 110–19
  sidesaddle, 175–76
  three-point (full-seat), 110–11, 123
  for trot, 81, 82–83
    incorrect, 155
    sitting, 85–86
  turning and, 78
  two-point (half-seat), 94, 110–111
  for walk, 74–75
Posting, 81–82
  diagonals in, 83–84
Poultices, 283–84, 311
Pre-training Level, 239
Protein, 264, 267
Proud flesh, 309, 310
Puncture wounds, 311
Punishment, 101

Quittor, 294

Rabies, 181
Races, 249–50
Radiographs, 259
Rails. *See also* Jumping.
  trotting over, 111, 112
Ratcatcher, 197, 198, 200, 203, 220, 231
Ratings, Pony Club, 222
Rearing, 97–98
Record, health, 290–91
Reducine, 294
Reins, 65. *See also* Hands, rider's.
  backward movement and, 80–81
  bolting and, 97

canter and, 91, 92–93
curb, 39, 40, 65
direct, 87, 88
dressage and, 140–41, 143
gallop and, 94–95
halt and, 77–78
indirect, 140–41
jumping and, 117
in one hand, 77–78
of opposition, 87, 140–41
running, 167
shortening, 72, 74
shying and, 97
side, 165, 166, 167
signaling with, 72
snaffle, 38, 39, 65
stops for, 43
trot and, 82
turning and, 78, 87–88, 156
Relaxation
  dressage and, 153
  jumping and, 116
Repetition of aids, 148
Respiratory disease, 304–5
Rhythm
  basic paces and, 151–52
  canter, 89, 90
Ringbone, 295–96
Rings
  bit, 35–37
  D, 34, 37, 45
  saddle, 45
Ringworm, 307–8
Rising (posting) trot, 94, 111, 114
Roads and tracks event, 237, 242
Roaring, 305
Rose Tree Foxhunting Club, 180
Roughage, 266, 268
Rubber pads, 50
Rub marks, 279
Running, 95

Saddles, 44–47
  buying, 50–51
  cleaning of, 51–54

Saddles *(Cont.)*
  for dressage, 135–36
  leather, 51
  longeing and, 166
  options for, 46–47
  pads for, 50
  placement of, 54
  for sidesaddle riding, 173
  types of, 44–47
Safety measures
  in foxhunting, 205
  in grooming, 22–23
  in jumping, 121
  for longeing, 171
  for stirrups, 48
Salt, 261
Salutes, 234
Sand crack, 294
Sawdust, 271, 272–73
Scabs, 310
Scent, foxhunting and, 188, 209, 212, 217
Schooling
  over ditches, 240, 241, 244
  ring, 224
Schools, riding, 16–17
Scratches, 27, 309–10
  heel, 308
Seat. *See also* Position; Saddles; Weight.
  dressage and, 135–36, 138
Serpentine, 133
Shanks, 24–25, 26
Shavings, wood, 271, 272, 273
Sheath, 280
  washing, 31
Sheepskin, 50, 279
Sheets, stable, 278–79
Shifting weight. *See* Weight, rider's.
Shoes, horse, 105, 284
  corns and, 293
  for foxhunting, 196
  nail pricks and, 293
Shoes, riding, 19, 20

Shoulder-in, 159, 161, 162–63
Shows, horse, 225–29
  classes in, 227–28, 229
  guidelines for, 226–27
  judges in, 223, 227–28, 229
  kit for, 227
  novices in, 226
  participation in, 223–25
  regulation of, 221–22
  types of, 225–26
  warming up for, 228
Shying, 96–97, 100–101
Sidebone, 296
Sidesaddle riding, 172–76
Sideways movement, 158–63
Signals. *See also* Aids.
  backward movement and, 80–81
  for canter, 92–93
  dressage and, 137
  for gallop, 94–95
  for halt, 76–80
  for lead, 92–93
  for trot, 83
  for turning, 78, 87–88
  for walk, 72–75
Sitting position, 66–69. *See also* Position.
Sitting trot, 85–86
Size of horse, 256
Skin
  diseases of, 306–9
  wounds of, 309–11
Skirt, sidesaddle, 173, 175
Slowing the pace, 142
Sluggish horse, 148
Snaffles, 34, 35–37
  in double bridle, 40
  for longeing, 165, 166
Soaps, saddle, 52–53
Soreness, muscle, 82
Sores, skin, 306–9
Soybean meal, 264
Spavin, 300
Speed in combined training, 237, 241, 243, 246

Index

Splints, 297–98
Sports, horse. *See* Combined training; Dressage; Foxhunting; Hunter trials; Shows.
Sprains, 297
Spread fences, 120
Spurs, 73, 138
 for foxhunting, 200
Stables, 271–74
 boarding, 260
Stadium jumping, 236, 237, 248
Stall
 cleaning of, 273–74, 288
Stazdry, 271, 272, 273
Steeplechase, 237, 242, 250
Stifle, 280
 lameness, 301
Stirrups, 47–48, 196
 adjustment of, 64
 dressage and, 134–35
 position and, 67
 riding without, 85–86
 sidesaddle, 176
Stocking up (of legs), 296–97
Stomach, horse's, 262
 pains, 303–4
Stops, rein, 43
Straight movement, 136, 143
Strapping, 32
Straps
 billet, 54
 sidesaddle, 173–74
Straw, 271–72, 273–74
Stringhalt, 300
Stumbling, 96
Supplements, feed, 265, 266, 270, 271
Supplement to Rules on Dressage and Combined Training, 231, 236–37, 239
Suppleness of horse, 153
Surcingle, longeing, 166
Surface wounds, 309–10
Sweet feed, 265–66, 269

Swellings. *See also* Puffs.
 skin (bruises), 311

Tack, 33–57. *See also* Bridles; Saddles.
 buying, 50–51
 care of, 51–54
 inspection of, 61–62
Tacking up, 54–57
Tail
 banging of, 276
 braiding of, 276
 grooming of, 28–29, 32
 mud knot for, 276
 pulling of, 275–76
Tanner's oil, 53–54
Teacher
 communication with, 71
 need for, 16
 selection of, 17–18
Teaching institutions, 16–17
Teeth, 35, 57, 286–87
Temperament of horse, 148
 feeding and, 263
Temperature, 281, 304
Tendons
 bowed, 297, 298
 filled, 296–97
Tests
 combined training, 236
 dressage, 130–31, 155, 229, 230, 231, 233
Tetanus, 302–3
 immunization, 286, 303
Thermometers, 281
Thoroughbred, 255, 257
 clipping of, 278
Thoroughpin, 299
Three-Day Event, 236, 238
Three-point position, 110–11, 123
Throatlatch (throatlash), 36, 38, 56
Thrush, 30, 292–93
Ticks, 289

Tieing up (fastening) horse, 25–26
Tieing-up (azoturia), 301–2
Timing
  canter and, 148–49
  in combined training, 246–47, 248
  in dressage, 147
  jumping and, 117, 123–24
Timothy hay, 264, 265, 268
Tiredness, signs of, 194
Tom Thumb Pelham, 40
Tongue, 189
Tourniquets, 310
Trail riding, 99–105
Training Level, 132, 229
Tranquilizers, 304
Transitions, 95
Trials, horse, 238. *See also* Combined training.
  hunter, 248–50
Trot, 81–84
  cavalletti and, 154
  jumping and, 111, 112, 114–15
  longeing and, 169, 170, 172
  rising, 94, 111, 114
  sidesaddle, 176
  sitting to, 85–86
  working, 132, 152
Tubing for worms, 287
Turning, 86–88
  on forehand, 156–58, 161
  hands and, 87–88, 144, 156
  legs and, 87–88, 144, 156
  signals for, 78, 87–88
  weight and, 79, 142, 156
Twitch for lip, 277
Two-point position, 94, 110–11

United States Combined Training Association, 222, 231, 238, 313
United States Pony Club, 222, 313

Vaccinations, 286, 303, 304
Veins, bleeding from, 310

Veterinarian, 283
  examination, buying horse and, 258–59
View holloa, 220
Virginia hound, 190
Vitamins, 265
Voice as aid, 138
  longeing and, 168

Walk, 71–75, 132, 151
  position for, 66–68
Warble, 308–9
Warming up, 99, 228
  for combined training, 246
Washing, 31. *See also* Cleaning; Grooming.
  galls and, 306
  of unclipped horse, 279
Water, 103, 227
  jumping into, 244, 247
  requirements for drinking, 261
Water brush, 29
Weeds, 269
  poisoning from, 307
Weight, horse's, feeding and, 263–265
Weight, rider's
  basic position and, 66–67
  turning and, 79, 142, 156
Welsh ponies, 276
Wheat bran, 265, 267
Wheeling, 96–97
Whip, 73, 74, 100
  dressage and, 137
  forward movement and, 146
  longeing and, 164, 168, 171, 172
  sidesaddle riding and, 176
Whippers-in, 182, 212, 216
Whistling, 305
Willingness for forward movement, 149–50
Wind, broken, 305–6
Windpuff (wind gall), 296, 299
Wire, 105
Wisping, 32

Index

Withers, 280
Woods, riding in, 103–4
Wood shavings, 271, 272, 273
Working gaits, 132, 152
Worms, 287–89
Wounds, 309–11

X rays, 259

Yielding, leg (sideways movement), 158–61
Yielding motion, aids and, 145
Yoke, 41, 42, 43

Zinc ointment, 308